remember

201 KOREAN VERBS

Fully Conjugated in All Aspects, Moods,
Tenses, and Formality Levels

by

Seok Choong Song

Professor of Linguistics

Michigan State U

don't

New York   London   Toronto   Sydney

All inquiries should be addressed to:

Barron's Educational Series, Inc.
250 Wireless Boulevard
Hauppauge, New York 11788

International Standard Book No. 0-8120-2567-9

Library of Congress Cataloging-in-Publication Data
Song, Seok C. (Seok Choong)
    201 Korean verbs, fully conjugated in all
the forms.

    Bibliography
    Includes index.
    1. Korean language--Verb--Tables. I. Title.
II. Title: Two hundred one Korean verbs.
PL921.S66   1988   495.7'82421   87-35119
ISBN 0-8120-2567-9

CONTENTS

There are very few treatments on the subject of verb conjugation in
Korean. If available, they are not accessible to ordinary readers and
beginning students. Though of excellent quality, they are highly sophis-
ticated and technical in nature and brief and schematic in description.
Korean verbs, at the same time, present some knotty problems to learners.

There are a number of irregular verbs whose conjugations deviate from
the norm and tax the student's memory. The agonies and frustrations on
the part of foreign students, trying to remember irregular forms, are
considerable. Under the circumstances, I did not hesitate to undertake the
task of compiling this table of Korean verb conjugations, when I was
approached by Barron's Educational Series with the plan to include Korean
in their 201 verb series.

The task of preparing this table was not an easy one. There is not a
single volume of Korean grammar in the English language available on the
market. In other words, there is no standard work to refer to in the matter
of formality levels and speech styles. The choice of which verbs to include
in the table was difficult. Just as difficult was the choice of proper
terminology for describing certain grammatical functions. Although there
are universal terms readily available for tenses, aspects, and moods, these
are not necessarily coterminous in all languages. These are only a few of
many problems a grammarian has to face in writing about a language like
Korean, which has not been fully codified.

I hope that the present volume will alleviate some of the difficulties
that beginning students inevitably experience and will facilitate the task
of learning Korean. If it succeeds in removing some of the stumbling

blocks that scare away beginning students, I feel that the long and difficult hours I have spent in trying to reach decisions will be amply rewarded.

With great pleasure, I acknowledge my indebtedness to my wife, Taekja, and my son, Clarence, for their help. Taekja has been a constant help in preparing the tables and also provided an additional typing help on weekends. Clarence helped me with the English-Korean index at the end. I also would like to thank Cynthia Sabin for typing the bulk of the manuscript.

PRONUNCIATION

A full treatment of the sound system of Korean would by itself require a book more voluminous than this one. What is presented here is schematic at best, and is intended to help students identify the sounds of letters used to spell Korean words. The description of Korean sounds in terms of symbols used to represent sounds of other languages is bound to be inadequate as well as inaccurate. The explanation of the letter-values in our Romanization must be taken as rough approximations. Students are encouraged to consult other works but the best way to learn to pronounce Korean is to listen to native speakers and imitate them as closely as possible.

I. VOWELS

Symbols	Nearest equivalent in American English or other European languages
a	'o' in 'h<u>o</u>t'
ae	'a' in 'c<u>a</u>t'
e	'e' in 'b<u>e</u>t'
i	'i' in 'mach<u>i</u>ne' but shorter
o	'o' in '<u>o</u>il'
ȯ	'a' in '<u>a</u>bout'
oe	'oe' in 'G<u>oe</u>the' in German but also pronounced as 'we' in '<u>we</u>t' by many
u	'oo' in 'g<u>oo</u>se' with lips rounded but shorter
u̇	'oo' in 'b<u>oo</u>k' with lips spread

NOTES: The difference between the Korean o and ȯ is parallel to that between the Korean u and u̇. The ones with a diacritical mark are unrounded whereas those without a diacritic are rounded. The Korean i and u are not as long as their counterparts in the English words <u>machine</u> and <u>goose</u> respectively.

II. CONSONANTS AND SEMI-VOWELS

The following symbols are used in describing phonetic environments or contexts in which consonants occur.

V=Vowels   C=Consonants   N=Nasals (n,m, and ng)   L=Liquids (l/r)

Symbols	Position in word	Nearest American English equivalent	Special remarks
p	initial consonant	'p' in '<u>p</u>in'	Less aspirated* than its English counterpart
	medial consonant between V, L or N and V	'b' in 'o<u>b</u>ey'	Fully voiced
	final consonant or before C	'p' in 'sto<u>p</u>'	Unreleased

* Aspirated consonants are produced with a distinct puff of breath following the release of closure.

pp	initial and medial consonant	'p' in 'spin'	Tight throat release; does not occur as final consonant
ph	initial and medial consonant	'ph' in 'uphill'	Strong aspiration
	final consonant or before C	'p' in 'stop'	Unreleased
t	initial consonant	't' in 'tin'	Less aspirated than its English counterpart
	medial consonant between V, L or N and V	'd' in 'ado'	Fully voiced
	final consonant or before C	't' in 'yet'	Unreleased
tt	initial and medial consonant	't' in 'stay'	Tight throated release; does not occur as final consonant
th	initial and medial consonant	'th' in 'hothouse'	Strong aspiration
	final consonant or before C	't' in 'yet'	Unreleased
k	initial consonant	'k' in 'kin'	Less aspirated than its English counterpart
	medial consonant between V, L or N and V	'g' in 'ago'	Fully voiced
	final consonant or before C	'c' in 'tic'	Unreleased
kk	initial and medial consonant	'k' in 'sky'	Tight throated release
	final consonant or before C	'c' in 'tic'	Unreleased
kh	initial and medial consonant	'ckh' in 'blockhead'	Strong aspiration

	final consonant or before C	'c' in 'ti<u>c</u>'	Unreleased
<u>c</u>	initial consonant	'c' in '<u>c</u>ello'	Less aspirated than its English counterpart
	medial consonant between V, L or N and V	'j' in re<u>j</u>oice'	Fully voiced
	final consonant or before C	't' in 'ye<u>t</u>'	Unreleased
<u>cc</u>	initial and medial consonant	'tch' in 'pi<u>tch</u>er'	Tight throated release; does not occur as final consonant
<u>ch</u>	initial and medial consonant	'chh' in 'hit<u>chh</u>ike'	Strong aspiration
	final consonant or before C	't' in 'ye<u>t</u>'	Unreleased
<u>s</u>	initial and medial consonant	's' in '<u>s</u>ing'	Weaker than its English counterpart
	before i and y	'sh' in '<u>sh</u>ip'	Tongue raised toward the palate
	final consonant or before C	't' in 'ye<u>t</u>'	Unreleased
<u>ss</u>	initial and medial consonant	'ss' in 'a<u>ss</u>ail'	With tension in the throat and tongue
	final consonant or before C	't' in 'ye<u>t</u>'	Unreleased
<u>m</u>	in all positions	'm' in '<u>mom</u>entum'	Like English 'm'
<u>n</u>	in all positions	'n' in '<u>N</u>ewto<u>n</u>ian'	Tongue tip behind upper teeth
<u>ng</u>	medial and final consonant	'ng' in 'si<u>ng</u>i<u>ng</u>'	Like English 'ng' as final consonant

<u>h</u>	initial and medial consonant	'h' in '<u>h</u>at'	
	final consonant or before C	't' in 'ye<u>t</u>'	Unreleased
<u>l</u>	final consonant or before C	'l' in 'tai<u>l</u>'	Does not occur as initial consonant in native Korean words
	medial consonant between Vs	'r' in 've<u>r</u>y' in British English	Made by a single stroke of tongue against the ridge behind the upper front teeth in a manner similar to the way 't' in 'wa<u>t</u>er' is made in American English

There are two semi-vowels in Korean, namely, <u>w</u> and <u>y</u>. They occur only before a vowel in word-initial or medial position.

<u>w</u>	initially and medially	'w' in '<u>w</u>ise'	Does not occur finally and before C
y	initially and medially	'y' in '<u>y</u>awn'	Does not occur finally and before C

III. SOME PRONUNCIATION RULES

It is not enough to know how each segment of a word is pronounced. When two words are brought together in a sequence, the neighboring sounds often interact to cause sound changes. Two neighboring sounds may become more alike. If an unpronounceable sequence of consonant clusters results, one consonant is omitted. Some segments become weaker and are optionally left out. Other segments become stronger and are produced with a greater tension in the throat. Given below are most common rules of assimilation and consonant cluster reduction as well as weakening and strengthening. Only those that occur within the verb paradigm are mentioned. The arrow in the rule is to be read as "become."

(1) ASSIMILATION

pn---->mn	apnita [amnida]
tn---->nn	sitne [sinne]
kn---->ngn	cókne [cóngne]

These rules have a wider application than they might seem to. As has already been pointed out (See II. Consonants and Semi-Vowels), c, ch, s, ss, th, and h all become t word-finally or before a consonant. Thus, when these sounds occur before n, they automatically become t and this in turn will be an input as shown below to the assimilation rule above.

cn---->tn---->nn	icne [inne]
chn--->tn---->nn	ccochne [cconne]
sn---->tn---->nn	cisne [cinne]
ssn--->tn---->nn	issne [inne]
thn--->tn---->nn	kathne [kanne]
hn---->tn---->nn	cohne [conne]

Similarly, ph and kk change to p and k respectively before n and then become subject to the assimilation rule as shown below.

phn--->pn---->mn	nophne [nomne]
kkn--->kn---->ngn	takkne [tangne]

(2) REINFORCEMENT

pc---->pcc	kupca [kupcca]
tc---->tcc	tatca [tatcca]
kc---->kcc	mókca [mókcca]
pk---->pkk	topkessta [topkketta]
tk---->tkk	mutkessta [mutkketta]
kk---->kkk	cukkessta [cukkketta]
pt---->ptt	ótupta [óduptta]
tt---->ttt	sitta [sittta]
kt---->ktt	cukta [cuktta]
ps---->pss	topse [topsse]
ts---->tss	tatse [tatsse]
ks---->kss	cókse [cóksse]

It should be noted that the output of these rules are subject to the consonant cluster reduction rules that will be given below. For instance, <u>kkk</u> and <u>ttt</u> will be reduced to <u>kk</u> and <u>tt</u> respectively. <u>t</u> also gets deleted before the reinforced consonants, reducing <u>tcc</u>, <u>tkk</u>, and <u>tss</u> to <u>cc</u>, <u>kk</u>, and <u>ss</u> respectively.

(3) WEAKENING

VhV---->VV	coha [coa]
nhV---->nV	manha [mana]
lhV---->lV	silhŏ [sirŏ]

The <u>h</u> between vowels or between a sonorant consonant such as <u>n</u> or <u>l</u> and a vowel becomes so weakened that it becomes inaudible in rapid speech, i.e., at the normal rate of speech in conversational situations.

(4) METATHESIS

hc---->ch	olhci [olchi]
ht---->th	cohta [cotha]
hk---->kh	manhkessŏ [mangkhessŏ]

When <u>h</u> is followed by consonants like <u>c</u>, <u>k</u>, and <u>t</u>, two segments interchange and then become one aspirated consonant.

(5) CONSONANT CLUSTER REDUCTION

lkc---->kc	ilkci [ikcci]
lms---->ms	talmsŭpnita [tamssŭmnida]
lpht---->ph	ŭlphtŏla [ŭpttŏra]
lhs---->ls	alhsŭpnita [alssŭmnida]
lthk---->lk	halthkessŏ [halkkessŏ]
lpc---->lc	yalpci [yalcci]
lpc---->pc	palpci [papcci]
nck---->nk	anckessta [angkketta]
nhc---->ns	kkunhse [kkunsse]
pst---->pt	ŏpsta [ŏptta]

These clusters are formed when a verb stem that ends in a consonant cluster of two is followed by an ending that begins with a consonant. These clusters are considered unpronounceable and simplification takes place. In the first three cases, the first consonant gets deleted, whereas

the next two drop the second. The cluster lpc usually deletes the second
consonant but an exception to this rule is the verb palp which deletes the

KOREAN ROMANIZATION

There are at least four different romanization systems currently in use. In
both North and South Korea, the use of an official romanization system,
sanctioned by each government, is strictly enforced. In the Western world,
two other prevalent systems peacefully coexist, serving various purposes
of different clienteles.

The Yale romanization, an innovative and convenient system, is preferred
by linguists for simplicity and consistency. With a very few exceptions,
most technical papers in linguistics that are being published today
countenance this system and perhaps will continue to do so. The
Korean-English Dictionary (1967) by Samuel E. Martin, Yang Ha Lee and
Sung-Un Chang, and Beginning Korean (1969) by S. E. Martin and Young-Sook
C. Lee, both published by the Yale University Press, adopt the Yale
romanization system. Martin's forthcoming work, A Reference Grammar of
Korean, will also be cast in the same mold and the Yale romanization is
here to stay.

The traditional and somewhat cumbersome system known as
McCune-Reischauer Romanization is still fervently adhered to by librarians
for the sole reason that the existing library catalogs employ this system.
Since a new romanization means a new catalog and the new catalog means
an additional expense, no libraries today can afford to change to a new
romanization. There is little hope that McCune-Reischauer Romanization,
despite its inconsistencies and obtrusive diacritical marks, will be
replaced in the near future.

Under the circumstances, the best thing for Koreanists to do is to
suggest a minor revision to help alleviate the inadequacies and
inconveniences of overly cluttered diacritical marks. I have adopted here
an eclectic system based on recommendations of Hawaii Korean
Romanization Workshop (1981). Following is the romanization adopted for
the present manual along with the four systems mentioned above.

Korean Symbol	201 Korean Verbs	Yale	McCune-Reischauer	S. Korea	N. Korea
ㅂ	p	p	p, b	b	p
ㅍ	ph	ph	p'	p	ph
ㅃ	pp	pp	pp	bb	pp
ㄷ	t	t	t, d	d	t
ㅌ	th	th	t'	t	th
ㄸ	tt	tt	tt	dd	tt
ㅅ	s	s	s	s	s
ㅆ	ss	ss	ss	ss	ss
ㅈ	c	c	ch, j	j	ts
ㅊ	ch	ch	ch'	ch	tsh
ㅉ	cc	cc	tch	jj	tss
ㄱ	k	k	k, g	g	k
ㅋ	kh	kh	k'	k	kh
ㄲ	kk	kk	kk	gg	kk
ㅁ	m	m	m	m	m
ㄴ	n	n	n	n	n
ㅇ	ng	ng	ng	ng	ng
ㄹ	l	l	l, r	l, r	r
ㅎ	h	h	h	h	h
ㅣ	i	i	i	i	i
ㅟ	wi	wi	wi	wi	wi
ㅔ	e	ey	e	e	e
ㅖ	ye	yey	ye	ye	ye
ㅞ	we	wey	we	we	we
ㅚ	oe	oy	oe	oe	oi
ㅐ	ae	ay	ae	ae	ai
ㅒ	yae	yay	yae	yae	yai
ㅙ	wae	way	wae	wae	wai
ㅡ	u̇	u	û	eu	û
ㅓ	ȯ	e	ô	eo	ô

xiv

ı	yŏ	ye	yô	yeo	yô
ㅓ	wŏ	we	wô	weo	wô
ㅏ	a	a	a	a	a
ㅑ	ya	ya	ya	ya	ya
ㅘ	wa	wa	wa	wa	wa
ㅜ	u	wu	u	u	u
ㅠ	yu	yu	yu	yu	yu
ㅗ	o	o	o	o	o
ㅛ	yo	yo	yo	yo	yo
ㅓ	ui	uy	ui	eui	ui

SPEECH LEVELS

Most European languages include grammatical categories like PERSON, NUMBER, and GENDER. For other languages, these categories are either non-existent or not overtly marked. On the surface, a sentence in Korean or Japanese often lacks a subject and consists solely of a predicate.

One peculiarity of some oriental languages is that they possess a highly developed system of honorifics. In Korean, speakers differentiate a formal from an informal speech situation. An honorific suffix is added to a verb stem to indicate the speaker's deference toward the person he is speaking about. Choice of speech levels depends upon various factors such as age, sex, familiarity, social status, and so on, of the speaker in relation to those of hearer and the referent of the subject of a sentence. The speaker's judgment, however, reflects the social views of Korean people. It is essential for students to develop a knowledge of Korean social custom in order to be able to speak the language properly. Since it is impossible to describe this aspect of Korean grammar fully in a limited space, I will simply provide some examples and indicate the circumstances under which they are used.

I. FORMALITY

The two sentences chaek úl ilksúpnita and chaek úl ilkne both mean 'I (you, he, she, we, or they) read a book,' but the first is more formal than the second. While the formal sentence can be used between two adults under any circumstances without giving offense, the second sentence is appropriate only in an informal situation between close friends. The INFORMAL is further divided into three different styles, FAMILIAR, INTIMATE, and CASUAL. The FORMAL level exhibits two distinct forms, POLITE and PLAIN, and this distinction further applies to all three styles of the INFORMAL. In other words, there are FAMILIAR polite, FAMILIAR plain, INTIMATE polite, INTIMATE plain, and CASUAL polite, CASUAL plain. In the following conjugation tables, only the plain forms of all three styles of the INFORMAL ending are listed. In INFORMAL speech, all that is needed to convert the plain form into the polite one is to add the particle yo at the end. Compare the following paradigms that contrast the polite with the plain forms of the INTIMATE style on the INFORMAL level.

INTIMATE

	Plain	Polite
Present	ilk-ó	ilk-ó-yo
Past	ilkóss-ó	ilkóss-ó-yo
Remote Past	ilkóssóss-ó	ilkóssóss-ó-yo
Future	ilkkess-ó	ilkkess-ó-yo
Past Future	ilkósskess-ó	ilkósskess-ó-yo

Because the polite and plain forms on the FORMAL level exhibit considerable difference, they are listed separately in the table.

II. DEFERENCE

While formality level expresses the speaker's attitude toward the person he is speaking to, the deference axis indicates the speaker's attitude toward the person he is speaking about. In Korean, the degree of deference is indicated by the honorific suffix (ú)si which is added directly after a verb stem. The two sentences chaek úl ilkúsió and chaek úl ilkó both mean

" He, she, and so on, read(s) a book," but are different in the degree of deference. The first sentence indicates that it is someone honored who is doing the reading. Again the process of forming the honorific verb stem is entirely regular and it is unnecessary to list each one separately, just as in the case of the polite forms on the INFORMAL level. In order to derive the honorific stem, simply add the honorific suffix si after a verb stem ending in a vowel segment. An alternative shape ùsi is added after a verb stem ending in a consonant segment. The honorific stem is used whenever the speech situation calls for it in all the styles, polite or plain, and on all levels. Compare the following paradigms, which contrast the honorific with the ordinary stem of the CASUAL style on the INFORMAL level.

CASUAL

	Ordinary	Honorific
Present	ilk-ci	ilkùsi-ci
Past	ilkóss-ci	ilkùsióss-ci
Remote Past	ilkóssóss-ci	ilkùsióssóss-ci
Future	ilkkess-ci	ilkùsikess-ci
Past Future	ilkósskess-ci	ilkùsiósskess-ci

III. STYLE

The speaker of Korean observes the speech situation in order to decide the level of formality, and then makes a choice in terms of degree of deference depending on the status of the subject of a sentence, that is, the person he is speaking about. Whether the speech situation is formal or informal, the speaker selects the polite or plain form in accordance with his status, age, and other social relations to those of the hearer. On the INFORMAL level, he has to decide on one of three speech styles. Speakers of European languages may be astounded by descriptions of the honorific system of Korean, and begin to wonder how Koreans go about making all these decision. For Korean speakers, however, it is a never-failing wonder that English speakers keep making unerring choices between definite and indefinite articles before a noun and, to make things worse, no article at

all sometimes. Every time a noun is mentioned, English speakers
differentiate singular from plural and then nouns that are always plural
from those that never take plural forms. The choice of a noun form in
German depends on its Number, Gender, and Case and it seems almost a
tour-de-force for Koreans that Germans are able to select the correct
forms. Korean is no more difficult or complicated than any other language,
and students will eventually be able to make these choices almost
automatically, just as students of German do in choosing the correct form
of a noun.

The choice of styles indicates, among other things, the attitude of the
speaker toward the statement he is making. The three sentences chaek úl
ilkne, chaek úl ilkó, and chaek úl ilkci all mean "I, you, he, and so on, read(s)
a book." Although the substance of the statement has, logically speaking,
the same truth-value, the speaker conveys different connotations by
choosing different styles. In the FAMILIAR, he is saying something like "I
tell you, I, you, he, and so on, am/are/is reading a book." In the CASUAL, he
is much less assertive and says "I, you, he, and so on, am/are/is reading a
book, I presume." The INTIMATE is somewhat neutral and colorless and may
be saying simply that "I/you/he, and so on, am/are/ is reading a book." The
plain form of the FAMILIAR speech is used between close friends among
adults or by adults when they are addressing those whose status is
socially inferior. The INTIMATE and CASUAL are used among young people
and children. Polite forms of all three speech styles, however, can be used
by the younger in addressing the older. FORMAL plain is the style used by
writers for public consumption of general readership. It is also used by
children among themselves.

In colloquial speech, abbreviated forms of ending such as ni and ti are
more commonly used in place of núnya and tónya in the Interrogative of the
FORMAL plain. In the FAMILIAR style, na is often substituted for núnka. I
have taken a conservative approach in listing more literary styles for the
benefit of students interested in learning to read Korean.

INFLECTIONAL CATEGORIES

The verbal ending in Korean contains various inflectional elements besides indicators of speech levels and styles discussed above. They can be arranged according to sequence positions in a table.

1. HONORIFIC

(ŭ)si

2. TENSE

Past	óss
Remote past	óss-óss
Future	kess
Past future	óss-kess

3. FORMALITY (polite)

súp/úp/p

4. ASPECT

Indicative	nún/ni/n
Retrospective	tón/ti/t
Subjunctive	si/s

5. MOOD/STYLE

Declarative	ta/la (Formal)
	e (Familiar)
Interrogative	kka/ya (Formal)
	ka (Familiar)
Propositive	ta (Formal polite)
	ca (Formal plain)
	e (Familiar)
Imperative	o (Formal polite)
	óla (Formal plain)
	ke (Familiar)

The INTIMATE and CASUAL styles on the INFORMAL level do not co-occur with Aspectual markers, and furthermore, they are not differentiated in terms of MOOD. The same shapes ǫ̇ and ci are used throughout in Declarative, Interrogative, Propositive, and Imperative Moods. In actual speech, however, different intonational patterns signal which of these moods are being combined with those styles indicators.

Now that all the inflectional categories have been mentioned and the forms that represent these categories have been listed, it will be shown below, in a simple and sketchy manner, how these elements are combined to form verbal endings.

There are three simple tenses: PRESENT, PAST, and FUTURE. The PRESENT is unmarked, that is, has no overt indicator. There are two complex tenses which are made up of combinations of simple tense markers: REMOTE PAST formed by a sequence of two PAST tense markers and PAST FUTURE, a combined form of PAST and FUTURE tense markers. Although the REMOTE PAST can be combined with the FUTURE, it is rarely used in actual speech except in combination with verbs of COMING and GOING. In the present conjugation table, it can be safely left out. The following paradigm exemplifies all the tense forms that are given in this manual. The symbol ∅ indicates zero.

Present	∅
Past	óss
Remote Past	óssóss
Future	kess
Past Future	ósskess

The FORMALITY indicator occurs only in the polite forms on the FORMAL level. Of the ASPECT markers, INDICATIVE and RETROSPECTIVE co-occur with the Declarative and Interrogative Moods, while SUBJUNCTIVE combines with the Propositive and Imperative. Since the regularity of the sequential arrangement of inflectional categories is best exemplified by the FORMAL polite, I will provide the full paradigm of the verb ilk 'read' on this level.

STEM	HON	TENSE	FORM	ASP	MOOD	FORMAL Polite
						INDICATIVE/Declarative
ilk	∅	∅	súp	ni	ta	ilksúpnita (Present)
ilk	∅	óss	úp	ni	ta	ilkóssúpnita (Past)
ilk	∅	óssóss	úp	ni	ta	ilkóssóssúpnita (Remote Past)
ilk	∅	kess	úp	ni	ta	ilkessúpnita (Future)
ilk	∅	ósskess	úp	ni	ta	ilkósskessúpnita (Future Past)

						RETROSPECTIVE/Interrogative
ilk	ø	ø	súp	ti	kka	ilksúptikka (Present)
ilk	ø	óss	úp	ti	kka	ilkóssúptikka (Past)
ilk	ø	óssóss	úp	ti	kka	ilkóssóssúptikka (Remote Past)
ilk	ø	kess	úp	ti	kka	ilkkessúptikka (Future)
ilk	ø	ósskess	úp	ti	kka	ilkósskessúptikka (Past Future)
						Propositive/Imperative
ilk	ø	ø	úp	si	ta	ilkúpsita (Propositive)
ilk	úsi	ø	p	si	o	ilkúsipsio (Imperative)

The only form that contains the honorific suffix is the Imperative form of the FORMAL polite. Although it is not obligatory, it is more natural and extremely common for the honorific suffix to accompany the Imperative on the FORMAL polite level. In the table of conjugation, the honorific suffix is enclosed in parentheses.

An irregular feature of the Declarative in the INDICATIVE on the FORMAL plain level is that the INDICATIVE marker is not allowed whenever a Tense marker is selected. In the Interrogative, the INDICATIVE and Tense markers are regularly combined, as on the FORMAL polite level. Compare the Declarative with the Interrogative paradigms on the FORMAL plain level. Since the Honorific and Formality markers are not relevant, they will be left out in the sequence positions.

STEM	TENSE	ASPECT	MOOD	INDICATIVE/Declarative
ilk	ø	nún	ta	ilknúnta (Present)
ilk	óss	ø	ta	ilkóssta (Past)
ilk	óssóss	ø	ta	ilkóssóssta (Remote Past)
ilk	kess	ø	ta	ilkkessta (Future)
ilk	ósskess	ø	ta	ilkósskessta (Past Future)
				INDICATIVE/Interrogative
ilk	ø	nún	ya	ilknúnya (Present)
ilk	óss	nún	ya	ilkóssnúnya (Past)
ilk	óssóss	nún	ya	ilkóssóssnúnya (Remote Past)
ilk	kess	nún	ya	ilkkessnúnya (Future)
ilk	ósskess	nún	ya	ilkósskessnúnya (Past Future)

As you can see clearly, the Indicative marker occurs only when the
Declarative Mood is in the Present. Once a Tense marker is chosen, the
Indicative marker is not allowed. Description verbs do not allow the
Indicative marker even when the Declarative Mood is in the Present.
Compare the Declarative Present of the Description verb aphú-ta wiht that
of Action/Process verb ilk-ta.

STEM	TENSE	ASPECT	MOOD	
aphú	ø	ø	ta	aphúta (Ind/Pres/Dec)
aphú	ø	n	ya	aphúnya (Ind/Pres/Inter)

Before presenting sample conjugation tables of regular verbs, let me
briefly touch upon the alternant shapes of suffixes that represent various
inflectional categories. The past tense has two shapes: óss and ass. The
latter occurs after a verb stem which contains the vowel a or o in its final
syllable. When the REMOTE PAST, which doubles the PAST tense form,
follows such a verb stem, only the vowel of the first syllable of the
REMOTE PAST tense form is affected. See the contrast of the Past and
Remote Past forms after three different stems.

STEM	PAST	REMOTE PAST	MOOD Decl	
al	ass		ta	alassta (Past)
al		assóss	ta	alassóssta (Remote past)
po	ass		ta	poassta (Past)
po		assóss	ta	poassóssta (Remote Past)
mók	óss		ta	mókóssta (Past)
mók		óssóss	ta	mókóssóssta (Remote Past)

The ASPECT markers also have several variant shapes: nún, ni and n for
the INDICATIVE and tón, tó, ti and t for the RETROSPECTIVE. Their pattern
of occurrence is quite similar. nún and tón occur on the FORMAL plain,

while <u>ni</u> and <u>ti</u> are used on the FORMAL polite level. <u>n</u> and <u>t</u> are used in the Declarative of the FAMILIAR style. <u>nún</u> and <u>tón</u> on the FORMAL plain are replaced by <u>n</u> and <u>tó</u> only in the Declarative under specific phonetic conditions. <u>n</u> is chosen when the preceding verb stem ends in a vowel segment, whereas <u>tó</u> occurs when the Declarative mood has the shape <u>la</u> instead of <u>ta</u>.

The FORMALITY indicator, which occurs only on the FORMAL Polite level, has three shapes: <u>súp, úp,</u> and <u>p</u>. In the Declarative and Interrogative Moods, <u>súp</u> occurs after a stem ending in a consonant or consonant cluster (except <u>ss</u>), <u>úp</u> after stem or tense forms ending in <u>ss</u> and, <u>p</u> after the stem ending in a vowel. See the following paradigm which illustrate the pattern of occurrence for the ASPECT and FORMALITY markers.

STEM	TENSE	FORM	ASPECT	MOOD	FORMAL Plain
mók	ø	ø	nún	ta	móknúnta (Ind/Dec)
ka	ø	ø	n	ta	kanta (Ind/Dec)
mók	ø	ø	tón	ya	móktónya (Ret/Int)
ka	ø	ø	tó	la	katóla (Ret/Dec)
					FAMILIAR Plain
mók	ø	ø	n	e	mókne (Ind/Dec)
ka	ø	ø	t	e	kate (Ret/Dec)
					FORMAL Polite
mók	ø	súp	ni	ta	móksúpnita (Ind/Dec)
mók	ø	súp	ti	ta	móksúptita (Ret/Dec)
iss	ø	úp	ni	kka	issúpnikka (Ind/Int)
ka	ass	úp	ti	ta	kassúptita (Ret/Dec)
o	ø	p	ni	ta	opnita (Ind/Dec)
o	ø	p	ti	kka	optikka (Ret/Int)
mók	ø	úp	si	ta	mókúpsita (Propos)
ka(si)	ø	p	si	o	kasipsio (Hon/Imper)

Finally, there are several different STYLE/MOOD markers. The simplest of them all, with no variant shapes, are ọ for INTIMATE and ci for CASUAL. The declarative in both the INDICATIVE and the RETROSPECTIVE is always tạ on the FORMAL level. However, in the RETROSPECTIVE, it is lạ on the FORMAL plain level. The Interrogative is kkạ on the FORMAL polite and yạ on the FORMAL plain. The Imperative and Propositive on the FORMAL polite are ọ and tạ and on the FORMAL plain ọlạ and cạ. The Declarative in the FAMILIAR is ẹ, while the Interrogative is kạ. The Imperative and Propositive in the same style are kẹ and ẹ. Since the subjunctive marker s always co-occurs with the Propositive ẹ, it will be convenient to remember the Propositive ending in the FAMILIAR as sẹ. Even when the same form is used to represent different functions, there is little danger of confusion, for they combine with other markers to keep one apart from others. See the following paradigm which illustrates all the MOOD/STYLE markers for the verb ilk 'read.'

STEM	TENSE/HON	FORMAL	ASPECT	MOOD/STYLE	FORMAL Plain
ilk	ø	ø	nún	ta	ilknúnta
ilk	ø	ø	tó	la	ilktóla
ilk	ø	ø	nún	ya	ilknúnya
ilk	ø	ø	tón	ya	ilktónya
ilk	úsi	p	ni	ta	ilkúsipnita
ilk	ø	súp	ti	ta	ilksúptita
ilk	ø	súp	ni	kka	ilksúpnikka
ilk	úsi	p	ti	kka	ilkúsiptikka
					FAMILIAR
ilk	ø	ø	n	e	ilkne
ilk	ø	ø	t	e	ilkte
ilk	úsi	ø	nún	ka	ilkúsinúnka
ilk	úsi	ø	tón	ka	ilkúsitónka
ilk	ø	ø	s	e	ilkse (Propos)

ilk	ø	ø	ø	ke	ilkke (Imper)
					FORMAL Polite
ilk	ø	úp	si	ta	ilkúpsita (Propos)
ilk	úsi	p	si	o	ilkúsipsio (Imper)
					FORMAL Plain
ilk	ø	ø	ø	ca	ilkca (Propos)
ilk	ø	ø	ø	óla	ilkóla (Imper)
					INFORMAL
ilk	ø	ø	ø	ó	ilkó (INTIMATE)
ilk	ø	ø	ø	ci	ilkci (CASUAL)

This exhausts all the elements in the inflectional categories. Regular verb stems are of two kinds, one ending in a consonant segment and the other ending in a vowel segment. Besides, there are irregular stems, which will be our next topic.

IRREGULAR VERBS

Before presenting the tables of verb conjugation, I will take a brief look at irregular verbs. A regular verb has only one uniform stem throughout the paradigm, whereas an irregular verb has alternating stem shapes, one occurring before one phonologically defineable group of suffixes and the other before another group. I will simply list the different classes of irregular verbs with a description of their characteristic features.

1. L-dropping stem. The stem-final l drops before suffixes beginning with the consonants n and s.

Ex. mal.ta: mal-ci, mal-ass-ta, mal-kess-ó but ma-n-ta instead of the
                expected *mal-nún-ta and ma-si-p-si-o instead of the
                expected *mal-úsi-p-si-o

Included in this class are: pul.ta 'to blow', al.ta 'to know', kal.ta 'to change', cwul.ta 'to decrease', phal.ta 'to sell', hól.ta 'to destroy' and so on.

2. S-dropping stem. The stem-final s̲ drops when a suffix beginning with a vowel segment is added.

Ex. cis.ta: cis-ci, cis-ke, cis-tón-ka but ci-óss-ta instead of the
    expected *cis-óss-ta and ci-óla instead of the expected
    *cis-óla

Included in this class are: is.ta 'to join', kús.ta 'to draw (a line)', cós.ta 'to stir', cwus.ta 'to pick up'. pus.ta 'to pour' and s on.

3. P~W alternating stem. The stem final p̲ changes to w̲ before a suffixes beginning with a vowel segment.

Ex. chup.ta: chup-súp-ni-ta, chup-kess-ci, chup-n-e but chuw-ó instead
    of the expected *, chup-ó, and chuw-óss-ta instead of the
    expected *chup-óss-ta

Included in this class are: tóp.ta 'to be warm', nup.ta 'to lie down', top.ta 'to help', kup.ta 'to roast' alúmtap.ta 'to be beautiful' and so on.

4. T~L alternating stem. The stem-final t̲ changes to l̲ before suffixes beginning with a vowel segment.

Ex. kót.ta: kót-nún-ta, kót-tó-la, kót-kess-n-e but kól-óla instead of
    the expected *kót-óla, and kól-óss-ta instead of the
    expected *kót-óss-ta

Included in this class are: tút.ta 'to hear', kkaetat.ta 'to realize', mut.ta 'to ask', sit.ta 'to load', put.ta 'to swell' and so on.

5. L-doubling stem. The stem final syllable lú drops the vowel and doubles the remaining l̲ before suffixes beginning with a vowel segment.

Ex. kalú.ta: kalú-p-ni-ta, kalú-ci, kalú-kess-ó but kall-ass-ta instead
    of the expected *kalú-óss-ta and kall-ala instead of the
    expected *kalú-óla

Included in this class are: kolú.ta 'to choose', nulú.ta 'to press down', calú.ta 'to cut', molú.ta 'not to know', pulú.ta 'to call' and so on.

6. Final vowel eliding stem. Some verbs have stems ending in high vowels such as ú and u which elide when a suffix beginning with ó is added.

Ex. ssú.ta: ssú-n-ta, ssú-p-ni-ta, ssú-kess-ci but ss-óla instead of the
　　　　expected *ssú-óla (or *ssw-óla) and ss-óss-tó-la instead of
　　　　the expected *ssú-óss-tó-la

phu.ta:　phu-p-ni-ta, phu-n-e, phu-kess-tón-ya but ph-óla instead of the
　　　　expected *phu-óla and ph-óss-ta instead of the expected
　　　　*phu-óss-ta

Included in this class are: kkú.ta 'extinguish', ttú.ta "to float" chilú.ta 'to
pay' and so on. Phu.ta is the only such verb whose stem vowel is u.

　7. Y inserting ha-stem. This verb stem can occur by itself as an action/
process verb. It is also used as a verb formative added to nouns and
noun-like stems to derive verbs of both action/process and description
types. Y is inserted between the stem ha and the suffix if the latter begins
with ó. The sequence hayó is contracted to hae in an ordinary speech. In
this book, the more literary hayó form is kept except in the Present
Declarative and Imperative forms of the Informal Intimate style.
Ex. ha.ta: ha-n-ta, ha-p-ni-ta, ha-tó-la but hae (<hay-ó) instead of the
　　　　expected *ha-ó and hay-óss-ta instead of the expected
　　　　*ha-óss-ta
This class has no members besides ha.

　HOW TO USE THIS BOOK MOST EFFECTIVELY
It is imperative that the reader understand how the verb conjugation
paradigms are organized in order to maximize the value of these tables.
Each table contains eight paradigms, four for the FORMAL Level and four
for the INFORMAL Level.
　Although both Plain and Polite forms of endings are provided for the
FORMAL Level, only the Plain forms for the INFORMAL Level are provided in
the paradigms. Because the Polite forms of INFORMAL Level can be derived
automatically by attaching yo at the end of the given forms, four more
paradigms can be added to the table. The following forms demonstrate how

this can be done with INFORMAL Intimate endings for the verb al.ta on
page 1:

	Plain	*Polite*
Present	al-a	al-a-yo
Past	alass-ó	alass-ó-yo
Remote Past	alassóss-ó	alassóss-ó-yo
Future	alkess-ó	alkess-ó-yo
Past Future	alasskess-ó	alasskess-ó-yo

INFORMAL Intimate and Casual endings have common moods. In other
words, they do not differentiate Declarative from Interrogative in spelling,
although different intonations are used in speech. For the FORMAL Level
and INFORMAL Familiar, four moods, Declarative, Interrogative,
Propositive, and Imperative have distinct forms and they are all listed in
the paradigm except for the Interrogative. The interrogative forms,
however, can be derived automatically by adding proper Interrogative
markers in place of the Declarative markers. The Interrogative marker is
provided side by side with the Declarative marker in the paradigm. Let us
take the FORMAL Polite Indicative paradigm as an example. The Present
tense lists the following: apni-ta/-kka. When you replace the Declarative
marker ta with the Interrogative marker kka, you derive Interrogative
forms in all the tenses.

FORMAL Polite

Indicative	*Declarative*	*Interrogative*
Present	apni-ta	apni-kka
Past	alassúpni-ta	alassúpni-kka
Remote Past	alassóssúpni-ta	alassóssúpni-kka
Future	alkessúpni-ta	alkessúpni-kka
Past Future	alasskessúpni-ta	alasskessúpni-kka

Thus, we can add six more paradigms in the Interrogative to the table.
Because honorific stems can be created automatically by adding the

honorific suffix (ú)si to a verb stem, you actually obtain thirty-six different verb conjugation paradigms for each page. The actual shape of the honorific stem is found in the Imperative form of FORMAL Polite Indicative ending: a(si)psi-o. The example below demonstrates how a new paradigm can be created using an honorifc stem in place of an ordinary stem.

INFORMAL Familiar	Ordinary stem	Honorific stem
Declarative		
Present	a-ne	a-si-ne
Past	al-ass-ne	a-si-óss-ne
Remote Past	al-assóss-n	a-si-óssóss-ne
Future	al-kess-ne	a-si-kess-ne
Past Future	al-asskess-ne	a-si-ósskess-ne

Now you are ready to turn to the table and make the maximal use of this handy reference.

AL.TA
to know, to understand

	FORMAL *Plain*	
	INDICATIVE	RETROSPECTIVE
DECLARATIVE/ *INTERROGATIVE*		
PRESENT	a-n.ta/-nùnya	al-tóla/-tónya
PAST	alass-ta	alass-tóla
REMOTE PAST	alassóss-ta	alassóss-tóla
FUTURE	alkess-ta	alkess-tóla
PAST FUTURE	alasskess-ta	alasskess-tóla
PROPOSITIVE	al-ca	
IMPERATIVE	al-ala	

	FORMAL *Polite*	
	INDICATIVE	RETROSPECTIVE
DECLARATIVE/ *INTERROGATIVE*		
PRESENT	apni-ta/-kka	apti-ta/-kka
PAST	alassùpni-ta	alassùpti-ta
REMOTE PAST	alassóssùpni-ta	alassóssùpti-ta
FUTURE	alkessùpni-ta	alkessùpti-ta
PAST FUTURE	alasskessùpni-ta	alasskessùpti-ta
PROPOSITIVE	apsi-ta	
IMPERATIVE	a(si)psi-o	

	INFORMAL *Familiar*	
	INDICATIVE	RETROSPECTIVE
DECLARATIVE/ *INTERROGATIVE*		
PRESENT	a-ne/-nùnka	al-te/-tónka
PAST	alass-ne	alass-te
REMOTE PAST	alassóss-ne	alassóss-te
FUTURE	alkess-ne	alkess-te
PAST FUTURE	alasskess-ne	alasskess-te
PROPOSITIVE	a-se	
IMPERATIVE	al-ke	

	INFORMAL *Intimate* INDICATIVE	INFORMAL *Casual* INDICATIVE
DECLARATIVE/ *INTERROGATIVE*		
PRESENT	al-a	al-ci
PAST	alass-ó	alass-ci
REMOTE PAST	alassóss-ó	alassóss-ci
FUTURE	alkess-ó	alkess-ci
PAST FUTURE	alasskess-ó	alasskess-ci
PROPOSITIVE *IMPERATIVE*	al-a	al-ci

CAUSATIVE: ALLI.TA	*PASSIVE:*
to make known, inform	

FORMAL *Plain*

	INDICATIVE	RETROSPECTIVE
DECLARATIVE/ *INTERROGATIVE*		
PRESENT	alh-nún.ta/-núnya	alh-tóla/-tónya
PAST	alhass-ta	alhass-tóla
REMOTE PAST	alhassóss-ta	alhassóss-tóla
FUTURE	alhkess-ta	alhkess-tóla
PAST FUTURE	alhasskess-ta	alhasskess-tóla

PROPOSITIVE
IMPERATIVE

FORMAL *Polite*

	INDICATIVE	RETROSPECTIVE
DECLARATIVE/ *INTERROGATIVE*		
PRESENT	alhsúpni-ta/-kka	alhsúpti-ta/-kka
PAST	alhassúpni-ta	alhassúpti-ta
REMOTE PAST	alhassóssúpni-ta	alhassóssúpti-ta
FUTURE	alhkessúpni-ta	alhkessúpti-ta
PAST FUTURE	alhasskessúpni-ta	alhasskessúpti-ta

PROPOSITIVE
IMPERATIVE

INFORMAL *Familiar*

	INDICATIVE	RETROSPECTIVE
DECLARATIVE/ *INTERROGATIVE*		
PRESENT	alh-ne/-núnka	alh-te/-tónka
PAST	alhass-ne	alhass-te
REMOTE PAST	alhassóss-ne	alhassóss-te
FUTURE	alhkess-ne	alhkess-te
PAST FUTURE	alhasskess-ne	alhasskess-te

PROPOSITIVE
IMPERATIVE

	INFORMAL *Intimate* INDICATIVE	INFORMAL *Casual* INDICATIVE
DECLARATIVE/ *INTERROGATIVE*		
PRESENT	alh-a	alh-ci
PAST	alhass-ó	alhass-ci
REMOTE PAST	alhassóss-ó	alhassóss-ci
FUTURE	alhkess-ó	alhkess-ci
PAST FUTURE	alhasskess-ó	alhasskess-ci

PROPOSITIVE
IMPERATIVE

CAUSATIVE: *PASSIVE:*

to hold (a baby, etc.) in one's arms, to embrace

FORMAL *Plain*

	INDICATIVE	RETROSPECTIVE
DECLARATIVE/ *INTERROGATIVE*		
PRESENT	an-nùn.ta/-nùnya	an-tóla/-tónya
PAST	anass-ta	anass-tóla
REMOTE PAST	anassóss-ta	anassóss-tóla
FUTURE	ankess-ta	ankess-tóla
PAST FUTURE	anasskess-ta	anasskess-tóla
PROPOSITIVE	an-ca	
IMPERATIVE	an-ala	

FORMAL *Polite*

	INDICATIVE	RETROSPECTIVE
DECLARATIVE/ *INTERROGATIVE*		
PRESENT	ansùpni-ta/-kka	ansùpti-ta/-kka
PAST	anassùpni-ta	anassùpti-ta
REMOTE PAST	anassóssùpni-ta	anassóssùpti-ta
FUTURE	ankessùpni-ta	ankessùpti-ta
PAST FUTURE	anasskessùpni-ta	anasskessùpti-ta
PROPOSITIVE	anùpsi-ta	
IMPERATIVE	anù(si)psi-o	

INFORMAL *Familiar*

	INDICATIVE	RETROSPECTIVE
DECLARATIVE/ *INTERROGATIVE*		
PRESENT	an-ne/-nùnka	an-te/-tónka
PAST	anass-ne	anass-te
REMOTE PAST	anassóss-ne	anassóss-te
FUTURE	ankess-ne	ankess-te
PAST FUTURE	anasskess-ne	anasskess-te
PROPOSITIVE	an-se	
IMPERATIVE	an-ke	

	INFORMAL *Intimate* INDICATIVE	INFORMAL *Casual* INDICATIVE
DECLARATIVE/ *INTERROGATIVE*		
PRESENT	an-a	an-ci
PAST	anass-ó	anass-ci
REMOTE PAST	anassóss-ó	anassóss-ci
FUTURE	ankess-ó	ankess-ci
PAST FUTURE	anasskess-ó	anasskess-ci
PROPOSITIVE *IMPERATIVE*	an-a	an-ci

CAUSATIVE: ANKI.TA
to let or have someone hold
in the arms

PASSIVE: ANKI.TA
to cuddle, nestle in
one's arms

to sit down, to squat   INTRANSITIVE   안다

FORMAL *Plain*

	INDICATIVE	RETROSPECTIVE
DECLARATIVE/ *INTERROGATIVE*		
PRESENT	anc-nún.ta/-núnya	anc-tóla/-tónya
PAST	ancass-ta	ancass-tóla
REMOTE PAST	ancassóss-ta	ancassóss-tóla
FUTURE	anckess-ta	anckess-tóla
PAST FUTURE	ancasskess-ta	ancasskess-tóla
PROPOSITIVE	anc-ca	
IMPERATIVE	anc-ala	

FORMAL *Polite*

	INDICATIVE	RETROSPECTIVE
DECLARATIVE/ *INTERROGATIVE*		
PRESENT	ancsúpni-ta/-kka	ancsúpti-ta/-kka
PAST	ancassúpni-ta	ancassúpti-ta
REMOTE PAST	ancassóssúpni-ta	ancassóssúpti-ta
FUTURE	anckessúpni-ta	anckessúpti-ta
PAST FUTURE	ancasskessúpni-ta	ancasskessúpti-ta
PROPOSITIVE	ancúpsi-ta	
IMPERATIVE	ancú(si)psi-o	

INFORMAL *Familiar*

	INDICATIVE	RETROSPECTIVE
DECLARATIVE/ *INTERROGATIVE*		
PRESENT	anc-ne/-núnka	anc-te/-tónka
PAST	ancass-ne	ancass-te
REMOTE PAST	ancassóss-ne	ancassóss-te
FUTURE	anckess-ne	anckess-te
PAST FUTURE	ancasskess-ne	ancasskess-te
PROPOSITIVE	anc-se	
IMPERATIVE	anc-ke	

	INFORMAL *Intimate* INDICATIVE	INFORMAL *Casual* INDICATIVE
DECLARATIVE/ *INTERROGATIVE*		
PRESENT	anc-a	anc-ci
PAST	ancass-ó	ancass-ci
REMOTE PAST	ancassóss-ó	ancassóss-ci
FUTURE	anckess-ó	anckess-ci
PAST FUTURE	ancasskess-ó	ancasskess-ci
PROPOSITIVE *IMPERATIVE*	anc-a	anc-ci

CAUSATIVE: ANCHI.TA   *PASSIVE:*
to seat,
to place (a person) in a seat

4

ANI'TA

아니다

not to be   COPULA(NEG)

FORMAL *Plain*

	INDICATIVE	RETROSPECTIVE
DECLARATIVE/		
INTERROGATIVE		
PRESENT	ani-ta/-nya	ani-tóla/-tónya
PAST	anióss-ta/-núnya	anióss-tóla
REMOTE PAST	aniόssόss-ta	aniόssόss-tόla
FUTURE	anikess-ta	anikess-tόla
PAST FUTURE	aniósskess-ta	aniósskess-tόla

PROPOSITIVE
IMPERATIVE

FORMAL *Polite*

	INDICATIVE	RETROSPECTIVE
DECLARATIVE/		
INTERROGATIVE		
PRESENT	anipni-ta/-kka	anipti-ta/-kka
PAST	anióssúpni-ta	anióssúpti-ta
REMOTE PAST	aniόssόssúpni-ta	aniόssόssúpti-ta
FUTURE	anikessúpni-ta	anikessúpti-ta
PAST FUTURE	aniósskessúpni-ta	aniósskessúpti-ta

PROPOSITIVE
IMPERATIVE

INFORMAL *Familiar*

	INDICATIVE	RETROSPECTIVE
DECLARATIVE/		
INTERROGATIVE		
PRESENT	ani-ne/-nka	ani-te/-tónka
PAST	anióss-ne/-núnka	anióss-te
REMOTE PAST	aniόssόss-ne	aniόssόss-te
FUTURE	anikess-ne	anikess-te
PAST FUTURE	aniósskess-ne	aniósskess-te

PROPOSITIVE
IMPERATIVE

	INFORMAL *Intimate*	INFORMAL *Casual*
	INDICATIVE	INDICATIVE
DECLARATIVE/		
INTERROGATIVE		
PRESENT	ani-ya	ani-ci
PAST	anióss-ό	anióss-ci
REMOTE PAST	aniόssόss-ό	aniόssόss-ci
FUTURE	anikess-ό	anikess-ci
PAST FUTURE	aniósskess-ό	aniósskess-ci

PROPOSITIVE
IMPERATIVE

CAUSATIVE: *PASSIVE:*

5

APHÙ.TA   아프다
to be painful, to be sore, to feel a pain   DESCRIPTIVE

FORMAL *Plain*

	INDICATIVE	RETROSPECTIVE
DECLARATIVE/ *INTERROGATIVE*		
PRESENT	aphù-ta/-nya	aphù-tóla/-tònya
PAST	aphass-ta/-nùnya	aphass-tóla
REMOTE PAST	aphassóss-ta	aphassóss-tóla
FUTURE	aphùkess-ta	aphùkess-tóla
PAST FUTURE	aphasskess-ta	aphasskess-tóla

PROPOSITIVE
IMPERATIVE

FORMAL *Polite*

	INDICATIVE	RETROSPECTIVE
DECLARATIVE/ *INTERROGATIVE*		
PRESENT	aphùpni-ta/-kka	aphùpti-ta/-kka
PAST	aphassùpni-ta	aphassùpti-ta
REMOTE PAST	aphassóssùpni-ta	aphassóssùpti-ta
FUTURE	aphùkessùpni-ta	aphùkessùpti-ta
PAST FUTURE	aphasskessùpni-ta	aphasskessùpti-ta

PROPOSITIVE
IMPERATIVE

INFORMAC *Familiar*

	INDICATIVE	RETROSPECTIVE
DECLARATIVE/ *INTERROGATIVE*		
PRESENT	aphù-ne/-ùnka	aphù-te/-tònka
PAST	aphass-ne/-nùnka	aphass-te
REMOTE PAST	aphassóss-ne	aphassóss-te
FUTURE	aphùkess-ne	aphùkess-te
PAST FUTURE	aphasskess-ne	aphasskess-te

PROPOSITIVE
IMPERATIVE

	INFORMAL *Intimate* INDICATIVE	INFORMAL *Casual* INDICATIVE
DECLARATIVE/ *INTERROGATIVE*		
PRESENT	aph-a	aphù-ci
PAST	aphass-ó	aphass-ci
REMOTE PAST	aphassóss-ó	aphassóss-ci
FUTURE	aphùkess-ó	aphùkess-ci
PAST FUTURE	aphasskess-ó	aphasskess-ci

PROPOSITIVE
IMPERATIVE

CAUSATIVE: *PASSIVE:*

to miss, to feel the lack of   DESCRIPTIVE

FORMAL *Plain*

	INDICATIVE	RETROSPECTIVE
DECLARATIVE/ *INTERROGATIVE*		
PRESENT	aswi-p.ta/-unya	aswip-tóla/-tònya
PAST	aswiwóss-ta/-núnya	aswiwóss-tóla
REMOTE PAST	aswiwóssóss-ta	aswiwóssóss-tóla
FUTURE	aswipkess-ta	aswipkess-tóla
PAST FUTURE	aswiwósskess-ta	aswiwósskess-tóla

PROPOSITIVE
IMPERATIVE

FORMAL *Polite*

	INDICATIVE	RETROSPECTIVE
DECLARATIVE/ *INTERROGATIVE*		
PRESENT	aswipsúpni-ta/-kka	aswipsúpti-ta/-kka
PAST	aswiwóssúpni-ta	aswiwóssúpti-ta
REMOTE PAST	aswiwóssóssúpni-ta	aswiwóssóssúpti-ta
FUTURE	aswipkessúpni-ta	aswipkessúpti-ta
PAST FUTURE	aswiwósskessúpni-ta	aswiwósskessúpti-ta

PROPOSITIVE
IMPERATIVE

INFORMAL *Familiar*

	INDICATIVE	RETROSPECTIVE
DECLARATIVE/ *INTERROGATIVE*		
PRESENT	aswi-p.ne/-unka	aswip-te/-tónka
PAST	aswiwóss-ne/-núnka	aswióss-te
REMOTE PAST	aswiwóssóss-ne	aswióssóss-te
FUTURE	aswipkess-ne	aswipkess-te
PAST FUTURE	aswiwósskess-ne	aswiósskess-te

PROPOSITIVE
IMPERATIVE

	INFORMAL *Intimate* INDICATIVE	INFORMAL *Casual* INDICATIVE
DECLARATIVE/ *INTERROGATIVE*		
PRESENT	aswiw-ó	aswip-ci
PAST	aswiwóss-ó	aswiwóss-ci
REMOTE PAST	aswiwóssóss-ó	aswiwóssóss-ci
FUTURE	aswipkess-ó	aswipkess-ci
PAST FUTURE	aswiwósskess-ó	aswiwósskess-ci

PROPOSITIVE
IMPERATIVE

CAUSATIVE: *PASSIVE:*

CA.TA   지다
to sleep   INTRANSITIVE

<hr>

FORMAL Plain

	INDICATIVE	RETROSPECTIVE
DECLARATIVE/		
INTERROGATIVE		
PRESENT	ca-n.ta/-núnya	ca-tóla/-tónya
PAST	cass-ta	cass-tóla
REMOTE PAST	cassóss-ta	cassóss-tóla
FUTURE	cakess-ta	cakess-tóla
PAST FUTURE	casskess-ta	casskess-tóla
PROPOSITIVE	ca-ca	
IMPERATIVE	ca-la ~ ca-kóla	

FORMAL Polite

	INDICATIVE	RETROSPECTIVE
DECLARATIVE/		
INTERROGATIVE		
PRESENT	capni-ta/-kka	capti-ta/-kka
PAST	cassúpni-ta	cassúpti-ta
REMOTE PAST	cassóssúpni-ta	cassóssúpti-ta
FUTURE	cakessúpni-ta	cakessúpti-ta
PAST FUTURE	casskessúpni-ta	casskessúpti-ta
PROPOSITIVE	capsi-ta	
IMPERATIVE	ca(si)psi-o	

INFORMAL Familiar

	INDICATIVE	RETROSPECTIVE
DECLARATIVE/		
INTERROGATIVE		
PRESENT	ca-ne/-núnka	ca-te/-tónka
PAST	cass-ne	cass-te
REMOTE PAST	cassóss-ne	cassóss-te
FUTURE	cakess-ne	cakess-te
PAST FUTURE	casskess-ne	casskess-te
PROPOSITIVE	ca-se	
IMPERATIVE	ca-ke	

	INFORMAL Intimate INDICATIVE	INFORMAL Casual INDICATIVE
DECLARATIVE/		
INTERROGATIVE		
PRESENT	ca	ca-ci
PAST	cass-ó	cass-ci
REMOTE PAST	cassóssó	cassóss-ci
FUTURE	cakess-ó	cakess-ci
PAST FUTURE	casskess-ó	casskes-ci
PROPOSITIVE	ca	ca-ci
IMPERATIVE		

<hr>

CAUSATIVE: CAEU.TA   *PASSIVE:*
           to put (a person) to sleep

FORMAL *Plain*		
	INDICATIVE	RETROSPECTIVE
DECLARATIVE/ INTERROGATIVE		
PRESENT	calú-n.ta/-núnya	calú-tóla/-tónya
PAST	callass-ta	callass-tóla
REMOTE PAST	callassóss-ta	callassóss-tóla
FUTURE	calúkess-ta	calúkess-tóla
PAST FUTURE	callasskess-ta	callasskess-tóla
PROPOSITIVE	calú-ca	
IMPERATIVE	call-ala	

FORMAL *Polite*		
	INDICATIVE	RETROSPECTIVE
DECLARATIVE/ INTERROGATIVE		
PRESENT	calúpni-ta/-kka	calúpti-ta/-kka
PAST	callassúpni-ta	callassúpti-ta
REMOTE PAST	callassóssúpni-ta	callassóssúpti-ta
FUTURE	calúkessúpni-ta	calúkessúpti-ta
PAST FUTURE	callasskessúpni-ta	callasskessúpti-ta
PROPOSITIVE	calúpsi-ta	
IMPERATIVE	calú(si)psi-o	

INFORMAL *Familiar*		
	INDICATIVE	RETROSPECTIVE
DECLARATIVE/ INTERROGATIVE		
PRESENT	calú-ne/-núnka	calú-te/tónka
PAST	callass-ne	callass-te
REMOTE PAST	callassóss-ne	callassóss-te
FUTURE	calúkess-ne	calúkess-te
PAST FUTURE	callasskess-ne	callasskess-te
PROPOSITIVE	calú-se	
IMPERATIVE	calú-ke	

	INFORMAL *Intimate* INDICATIVE	INFORMAL *Casual* INDICATIVE
DECLARATIVE/ INTERROGATIVE		
PRESENT	call-a	calú-ci
PAST	callass-ó	callass-ci
REMOTE PAST	callassóss-ó	callassóss-ci
FUTURE	calúkess-ó	calúkess-ci
PAST FUTURE	càllasskess-ó	callasskess-ci
PROPOSITIVE *IMPERATIVE*	call-a	calú-ci

CAUSATIVE: *PASSIVE:* CALLI.TA
to be cut

	FORMAL *Plain*	
	INDICATIVE	RETROSPECTIVE
DECLARATIVE/		
INTERROGATIVE		
PRESENT	capsusi-n.ta/-núnya	capsusi-tóla/-tónya
PAST	capsusióss-ta	capsusióss-tóla
REMOTE PAST	capsusióssóss-ta	capsusióssóss-tóla
FUTURE	capsusikess-ta	capsusikess-tóla
PAST FUTURE	capsusiósskess-ta	capsusiósskess-tóla

PROPOSITIVE
IMPERATIVE

	FORMAL *Polite*	
	INDICATIVE	RETROSPECTIVE
DECLARATIVE/		
INTERROGATIVE		
PRESENT	capsusipni-ta/-kka	capsusipti-ta/-kka
PAST	capsusióssúpni-ta	capsusióssúpti-ta
REMOTE PAST	capsusióssóssúpni-ta	capsusióssóssúpti-ta
FUTURE	capsusikessúpni-ta	capsusikessúpti-ta
PAST FUTURE	capsusiósskessúpni-ta	capsusiósskessúpti-ta
PROPOSITIVE	capsusipsi-ta	
IMPERATIVE	capusipsi-o	

	INFORMAL *Familiar*	
	INDICATIVE	RETROSPECTIVE
DECLARATIVE/		
INTERROGATIVE		
PRESENT	capsusi-ne/-núnka	capsusi-te/-tónka
PAST	capsusióss-ne	capsusióss-te
REMOTE PAST	capsusióssóss-ne	capsusióssóss-te
FUTURE	capsusikess-ne	capsusikess-te
PAST FUTURE	capsusiósskess-ne	capsusiósskess-te

PROPOSITIVE
IMPERATIVE

	INFORMAL *Intimate*	INFORMAL *Casual*
	INDICATIVE	INDICATIVE
DECLARATIVE/		
INTERROGATIVE		
PRESENT	capsusi-ó	capsusi-ci
PAST	capsusióss-ó	capsusióss-ci
REMOTE PAST	capsusióssóss-ó	capsusióssóss-ci
FUTURE	capsusikess-ó	capsusikess-ci
PAST FUTURE	capsusiósskess-ó	capsusiósskess-ci
PROPOSITIVE *IMPERATIVE*	capsusi-ó	capsusi-ci

CAUSATIVE: PASSIVE:

CI.TA   지다
1) to carry on the back, to bear TRANSITIVE   2) to lose, to be defeated INTRANSITIVE

FORMAL *Plain*

	INDICATIVE	RETROSPECTIVE
DECLARATIVE/ INTERROGATIVE		
PRESENT	cin-n.ta/-núnya	ci-tóla/-tónya
PAST	cyóss-ta	cyóss-tóla
REMOTE PAST	cyóssóss-ta	cyóssóss-tóla
FUTURE	cikess-ta	cikess-tóla
PAST FUTURE	cyósskess-ta	cyósskess-tóla
PROPOSITIVE	ci-ca	
IMPERATIVE	cy-ó.la	

FORMAL *Polite*

	INDICATIVE	RETROSPECTIVE
DECLARATIVE/ INTERROGATIVE		
PRESENT	cipni-ta/-kka	cipti-ta/-kka
PAST	cyóssúpni-ta	cyóssúpti-ta
REMOTE PAST	cyóssóssúpni-ta	cyóssóssúpti-ta
FUTURE	cikessúpni-ta	cikessúpti-ta
PAST FUTURE	cyósskessúpni-ta	cyósskessúpti-ta
PROPOSITIVE	cipsi-ta	
IMPERATIVE	ci(si)psi-o	

INFORMAL *Familiar*

	INDICATIVE	RETROSPECTIVE
DECLARATIVE/ INTERROGATIVE		
PRESENT	ci-ne/-núnka	ci-te/-tónka
PAST	cyóss-ne	cyóss-te
REMOTE PAST	cyóssóss-ne	cyóssóss-te
FUTURE	cikess-ne	cikess-te
PAST FUTURE	cyósskess-ne	cyósskess-te
PROPOSITIVE	ci-se	
IMPERATIVE	ci-ke	

	INFORMAL *Intimate* INDICATIVE	INFORMAL *Casual* INDICATIVE
DECLARATIVE/ INTERROGATIVE		
PRESENT	cy-ó	ci-ci
PAST	cyóss-ó	cyóss-ci
REMOTE PAST	cyóssóss-ó	cyóssóss-ci
FUTURE	cikess-ó	cikess-ci
PAST FUTURE	cyósskess-ó	cyósskess-ci
PROPOSITIVE		
IMPERATIVE	cy-ó	ci-ci

CAUSATIVE: CIU.TA   *PASSIVE:*
         1) to make a person carry on
            his back, 2) to defeat
*Like CI.TA are KKOKKO-CITA, NOMO-CITA, PULO-CITA, SSULO-CITA, etc.

11

CIS.TA   짓다
to make, to fashion, to build

FORMAL *Plain*

DECLARATIVE/ *INTERROGATIVE*	INDICATIVE	RETROSPECTIVE
PRESENT	cis-nún.ta/-núnya	cis-tóla/-tònya
PAST	cióss-ta	cióss-tóla
REMOTE PAST	cióssóss-ta	cióssóss-tóla
FUTURE	ciskess-ta	ciskess-tóla
PAST FUTURE	ciósskess-ta	ciósskess-tóla
PROPOSITIVE	cis-ca	
IMPERATIVE	ci-óla	

FORMAL *Polite*

DECLARATIVE/ *INTERROGATIVE*	INDICATIVE	RETROSPECTIVE
PRESENT	cissúpni-ta/-kka	cissúpti-ta/-kka
PAST	cióssúpni-ta	cióssúpti-ta
REMOTE PAST	cióssóssúpni-ta	cióssóssúpti-ta
FUTURE	ciskessúpni-ta	ciskessúpti-ta
PAST FUTURE	ciósskessúpni-ta	ciósskessúpti-ta
PROPOSITIVE	ciúpsi-ta	
IMPERATIVE	ciú(si)spi-o	

INFORMAL *Familiar*

DECLARATIVE/ *INTERROGATIVE*	INDICATIVE	RETROSPECTIVE
PRESENT	cis-ne/-núnka	cis-te/-tònka
PAST	cióss-ne	cióss-te
REMOTE PAST	cióssóss-ne	cióssóss-te
FUTURE	ciskess-ne	ciskess-te
PAST FUTURE	ciósskess-ne	ciósskess-te
PROPOSITIVE	cis-se	
IMPERATIVE	cis-ke	

DECLARATIVE/ *INTERROGATIVE*	INFORMAL *Intimate* INDICATIVE	INFORMAL *Casual* INDICATIVE
PRESENT	ci-ó	cis-ci
PAST	cióss-ó	cióss-ci
REMOTE PAST	cióssóss-ó	cióssóss-ci
FUTURE	ciskess-ó	ciskess-ci
PAST FUTURE	ciósskess-ó	ciósskess-ci
PROPOSITIVE *IMPERATIVE*	ci-ó	cis-ci

CAUSATIVE: *PASSIVE:*

to be good, fine   DESCRIPTIVE

FORMAL *Plain*

	INDICATIVE	RETROSPECTIVE
DECLARATIVE/ *INTERROGATIVE*		
PRESENT	coh-ta/-únya	coh-tóla/-tónya
PAST	cohass-ta/-núnya	cohass-tóla
REMOTE PAST	cohassóss-ta	cohassóss-tola
FUTURE	cohkess-ta	cohkess-tóla
PAST FUTURE	cohasskess-ta	cohasskess-tóla

PROPOSITIVE
IMPERATIVE

FORMAL *Polite*

	INDICATIVE	RETROSPECTIVE
DECLARATIVE/ *INTERROGATIVE*		
PRESENT	cohsúpni-ta/-kka	cohsúpti-ta/-kka
PAST	cohassúpni-ta	cohassúpti-ta
REMOTE PAST	cohassóssúpni-ta	cohassóssúpti-ta
FUTURE	cohkessúpni-ta	cohkessúpti-ta
PAST FUTURE	cohasskessúpni-ta	cohasskessúpti-ta

PROPOSITIVE
IMPERATIVE

INFORMAL *Familiar*

	INDICATIVE	RETROSPECTIVE
DECLARATIVE/ *INTERROGATIVE*		
PRESENT	coh-ne/-únka	coh-te/-tónka
PAST	cohass-ne/-núnka	cohass-te
REMOTE PAST	cohassóss-ne	cohassóss-te
FUTURE	cohkess-ne	cohkess-te
PAST FUTURE	cohasskess-ne	cohasskess-te

PROPOSITIVE
IMPERATIVE

	INFORMAL *Intimate* INDICATIVE	INFORMAL *Casual* INDICATIVE
DECLARATIVE/ *INTERROGATIVE*		
PRESENT	coh-a	coh-ci
PAST	cohass-ó	cohass-ci
REMOTE PAST	cohassóss-ó	cohassóss-ci
FUTURE	cohkess-ó	cohkess-ci
PAST FUTURE	cohasskess-ó	cohasskess-ci

PROPOSITIVE
IMPERATIVE

CAUSATIVE: *PASSIVE:*

to tighten, to strangle, to press (someone) about (something)

FORMAL *Plain*

	INDICATIVE	RETROSPECTIVE
DECLARATIVE/ *INTERROGATIVE*		
PRESENT	colú-n.ta/-núnya	colú-tóla/-tónya
PAST	collass-ta	collass-tóla
REMOTE PAST	collassóss-ta	collassóss-tóla
FUTURE	colúkess-ta	colúkess-tóla
PAST FUTURE	collasskess-ta	collasskess-tóla
PROPOSITIVE	colú-ca	
IMPERATIVE	coll-ala	

FORMAL *Polite*

	INDICATIVE	RETROSPECTIVE
DECLARATIVE/ *INTERROGATIVE*		
PRESENT	colúpni-ta/-kka	colúpti-ta/-kka
PAST	collassúpni-ta	collassúpti-ta
REMOTE PAST	collassóssúpni-ta	collassóssúpti-ta
FUTURE	colúkessúpni-ta	colúkessúpti-ta
PAST FUTURE	collasskessúpni-ta	collasskessúpti-ta
PROPOSITIVE	çolúpsi-ta	
IMPERATIVE	colú(si)psi-o	

INFORMAL *Familiar*

	INDICATIVE	RETROSPECTIVE
DECLARATIVE/ *INTERROGATIVE*		
PRESENT	colú-ne/-núnka	colú-te/-tónka
PAST	collas-ne	collass-te
REMOTE PAST	collassóss-ne	collassóss-te
FUTURE	colúkess-ne	colúkess-te
PAST FUTURE	collasskess-ne	collasskess-te
PROPOSITIVE	colú-se	
IMPERATIVE	colú-ke	

	INFORMAL *Intimate* INDICATIVE	INFORMAL *Casual* INDICATIVE
DECLARATIVE/ *INTERROGATIVE*		
PRESENT	coll-a	colú-ci
PAST	collass-ó	collass-ci
REMOTE PAST	collassóss-ó	collassóss-ci
FUTURE	colúkess-o	colúkess-ci
PAST FUTURE	collasskess-ó	collasskess-ci
PROPOSITIVE *IMPERATIVE*	coll-a	colú-ci

CAUSATIVE:

PASSIVE: COLLI.TA
to get tightened,
to get pestered

FORMAL *Plain*

	INDICATIVE	RETROSPECTIVE
DECLARATIVE/ *INTERROGATIVE*		
PRESENT	cók-ta/-únya	cók-tóla/-tónya
PAST	cókóss-ta/-núnya	cókóss-tóla
REMOTE PAST	cókóssóss-ta	cókóssóss-tóla
FUTURE	cókkess-ta	cókkess-tóla
PAST FUTURE	cókósskess-ta	cókósskess-tóla

PROPOSITIVE
IMPERATIVE

FORMAL *Polite*

	INDICATIVE	RETROSPECTIVE
DECLARATIVE/ *INTERROGATIVE*		
PRESENT	cóksúpni-ta/-kka	cóksúpti-ta/-kka
PAST	cókóssúpni-ta	cókóssúpti-ta
REMOTE PAST	cókóssóssúpni-ta	cókóssóssúpti-ta
FUTURE	cókkessúpni-ta	cókkessúpti-ta
PAST FUTURE	cókósskessúpni-ta	cókósskessúpti-ta

PROPOSITIVE
IMPERATIVE

INFORMAL *Familiar*

	INDICATIVE	RETROSPECTIVE
DECLARATIVE/ *INTERROGATIVE*		
PRESENT	cók-ne/-únka	cók-te/-tónka
PAST	cókóss-ne/-núnka	cókóss-te
REMOTE PAST	cókóssóss-ne	cókóssóss-te
FUTURE	cókkess-ne	cókkess-te
PAST FUTURE	cókósskess-ne	cókósskess-te

PROPOSITIVE
IMPERATIVE

	INFORMAL *Intimate* INDICATIVE	INFORMAL *Casual* INDICATIVE
DECLARATIVE/ *INTERROGATIVE*		
PRESENT	cók-ó	cók-ci
PAST	cókóss-ó	cókóss-ci
REMOTE PAST	cókóssóss-ó	cókóssóss-ci
FUTURE	cókkess-ó	cókkess-ci
PAST FUTURE	cókósskess-ó	cókósskess-ci

PROPOSITIVE
IMPERATIVE

CAUSATIVE: *PASSIVE:*

FORMAL *Plain*

	INDICATIVE	RETROSPECTIVE
DECLARATIVE/ *INTERROGATIVE*		
PRESENT	còk-nún.ta/-núnya	còk-tóla/-tónya
PAST	còkòss-ta	còkòss-tóla
REMOTE PAST	còkòssòss-ta	còkòssòss-tóla
FUTURE	còkkess-ta	còkkess-tóla
PAST FUTURE	còkòsskess-ta	còkòsskess-tóla
PROPOSITIVE	còk-ca	
IMPERATIVE	còk-óla	

FORMAL *Polite*

	INDICATIVE	RETROSPECTIVE
DECLARATIVE/ *INTERROGATIVE*		
PRESENT	còksúpni-ta/-kka	còksúpti-ta/-kka
PAST	còkòssúpni-ta	còkòssúpti-ta
REMOTE PAST	còkòssòssúpni-ta	còkòssòssúpti-ta
FUTURE	còkkessúpni-ta	còkkessúpti-ta
PAST FUTURE	còkòsskessúpni-ta	còkòsskessúpti-ta
PROPOSITIVE	còkúpsi-ta	
IMPERATIVE	còkù(si)psi-o	

INFORMAL *Familiar*

	INDICATIVE	RETROSPECTIVE
DECLARATIVE/ *INTERROGATIVE*		
PRESENT	còk-ne/-núnka	còk-te/-tónka
PAST	còkòss-ne	còkòss-te
REMOTE PAST	còkòssòss-ne	còkòssòss-te
FUTURE	còkkess-ne	còkkess-te
PAST FUTURE	còkòsskess-ne	còkòsskess-te
PROPOSITIVE	còk-se	
IMPERATIVE	còk-ke	

	INFORMAL *Intimate* INDICATIVE	INFORMAL *Casual* INDICATIVE
DECLARATIVE/ *INTERROGATIVE*		
PRESENT	còk-ó	còk-ci
PAST	còkòss-ó	còkòss-ci
REMOTE PAST	còkòssòss-ó	còkòssòss-ci
FUTURE	còkkess-ó	còkkess-ci
PAST FUTURE	còkòsskess-ó	còkòsskess-ci
PROPOSITIVE *IMPERATIVE*	còk-ó	còk-ci

CAUSATIVE:	*PASSIVE:* CÒKHI.TA to be written

FORMAL *Plain*

	INDICATIVE	RETROSPECTIVE
DECLARATIVE/ *INTERROGATIVE*		
PRESENT	cólm-ta/-únya	cólm-tóla/-tónya
PAST	cólmóss-ta/-núnya	cólmóss-tóla
REMOTE PAST	cólmóssóss-ta	cólmóssóss-tóla
FUTURE	cólmkess-ta	cólmkess-tóla
PAST FUTURE	cólmósskess-ta	cólmósskess-tóla

PROPOSITIVE
IMPERATIVE

FORMAL *Polite*

	INDICATIVE	RETROSPECTIVE
DECLARATIVE/ *INTERROGATIVE*		
PRESENT	cólmsúpni-ta/-kka	cólmsúpti-ta/-kka
PAST	cólmóssúpni-ta	cólmóssúpti-ta
REMOTE PAST	cólmóssóssúpni-ta	cólmóssóssúpti-ta
FUTURE	cólmkessúpni-ta	cólmkessúpti-ta
PAST FUTURE	cólmósskessúpni-ta	cólmósskessúpti-ta

PROPOSITIVE
IMPERATIVE

INFORMAL *Familiar*

	INDICATIVE	RETROSPECTIVE
DECLARATIVE/ *INTERROGATIVE*		
PRESENT	cólm-ne/-únka	cólm-te/-tónka
PAST	cólmóss-ne/-núnka	cólmóss-te
REMOTE PAST	cólmóssóss-ne	cólmóssóss-te
FUTURE	cólmkess-ne	cólmkess-te
PAST FUTURE	cólmósskess-ne	cólmósskess-te

PROPOSITIVE
IMPERATIVE

	INFORMAL *Intimate* INDICATIVE	INFORMAL *Casual* INDICATIVE
DECLARATIVE/ *INTERROGATIVE*		
PRESENT	cólm-ó	cólm-ci
PAST	cólmóss-ó	cólmóss-ci
REMOTE PAST	cólmóssóss-ó	cólmóssóss-ci
FUTURE	cólmkess-ó	cólmkess-ci
PAST FUTURE	cólmósskess-ó	cólmósskess-ci

PROPOSITIVE
IMPERATIVE

CAUSATIVE: *PASSIVE:*

FORMAL *Plain*

	INDICATIVE	RETROSPECTIVE
DECLARATIVE/ *INTERROGATIVE*		
PRESENT	cómcanh-ta/-únya	cómcanh-tóla/-tónya
PAST	cómcanhass-ta/-núnya	cómcanhass-tóla
REMOTE PAST	cómcanhassóss-ta	cómcanhassóss-tóla
FUTURE	cómcanhkess-ta	cómcanhkess-tóla
PAST FUTURE	cómcanhasskess-ta	cómcanhasskess-tóla

PROPOSITIVE
IMPERATIVE

FORMAL *Polite*

	INDICATIVE	RETROSPECTIVE
DECLARATIVE/ *INTERROGATIVE*		
PRESENT	cómcanhsúpni-ta/-kka	cómcanhsúpti-ta/-kka
PAST	cómcanhassúpni-ta	cómcanhassúpti-ta
REMOTE PAST	cómcanhassóssúpni-ta	cómcanhassóssúpti-ta
FUTURE	cómcanhkessúpni-ta	cómcanhkessúpti-ta
PAST FUTURE	cómcanhasskessúpni-ta	cómcanhasskessúpti-ta

PROPOSITIVE
IMPERATIVE

INFORMAL *Familiar*

	INDICATIVE	RETROSPECTIVE
DECLARATIVE/ *INTERROGATIVE*		
PRESENT	cómcanh-ne/-únka	cómcanh-te/-tónka
PAST	cómcanhass-ne/-núnka	cómcanhass-te
REMOTE PAST	cómcanhassóss-ne	cómcanhassóss-te
FUTURE	cómcanhkess-ne	cómcanhkess-te
PAST FUTURE	cómcanhasskess-ne	cómcanhasskess-te

PROPOSITIVE
IMPERATIVE

	INFORMAL *Intimate* INDICATIVE	INFORMAL *Casual* INDICATIVE
DECLARATIVE/ *INTERROGATIVE*		
PRESENT	cómcanh -a	cómcanh-ci
PAST	cómcanhass-ó	cómcanhass-ci
REMOTE PAST	cómcanhassóss-ó	cómcanhassóss-ci
FUTURE	cómcanhkess-ó	cómcanhkess-ci
PAST FUTURE	cómcanhasskess-ó	cómcanhasskess-ci

PROPOSITIVE
IMPERATIVE

CAUSATIVE: *PASSIVE:*

FORMAL *Plain*

	INDICATIVE	RETROSPECTIVE
DECLARATIVE/ *INTERROGATIVE*		
PRESENT	cós-nán.ta/-nánya	cós-tóla/-tónya
PAST	cóss-ta	cóss-tóla
REMOTE PAST	cóssóss-ta	cóssóss-tóla
FUTURE	cóskess-ta	cóskess-tóla
PAST FUTURE	cósskess-ta	cósskess-tóla
PROPOSITIVE	cós-ca	
IMPERATIVE	có-óla	

FORMAL *Polite*

	INDICATIVE	RETROSPECTIVE
DECLARATIVE/ *INTERROGATIVE*		
PRESENT	cós.súpni-ta/-kka	cós.súpti-ta/-kka
PAST	cóssúpni-ta	cóssúpti-ta
REMOTE PAST	cóssóssúpni-ta	cóssóssúpti-ta
FUTURE	cóskessúpni-ta	cóskessúpti-ta
PAST FUTURE	cósskessúpni-ta	cósskessúpti-ta
PROPOSITIVE	cóúpsi-ta	
IMPERATIVE	cóú(si)psi-o	

INFORMAL *Familiar*

	INDICATIVE	RETROSPECTIVE
DECLARATIVE/ *INTERROGATIVE*		
PRESENT	cós-ne/-nánka	cós-te/-tónka
PAST	cóss-ne	cóss-te
REMOTE PAST	cóssóss-ne	cóssóss-te
FUTURE	cóskess-ne	cóskess-te
PAST FUTURE	cósskess-ne	cósskess-te
PROPOSITIVE	cós-se	
IMPERATIVE	cós-ke	

	INFORMAL *Intimate* INDICATIVE	INFORMAL *Casual* INDICATIVE
DECLARATIVE/ *INTERROGATIVE*		
PRESENT	có	cós-ci
PAST	cóss-ó	cóss-ci
REMOTE PAST	cóssóss-ó	cóssóss-ci
FUTURE	cóskess-ó	cóskess-ci
PAST FUTURE	cósskess-ó	cósskess-ci
PROPOSITIVE *IMPERATIVE*	có	cós-ci

CAUSATIVE: *PASSIVE:*

CUK.TA   죽다
to die   INTRANSITIVE

FORMAL *Plain*

	INDICATIVE	RETROSPECTIVE
DECLARATIVE/ *INTERROGATIVE*		
PRESENT	cuk-nún.ta/-núnya	cuk-tóla/-tónya
PAST	cukóss-ta	cukóss-tóla
REMOTE PAST	cukóssóss-ta	cukóssóss-tóla
FUTURE	cukkess-ta	cukkess-tóla
PAST FUTURE	cukósskess-ta	cukósskess-tóla
PROPOSITIVE	cuk-ca	
IMPERATIVE	cuk-óla	

FORMAL *Polite*

	INDICATIVE	RETROSPECTIVE
DECLARATIVE/ *INTERROGATIVE*		
PRESENT	cuksúpni-ta/-kka	cuksúpti-ta/-kka
PAST	cukóssúpni-ta	cukóssúpti-ta
REMOTE PAST	cukóssóssúpni-ta	cukóssóssúpti-ta
FUTURE	cukkessúpni-ta	cukkessúpti-ta
PAST FUTURE	cukósskessúpni-ta	cukósskessúpti-ta
PROPOSITIVE	cukúpsita	
IMPERATIVE	cukú(si)psi-o	

INFORMAL *Familiar*

	INDICATIVE	RETROSPECTIVE
DECLARATIVE/ *INTERROGATIVE*		
PRESENT	cuk-ne/-núnka	cuk-te/-tónka
PAST	cukóss-ne	cukóss-te
REMOTE PAST	cukóssóss-ne	cukóssóss-te
FUTURE	cukkess-ne	cukkess-te
PAST FUTURE	cukósskess-ne	cukósskess-te
PROPOSITIVE	cuk-se	
IMPERATIVE	cuk-ke	

	INFORMAL *Intimate* INDICATIVE	INFORMAL *Casual* INDICATIVE
DECLARATIVE/ *INTERROGATIVE*		
PRESENT	cuk-ó	cuk-ci
PAST	cukóss-ó	cukóss-ci
REMOTE PAST	cukóssóss-ó	cukóssóss-ci
FUTURE	cukkess-ó	cukkess-ci
PAST FUTURE	cukósskess-ó	cukósskess-ci
PROPOSITIVE *IMPERATIVE*	cuk-ó	cuk-ci

CAUSATIVE: CUKI.TA   *PASSIVE:*
                 to kill

FORMAL *Plain*

	INDICATIVE	RETROSPECTIVE
DECLARATIVE/ *INTERROGATIVE*		
PRESENT	cu-n.ta/-núnya	cul-tóla/-tónya
PAST	culóss-ta	culóss-tóla
REMOTE PAST	culóssóss-ta	culóssóss-tóla
FUTURE	culkess-ta	culkes-tóla
PAST FUTURE	culósskess-ta	culósskess-tóla

PROPOSITIVE
IMPERATIVE

FORMAL *Polite*

	INDICATIVE	RETROSPECTIVE
DECLARATIVE/ *INTERROGATIVE*		
PRESENT	cupni-ta/-kka	cupti-ta/-kka
PAST	culóssúpni-ta	culóssúpti-ta
REMOTE PAST	culóssóssúpni-ta	culóssóssúpti-ta
FUTURE	culkessúpni-ta	culkessúpti-ta
PAST FUTURE	culósskessúpni-ta	culósskessúpti-ta

PROPOSITIVE
IMPERATIVE

INFORMAL *Familiar*

	INDICATIVE	RETROSPECTIVE
DECLARATIVE/ *INTERROGATIVE*		
PRESENT	cu-ne/-núnka	cul-te/-tónka
PAST	culóss-ne	culóss-te
REMOTE PAST	culóssóss-ne	culóssóss-te
FUTURE	culkess-ne	culkess-te
PAST FUTURE	culósskess-ne	culósskess-te

PROPOSITIVE
IMPERATIVE

	INFORMAL *Intimate* INDICATIVE	INFORMAL *Casual* INDICATIVE
DECLARATIVE/ *INTERROGATIVE*		
PRESENT	cul-ó	cul-ci
PAST	culóss-ó	culóss-ci
REMOTE PAST	culóssóss-ó	culóssóss-ci
FUTURE	culkess-ó	culkess-ci
PAST FUTURE	culósskess-ó	culósskess-ci

PROPOSITIVE
IMPERATIVE

CAUSATIVE: CULI.TA   *PASSIVE:*
                   to reduce, to decrease
                   to shorten

FORMAL *Plain*

	INDICATIVE	RETROSPECTIVE
DECLARATIVE/ *INTERROGATIVE*		
PRESENT	cup-nṹn.ta/-nṹnya	cup-tóla/-tónya
PAST	cuwóss-ta	cuwóss-tóla
REMOTE PAST	cuwóssóss-ta	cuwóssóss-tóla
FUTURE	cupkess-ta	cupkess-tóla
PAST FUTURE	cuwósskess-ta	cuwósskess-tóla
PROPOSITIVE	cup-ca	
IMPERATIVE	cuw-ó.la	

FORMAL *Polite*

	INDICATIVE	RETROSPECTIVE
DECLARATIVE/ *INTERROGATIVE*		
PRESENT	cupsṹpni-ta/-kka	cupsṹpti-ta/-kka
PAST	cuwóssṹpni-ta	cuwóssṹpti-ta
REMOTE PAST	cuwóssóssṹpni-ta	cuwóssóssṹpti-ta
FUTURE	cupkessṹpni-ta	cupkessṹpti-ta
PAST FUTURE	cuwósskessṹpni-ta	cuwósskessṹpti-ta
PROPOSITIVE	cuupsi-ta	
IMPERATIVE	cuu(si)psi-o	

INFORMAL *Familiar*

	INDICATIVE	RETROSPECTIVE
DECLARATIVE/ *INTERROGATIVE*		
PRESENT	cup-ne/-nṹnka	cup-te/-tónka
PAST	cuwóss-ne	cuwóss-te
REMOTE PAST	cuwóssóss-ne	cuwóssóss-te
FUTURE	cupkess-ne	cupkess-te
PAST FUTURE	cuwósskess-ne	cuwósskess-te
PROPOSITIVE	cup-se	
IMPERATIVE	cup-ke	

	INFORMAL *Intimate* INDICATIVE	INFORMAL *Casual* INDICATIVE
DECLARATIVE/ *INTERROGATIVE*		
PRESENT	cuw-ó	cup-ci
PAST	cuwóss-ó	cuwóss-ci
REMOTE PAST	cuwóssóss-ó	cuwóssóss-ci
FUTURE	cupkess-ó	cupkess-ci
PAST FUTURE	cuwósskess-ó	cuwósskess-ci
PROPOSITIVE *IMPERATIVE*	cuw-ó	cup-ci

CAUSATIVE:	*PASSIVE:*

FORMAL *Plain*

	INDICATIVE	RETROSPECTIVE
DECLARATIVE/ *INTERROGATIVE*		
PRESENT	cca-ta/-nya	cca-tóla/-tónya
PAST	ccass-ta/-nya	ccass-tóla
REMOTE PAST	ccassóss-ta	ccassóss-tóla
FUTURE	ccakess-ta	ccakess-tóla
PAST FUTURE	ccasskess-ta	ccasskess-tóla

PROPOSITIVE
IMPERATIVE

FORMAL *Polite*

	INDICATIVE	RETROSPECTIVE
DECLARATIVE/ *INTERROGATIVE*		
PRESENT	ccapni-ta/-kka	ccapti-ta/-kka
PAST	ccassúpni-ta	ccassúpti-ta
REMOTE PAST	ccassóssúpni-ta	ccassóssúpti-ta
FUTURE	ccakessúpni-ta	ccakessúpti-ta
PAST FUTURE	ccasskessúpni-ta	ccasskessúpti-ta

PROPOSITIVE
IMPERATIVE

INFORMAL *Familiar*

	INDICATIVE	RETROSPECTIVE
DECLARATIVE/ *INTERROGATIVE*		
PRESENT	cca-ne/-nka	cca-te/-tónka
PAST	ccass-ne/-núnka	ccass-te
REMOTE PAST	ccassóss-ne	ccassóss-te
FUTURE	ccakess-ne	ccakess-te
PAST FUTURE	ccasskess-ne	ccasskess-te

PROPOSITIVE
IMPERATIVE

	INFORMAL *Intimate* INDICATIVE	INFORMAL *Casual* INDICATIVE
DECLARATIVE/ *INTERROGATIVE*		
PRESENT	cca	cca-ci
PAST	ccass-ó	ccass-ci
REMOTE PAST	ccassóss-ó	ccassóss-ci
FUTURE	ccakess-ó	ccakess-ci
PAST FUTURE	ccasskess-ó	ccasskess-ci

PROPOSITIVE
IMPERATIVE

CAUSATIVE: *PASSIVE:*

1) to piece together, to assemble 2) to squeeze, to press 　　　　　 짜다

FORMAL *Plain*

	INDICATIVE	RETROSPECTIVE
DECLARATIVE/ *INTERROGATIVE*		
PRESENT	cca-n.ta/-núnya	cca-tóla/-tónya
PAST	ccass-ta	ccass-tóla
REMOTE PAST	ccassóss-ta	ccassóss-tóla
FUTURE	ccakess-ta	ccakess-tóla
PAST FUTURE	ccasskess-ta	ccasskess-tóla
PROPOSITIVE	cca-ca	
IMPERATIVE	cca-la	

FORMAL *Polite*

	INDICATIVE	RETROSPECTIVE
DECLARATIVE/ *INTERROGATIVE*		
PRESENT	ccapni-ta/-kka	ccapti-ta/-kka
PAST	ccassúpni-ta	ccassúpti-ta
REMOTE PAST	ccassóssúpni-ta	ccassóssúpti-ta
FUTURE	ccakessúpni-ta	ccakessúpti-ta
PAST FUTURE	ccasskessúpni-ta	ccasskessúpti-ta
PROPOSITIVE	ccapsi-ta	
IMPERATIVE	cca(si)psi-o	

INFORMAL *Familiar*

	INDICATIVE	RETROSPECTIVE
DECLARATIVE/ *INTERROGATIVE*		
PRESENT	cca-ne/-núnka	cca-te/-tónka
PAST	ccass-ne	ccass-te
REMOTE PAST	ccassóss-ne	ccassóss-te
FUTURE	ccakess-ne	ccakess-te
PAST FUTURE	ccasskess-ne	ccasskess-te
PROPOSITIVE	cca-se	
IMPERATIVE	cca-ke	

	INFORMAL *Intimate* INDICATIVE	INFORMAL *Casual* INDICATIVE
DECLARATIVE/ *INTERROGATIVE*		
PRESENT	cca	cca-ci
PAST	ccass-ó	ccass-ci
REMOTE PAST	ccassóss-ó	ccassóss-ci
FUTURE	ccakess-ó	ccakess-ci
PAST FUTURE	ctasskess-ó	ccasskess-ci
PROPOSITIVE *IMPERATIVE*	cca	cca-ci

CAUSATIVE: 　　　　　　　　　　　 *PASSIVE:* CCAI.TA
　　　　　　　　　　　　　　　　　　 to get pieced together,
　　　　　　　　　　　　　　　　　　 assembled

FORMAL *Plain*

	INDICATIVE	RETROSPECTIVE
DECLARATIVE/		
INTERROGATIVE		
PRESENT	ccalp-ta/-únya	ccalp-tóla/-tónya
PAST	ccalpass-ta/-núnya	ccalpass-tóla
REMOTE PAST	ccalpassóss-ta	ccalpassóss-tóla
FUTURE	ccalpkess-ta	ccalpkess-tóla
PAST FUTURE	ccalpasskess-ta	ccalpasskess-tóla

PROPOSITIVE
IMPERATIVE

FORMAL *Polite*

	INDICATIVE	RETROSPECTIVE
DECLARATIVE/		
INTERROGATIVE		
PRESENT	ccalpsúpni-ta/-kka	ccalpsúti-ta/-kka
PAST	ccalpassúpni-ta	ccalpassúpti-ta
REMOTE PAST	ccalpassóssúpni-ta	ccalpassóssúpti-ta
FUTURE	ccalpkessúpni-ta	ccalpkessúpti-ta
PAST FUTURE	ccalpasskessúpni-ta	ccalpasskessúpti-ta

PROPOSITIVE
IMPERATIVE

INFORMAL *Familiar*

	INDICATIVE	RETROSPECTIVE
DECLARATIVE/		
INTERROGATIVE		
PRESENT	ccalp-ne/-únka	ccalp-te/-tónka
PAST	ccalpass-ne/-núnka	ccalpass-te
REMOTE PAST	ccalpassóss-ne	ccalpassóss-te
FUTURE	ccalpkess-ne	ccalkess-te
PAST FUTURE	ccalpasskess-ne	ccalpasskess-te

PROPOSITIVE
IMPERATIVE

	INFORMAL *Intimate* INDICATIVE	INFORMAL *Casual* INDICATIVE
DECLARATIVE/		
INTERROGATIVE		
PRESENT	ccalp-a	ccalp-ci
PAST	ccalpass-ó	ccalpass-ci
REMOTE PAST	ccalpassóss-ó	ccalpassóss-ci
FUTURE	ccalpkess-ó	ccalpkess-ci
PAST FUTURE	c'calpasskess-ó	ccalpasskess-ci

PROPOSITIVE
IMPERATIVE

CAUSATIVE: *PASSIVE:*

to pierce, to prick, to stab

FORMAL Plain

	INDICATIVE	RETROSPECTIVE
DECLARATIVE/ *INTERROGATIVE*		
PRESENT	ccilú-n.ta/-núnya	ccilú-tóla/-tónya
PAST	ccillóss-ta	ccillóss-tóla
REMOTE PAST	ccillóssóss-ta	ccillóssóss-tóla
FUTURE	ccilúkess-ta	ccilúkess-tóla
PAST FUTURE	ccillósskess-ta	ccillósskess-tóla
PROPOSITIVE	ccilú-ca	
IMPERATIVE	ccill-óla	

FORMAL Polite

	INDICATIVE	RETROSPECTIVE
DECLARATIVE/ *INTERROGATIVE*		
PRESENT	ccilúpni-ta/-kka	ccilúpti-ta/-kka
PAST	ccillóssúpni-ta	ccillóssúpti-ta
REMOTE PAST	ccillóssóssúpni-ta	ccillóssóssúpti-ta
FUTURE	ccilúkessúpni-ta	ccilúkessúpti-ta
PAST FUTURE	ccillósskessúpni-ta	ccillósskessúpti-ta
PROPOSITIVE	ccilúpsi-ta	
IMPERATIVE	ccilú(si)psi-o	

INFORMAL Familiar

	INDICATIVE	RETROSPECTIVE
DECLARATIVE/ *INTERROGATIVE*		
PRESENT	ccilú-ne/-núnka	ccilú-te/-tónka
PAST	ccillóss-ne	ccillóss-te
REMOTE PAST	ccillóssóss-ne	ccillóssóss-te
FUTURE	ccilúkess-ne	ccilúkess-te
PAST FUTURE	ccillósskess-ne	ccillósskess-te
PROPOSITIVE	ccilú-se	
IMPERATIVE	ccilú-ke	

	INFORMAL *Intimate* INDICATIVE	INFORMAL *Casual* INDICATIVE
DECLARATIVE/ *INTERROGATIVE*		
PRESENT	ccill-ó	ccilú-ci
PAST	ccillóss-ó	ccillóss-ci
REMOTE PAST	ccillóssóss-ó	ccillóssóss-ci
FUTURE	ccilúkess-ó	ccilúkess-ci
PAST FUTURE	ccillósskess-ó	ccillósskess-ci
PROPOSITIVE *IMPERATIVE*	ccill-ó	ccilú-ci

CAUSATIVE:　　　　　　　　　　　*PASSIVE:* CCILLI.TA
　　　　　　　　　　　　　　　　　　　to get pierced

FORMAL *Plain*

	INDICATIVE	RETROSPECTIVE
DECLARATIVE/ *INTERROGATIVE*		
PRESENT	ccoch-nún.ta/-núnya	ccoch-tóla/-tónya
PAST	ccochass-ta	ccochass-tóla
REMOTE PAST	ccochassóss-ta	ccochassóss-tóla
FUTURE	ccochkess-ta	ccochkess-tóla
PAST FUTURE	ccochasskess-ta	ccochasskess-tóla
PROPOSITIVE	ccoch-ca	
IMPERATIVE	ccoch-ala	

FORMAL *Polite*

	INDICATIVE	RETROSPECTIVE
DECLARATIVE/ *INTERROGATIVE*		
PRESENT	ccochsúpni-ta/-kka	ccochsúpti-ta/-kka
PAST	ccochassúpni-ta	ccochassúpti-ta
REMOTE PAST	ccochassóssúpni-ta	ccochassóssúpti-ta
FUTURE	ccochkessúpni-ta	ccochkessúpti-ta
PAST FUTURE	ccochasskessúpni-ta	ccochasskessúpti-ta
PROPOSITIVE	ccochúpsi-ta	
IMPERATIVE	ccochú(si)psi-o	

INFORMAL *Familiar*

	INDICATIVE	RETROSPECTIVE
DECLARATIVE/ *INTERROGATIVE*		
PRESENT	ccoch-ne/-núnka	ccoch-te/-tónka
PAST	ccochass-ne	ccochass-te
REMOTE PAST	ccochassóss-ne	ccochassóss-te
FUTURE	ccochkess-ne	ccochkess-te
PAST FUTURE	ccochasskess-ne	ccochasskess-te
PROPOSITIVE	ccoch-se	
IMPERATIVE	ccoch-ke	

	INFORMAL *Intimate* INDICATIVE	INFORMAL *Casual* INDICATIVE
DECLARATIVE/ *INTERROGATIVE*		
PRESENT	ccoch-a	ccoch-ci
PAST	ccochass-ó	ccochass-ci
REMOTE PAST	ccochassóss-ó	ccochassóss-ci
FUTURE	ccochkess-ó	ccochkess-ci
PAST FUTURE	·ccochasskess-ó	ccochasskess-ci
PROPOSITIVE *IMPERATIVE*	ccoch-a	ccoch-ci

CAUSATIVE: *PASSIVE:* CCOCHKI.TA
                                         to get driven out,
                                         to get pursued

CHA.TA
to be cold, to be chilly (of a physical object)   DESCRIPTIVE

FORMAL *Plain*

	INDICATIVE	RETROSPECTIVE
DECLARATIVE/ *INTERROGATIVE*		
PRESENT	cha-ta/-nya	cha-tóla/-tónya
PAST	chass-ta/-núnya	chass-tóla
REMOTE PAST	chassóss-ta	chassóss-tóla
FUTURE	chakess-ta	chakess-tóla
PAST FUTURE	chasskess-ta	chasskess-tóla

PROPOSITIVE
IMPER TIVE

FORMAL *Polite*

	INDICATIVE	RETROSPECTIVE
DECLARATIVE/ *INTERROGATIVE*		
PRESENT	chapni-ta/-kka	chapti-ta/-kka
PAST	chassúpni-ta	chassúpti-ta
REMOTE PAST	chassóssúpni-ta	chassóssúpti-ta
FUTURE	chakessúpni-ta	chakessúpti-ta
PAST FUTURE	chasskessúpni-ta	chasskessúti-ta

PROPOSITIVE
IMPERATIVE

INFORMAL *Familiar*

	INDICATIVE	RETROSPECTIVE
DECLARATIVE/ *INTERROGATIVE*		
PRESENT	cha-ne/-nka	cha-te/-tónka
PAST	chass-ne/-núnka	chass-te
REMOTE PAST	chassóss-ne	chassóss-te
FUTURE	chakess-ne	chakess-te
PAST FUTURE	chasskess-ne	chasskess-te

PROPOSITIVE
IMPERATIVE

	INFORMAL *Intimate* INDICATIVE	INFORMAL *Casual* INDICATIVE
DECLARATIVE/ *INTERROGATIVE*		
PRESENT	cha	cha-ci
PAST	chass-ó	chass-ci
REMOTE PAST	chassóss-ó	chassóss-ci
FUTURE	chakess-ó	chakess-ci
PAST FUTURE	chasskess-ó	chasskess-ci

PROPOSITIVE
IMPERATIVE

CAUSATIVE: *PASSIVE:*

28

1) to kick 2) to put on, to wear

FORMAL *Plain*

	INDICATIVE	RETROSPECTIVE
DECLARATIVE/ *INTERROGATIVE*		
PRESENT	cha-n.ta/-núnya	cha-tóla/-tónya
PAST	chass-ta	chass-tóla
REMOTE PAST	chassóss-ta	chassóss-tóla
FUTURE	chakess-ta	chakess-tóla
PAST FUTURE	chasskess-ta	chasskess-tóla
PROPOSITIVE	cha-ca	
IMPERATIVE	cha-la	

FORMAL *Polite*

	INDICATIVE	RETROSPECTIVE
DECLARATIVE/ *INTERROGATIVE*		
PRESENT	chapni-ta/-kka	chapti-ta/-kka
PAST	chassúpni-ta	chassúpti-ta
REMOTE PAST	chassóssúpni-ta	chassóssúpti-ta
FUTURE	chakessúpni-ta	chakessúpti-ta
PAST FUTURE	chasskessúpni-ta	chasskessúpti-ta
PROPOSITIVE	chapsi-ta	
IMPERATIVE	cha(si)psi-o	

INFORMAL *Familiar*

	INDICATIVE	RETROSPECTIVE
DECLARATIVE/ *INTERROGATIVE*		
PRESENT	cha-ne/-núnka	cha-te/-tónka
PAST	chass-ne	chass-te
REMOTE PAST	chassóss-ne	chassóss-te
FUTURE	chakess-ne	chakess-te
PAST FUTURE	chasskess-ne	chasskess-te
PROPOSITIVE	cha-se	
IMPERATIVE	cha-ke	

	INFORMAL *Intimate* INDICATIVE	INFORMAL *Casual* INDICATIVE
DECLARATIVE/ *INTERROGATIVE*		
PRESENT	cha	cha-ci
PAST	chass-ó	chass-ci
REMOTE PAST	chassóss-ó	chassóss-ci
FUTURE	chakess-ó	chakess-ci
PAST FUTURE	chasskess-ó	chasskess-ci
PROPOSITIVE *IMPERATIVE*	cha	cha-ci

CAUSATIVE: CHAEU.TA
to make/let one wear

PASSIVE: CHAE.TA
to get kicked

CHAC.TA
to search for, to look for
찾다

<table>
<tr><td colspan="3" align="center">FORMAL Plain</td></tr>
<tr><td></td><td>INDICATIVE</td><td>RETROSPECTIVE</td></tr>
<tr><td>DECLARATIVE/
INTERROGATIVE</td><td></td><td></td></tr>
<tr><td>PRESENT</td><td>chac-nún.ta/-núnya</td><td>chac-tóla/-tónya</td></tr>
<tr><td>PAST</td><td>chacass-ta</td><td>chacass-tóla</td></tr>
<tr><td>REMOTE PAST</td><td>chacassóss-ta</td><td>chacassóss-tóla</td></tr>
<tr><td>FUTURE</td><td>chackess-ta</td><td>chackess-tóla</td></tr>
<tr><td>PAST FUTURE</td><td>chacasskess-ta</td><td>chacasskess-tóla</td></tr>
<tr><td>PROPOSITIVE</td><td>chac-ca</td><td></td></tr>
<tr><td>IMPERATIVE</td><td>chac-ala</td><td></td></tr>
</table>

<table>
<tr><td colspan="3" align="center">FORMAL Polite</td></tr>
<tr><td></td><td>INDICATIVE</td><td>RETROSPECTIVE</td></tr>
<tr><td>DECLARATIVE/
INTERROGATIVE</td><td></td><td></td></tr>
<tr><td>PRESENT</td><td>chacsúpni-ta/-kka</td><td>chacsúpti-ta/-kka</td></tr>
<tr><td>PAST</td><td>chacassúpni-ta</td><td>chacassúpti-ta</td></tr>
<tr><td>REMOTE PAST</td><td>chacassóssúpni-ta</td><td>chacassóssúpti-ta</td></tr>
<tr><td>FUTURE</td><td>chackessúpni-ta</td><td>chackessúpti-ta</td></tr>
<tr><td>PAST FUTURE</td><td>chacasskessúpni-ta</td><td>chacasskessúpti-ta</td></tr>
<tr><td>PROPOSITIVE</td><td>chacúpsi-ta</td><td></td></tr>
<tr><td>IMPERATIVE</td><td>chacú(si)psi-o</td><td></td></tr>
</table>

<table>
<tr><td colspan="3" align="center">INFORMAL Familiar</td></tr>
<tr><td></td><td>INDICATIVE</td><td>RETROSPECTIVE</td></tr>
<tr><td>DECLARATIVE/
INTERROGATIVE</td><td></td><td></td></tr>
<tr><td>PRESENT</td><td>chac-ne/-núnka</td><td>chac-te/-tónka</td></tr>
<tr><td>PAST</td><td>chacass-ne</td><td>chacass-te</td></tr>
<tr><td>REMOTE PAST</td><td>chacassóss-ne</td><td>chacassóss-te</td></tr>
<tr><td>FUTURE</td><td>chackess-ne</td><td>chackess-te</td></tr>
<tr><td>PAST FUTURE</td><td>chacasskess-ne</td><td>chacasskess-te</td></tr>
<tr><td>PROPOSITIVE</td><td>chac-se</td><td></td></tr>
<tr><td>IMPERATIVE</td><td>chac-ke</td><td></td></tr>
</table>

<table>
<tr><td></td><td>INFORMAL Intimate
INDICATIVE</td><td>INFORMAL Casual
INDICATIVE</td></tr>
<tr><td>DECLARATIVE/
INTERROGATIVE</td><td></td><td></td></tr>
<tr><td>PRESENT</td><td>chac-a</td><td>chac-ci</td></tr>
<tr><td>PAST</td><td>chacass-ó</td><td>chacass-ci</td></tr>
<tr><td>REMOTE PAST</td><td>chacassóss-ó</td><td>chacassóss-ci</td></tr>
<tr><td>FUTURE</td><td>chackess-ó</td><td>chackess-ci</td></tr>
<tr><td>PAST FUTURE</td><td>chacasskess-ó</td><td>chacasskess-ci</td></tr>
<tr><td>PROPOSITIVE
IMPERATIVE</td><td>chac-a</td><td>chac-ci</td></tr>
</table>

CAUSATIVE: PASSIVE:

CHALI.TA
to prepare, to make ready   차리다

FORMAL *Plain*

	INDICATIVE	RETROSPECTIVE
DECLARATIVE/ *INTERROGATIVE*		
PRESENT	chali-n.ta/-nùnya	chali-tóla/-tónya
PAST	chalyóss-ta	chalyóss-tóla
REMOTE PAST	chalyóssóss-ta	chalyóssóss-tóla
FUTURE	chalikess-ta	chalikess-tóla
PAST FUTURE	chalyósskess-ta	chalyósskess-tóla
PROPOSITIVE	chali-ca	
IMPERATIVE	chaly-ó.la	

FORMAL *Polite*

	INDICATIVE	RETROSPECTIVE
DECLARATIVE/ *INTERROGATIVE*		
PRESENT	chalipni-ta/-kka	chalipti-ta/-kka
PAST	chalyóssùpni-ta	chalyóssùpti-ta
REMOTE PAST	chalyóssóssùpni-ta	chalyóssóssùpti-ta
FUTURE	chalikessùpni-ta	chalikessùpti-ta
PAST FUTURE	chalyósskessùpni-ta	chalyósskessùpti-ta
PROPOSITIVE	chalipsi-ta	
IMPERATIVE	chali(si)psi-o	

INFORMAL *Familiar*

	INDICATIVE	RETROSPECTIVE
DECLARATIVE/ *INTERROGATIVE*		
PRESENT	chali-ne/-nùnka	chali-te/-tónka
PAST	chalyóss-ne	chalyóss-te
REMOTE PAST	chalyóssóss-ne	chalyóssóss-te
FUTURE	chalikess-ne	chalikess-te
PAST FUTURE	chalyósskess-ne	chalyósskess-te
PROPOSITIVE	chali-se	
IMPERATIVE	chali-ke	

	INFORMAL *Intimate* INDICATIVE	INFORMAL *Casual* INDICATIVE
DECLARATIVE/ *INTERROGATIVE*		
PRESENT	cha.ly-ó	chali-ci
PAST	chalyóss-ó	chalyóss-ci
REMOTE PAST	chalyóssóss-ó	chalyóssóss-ci
FUTURE	chalikess-ó	chalikess-ci
PAST FUTURE	chalyósskess-ó	chalyósskess-ci
PROPOSITIVE *IMPERATIVE*	cha.ly-ó	chali-ci

CAUSATIVE: *PASSIVE:*

31

FORMAL *Plain*

	INDICATIVE	RETROSPECTIVE
DECLARATIVE/ *INTERROGATIVE*		
PRESENT	cham-nún.'ta/-núnya	cham-tóla/-tónya
PAST	chamass-ta	chamass-tóla
REMOTE PAST	chamassóss-ta	chamassóss-tóla
FUTURE	chamkess-ta	chamkess-tóla
PAST FUTURE	chamasskess-ta	chamasskess-tóla
PROPOSITIVE	cham-ca	
IMPERATIVE	cham-ala	

FORMAL *Polite*

	INDICATIVE	RETROSPECTIVE
DECLARATIVE/ *INTERROGATIVE*		
PRESENT	chamsúpni-ta/-kka	chamsúpti-ta/-kka
PAST	chamassúpni-ta	chamassúpti-ta
REMOTE PAST	chamassóssúpni-ta	chamassóssúpti-ta
FUTURE	chamkessúpni-ta	chamkessúpti-ta
PAST FUTURE	chamasskessúpni-ta	chamasskessúpti-ta
PROPOSITIVE	chamúpsita	
IMPERATIVE	chamú(si)psi-o	

INFORMAL *Familiar*

	INDICATIVE	RETROSPECTIVE
DECLARATIVE/ *INTERROGATIVE*		
PRESENT	cham-ne/-núnka	cham-te/-tónka
PAST	chamass-ne	chamass-te
REMOTE PAST	chamassóss-ne	chamassóss-te
FUTURE	chamkess-ne	chamkess-te
PAST FUTURE	chamasskess-ne	chamasskess-te
PROPOSITIVE	cham-se	
IMPERATIVE	cham-ke	

	INFORMAL *Intimate* INDICATIVE	INFORMAL *Casual* INDICATIVE
DECLARATIVE/ *INTERROGATIVE*		
PRESENT	cham-a	cham-ci
PAST	chamass-ó	chamass-ci
REMOTE PAST	chamassóss-ó	chamassóss-ci
FUTURE	chamkess-ó	chamkess-ci
PAST FUTURE	chamasskess-ó	chamasskess-ci
PROPOSITIVE *IMPERATIVE*	cham-a	cham-ci

CAUSATIVE: *PASSIVE:*

FORMAL *Plain*

	INDICATIVE	RETROSPECTIVE
DECLARATIVE/ *INTERROGATIVE*		
PRESENT	chiu-n.ta/-núnya	chiu-tóla/-tònya
PAST	chiwóss-ta	chiwóss-tóla
REMOTE PAST	chiwóssóss-ta	chiwóssóss-tóla
FUTURE	chiukess-ta	chiukess-tóla
PAST FUTURE	chiwósskess-ta	chiwósskess-tóla
PROPOSITIVE	chiu-ca	
IMPERATIVE	chiw-ó.la	

FORMAL *Polite*

	INDICATIVE	RETROSPECTIVE
DECLARATIVE/ *INTERROGATIVE*		
PRESENT	chiupni-ta/-kka	chiupti-ta/-kka
PAST	chiwóssúpni-ta	chiwóssúpti-ta
REMOTE PAST	chiwóssóssúpni-ta	chiwóssóssúpti-ta
FUTURE	chiukessúpni-ta	chiukessúpti-ta
PAST FUTURE	chiwósskessúpni-ta	chiwósskessúpti-ta
PROPOSITIVE	chiupsi-ta	
IMPERATIVE	chiu(si)psi-o	

INFORMAL *Familiar*

	INDICATIVE	RETROSPECTIVE
DECLARATIVE/ *INTERROGATIVE*		
PRESENT	chiu-ne/-núnka	chiu-te/-tónka
PAST	chiwóss-ne	chiwóss-te
REMOTE PAST	chiwóssóss-ne	chiwóssóss-te
FUTURE	chiukess-ne	chiukess-te
PAST FUTURE	chiwósskess-ne	chiwósskess-te
PROPOSITIVE	chiu-se	
IMPERATIVE	chiu-ke	

	INFORMAL *Intimate* INDICATIVE	INFORMAL *Casual* INDICATIVE
DECLARATIVE/ *INTERROGATIVE*		
PRESENT	chi.w-ó	chiu-ci
PAST	chiwóss-ó	chiwóss-ci
REMOTE PAST	chiwóssóss-ó	chiwóssóss-ci
FUTURE	chiukess-ó	chiukess-ci
PAST FUTURE	chiwósskess-ó	chiwósskess-ci
PROPOSITIVE *IMPERATIVE*	chi.w-ó	chiu-ci

CAUSATIVE: *PASSIVE:*

CHUP.TA   춥다
to be cold, to be chilly (of the weather)   DESCRIPTIVE

FORMAL Plain

	INDICATIVE	RETROSPECTIVE
DECLARATIVE/		
INTERROGATIVE		
PRESENT	chu-p.ta/-unya	chup-tóla/-tónya
PAST	chuwóss-ta/-núnya	chuwóss-tóla
REMOTE PAST	chuwóssóss-ta	chuwóssóss-tóla
FUTURE	chupkess-ta	chupkess-tóla
PAST FUTURE	chuwósskess-ta	chuwósskess-tóla

PROPOSITIVE
IMPERATIVE

FORMAL Polite

	INDICATIVE	RETROSPECTIVE
DECLARATIVE/		
INTERROGATIVE		
PRESENT	chupsúpni-ta/-kka	chupsúpti-ta/-kka
PAST	chuwóssúpni-ta	chuwóssúpti-ta
REMOTE PAST	chuwóssóssúpni-ta	chuwóssóssúpti-ta
FUTURE	chupkessúpni-ta	chupkessúpti-ta
PAST FUTURE	chuwósskessúpni-ta	chuwósskessúpti-ta

PROPOSITIVE
IMPERATIVE

INFORMAL Familiar

	INDICATIVE	RETROSPECTIVE
DECLARATIVE/		
INTERROGATIVE		
PRESENT	chu-p.ne/-unka	chup-te/-tónka
PAST	chuwóss-ne/-núnka	chuwóss-te
REMOTE PAST	chuwóssóss-ne	chuwóssóss-te
FUTURE	chuupkess-ne	chupkess-te
PAST FUTURE	chuwósskess-ne	chuwósskess-te

PROPOSITIVE
IMPERATIVE

	INFORMAL *Intimate* INDICATIVE	INFORMAL *Casual* INDICATIVE
DECLARATIVE/		
INTERROGATIVE		
PRESENT	chu.w-ó	chup-ci
PAST	chuwóss-ó	chuwóss-ci
REMOTE PAST	chuwóssóss-ó	chuwóssósss-ci
FUTURE	chupkess-ó	chupkess-ci
PAST FUTURE	chuwósskess-ó	chuwósskess-ci

PROPOSITIVE
IMPERATIVE

    CAUSATIVE: *PASSIVE:*

FORMAL *Plain*

	INDICATIVE	RETROSPECTIVE
DECLARATIVE/ *INTERROGATIVE*		
PRESENT	ha-n.ta/-núnya	ha-tóla/-tónya
PAST	hayóss-ta	hayóss-tóla
REMOTE PAST	hayóssóss-ta	hayóssóss-tóla
FUTURE	hakess-ta	hakess-tóla
PAST FUTURE	hayósskess-ta	hayósskess-tóla
PROPOSITIVE	ha-ca	
IMPERATIVE	hay-ó.la	

FORMAL *Polite*

	INDICATIVE	RETROSPECTIVE
DECLARATIVE/ *INTERROGATIVE*		
PRESENT	hapni-ta/-kka	hapti-ta/-kka
PAST	hayóssúpni-ta	hayóssúpti-ta
REMOTE PAST	hayóssóssúpni-ta	hayóssóssúpti-ta
FUTURE	hakessúpni-ta	hakessúpti-ta
PAST FUTURE	hayósskessúpni-ta	hayósskessúpti-ta
PROPOSITIVE	hapsi-ta	
IMPERATIVE	ha(si)psi-o	

INFORMAL *Familiar*

	INDICATIVE	RETROSPECTIVE
DECLARATIVE/ *INTERROGATIVE*		
PRESENT	ha-ne/-núnka	ha-te/-tónka
PAST	hayóss-ne	hayóss-te
REMOTE PAST	hayóssóss-ne	hayóssóss-te
FUTURE	hakess-ne	hakess-te
PAST FUTURE	hayósskess-ne	hayósskess-te
PROPOSITIVE	ha-se	
IMPERATIVE	ha-ke	

	INFORMAL *Intimate* INDICATIVE	INFORMAL *Casual* INDICATIVE
DECLARATIVE/ *INTERROGATIVE*		
PRESENT	hae	ha-ci
PAST	hayóss-ó	hayóss-ci
REMOTE PAST	hayóssóss-ó	hayóssóss-ci
FUTURE	hakess-ó	hakess-ci
PAST FUTURE	hayósskess-ó	hayósskess-ci
PROPOSITIVE *IMPERATIVE*	hae	ha-ci

CAUSATIVE: *PASSIVE:*

FORMAL *Plain*

	INDICATIVE	RETROSPECTIVE
DECLARATIVE/ *INTERROGATIVE*		
PRESENT	halkhwi-n.ta/-nủnya	halkwi-tỏla/-tỏnya
PAST	halkhwiỏss-ta	halkhwiỏss-tỏla
REMOTE PAST	halkhwiỏssỏss-ta	halkhwiỏssỏss-tỏla
FUTURE	halkhwikess-ta	halkhwikess-tỏla
PAST FUTURE	halkhwiỏsskess-ta	halkhwiỏsskess-tỏla
PROPOSITIVE	halkhwi-ca	
IMPERATIVE	halkhwi-ỏla	

FORMAL *Polite*

	INDICATIVE	RETROSPECTIVE
DECLARATIVE/ *INTERROGATIVE*		
PRESENT	halkhwipni-ta/-kka	halkhwipti-ta/-kka
PAST	halkhwiỏssủpni-ta	halkhwiỏssủpti-ta
REMOTE PAST	halkhwiỏssỏssủpni-ta	halkhwiỏssỏssủpti-ta
FUTURE	halkhwikessủpni-ta	halkhwikessủpti-ta
PAST FUTURE	halkhwiỏsskessủpni-ta	halkhwiỏsskessủpti-ta
PROPOSITIVE	halkhwipsi-ta	
IMPERATIVE	halkhwi(si)psi-o	

INFORMAL *Familiar*

	INDICATIVE	RETROSPECTIVE
DECLARATIVE/ *INTERROGATIVE*		
PRESENT	halkhwi-ne/-nủnka	halkhwi-te/-tỏnka
PAST	halkhwiỏss-ne	halkhwiỏss-te
REMOTE PAST	halkhwiỏssỏss-ne	halkhwiỏssỏss-te
FUTURE	halkhwikess-ne	halkhwikess-te
PAST FUTURE	halkhwiỏsskess-ne	halkhwiỏsskess-te
PROPOSITIVE	halkhwi-se	
IMPERATIVE	halkhwi-ke	

	INFORMAL *Intimate* INDICATIVE	INFORMAL *Casual* INDICATIVE
DECLARATIVE/ *INTERROGATIVE*		
PRESENT	halkhwi-ỏ	halkhwi-ci
PAST	halkhwiỏss-ỏ	halkhwiỏss-ci
REMOTE PAST	halkhwiỏssỏss-ỏ	halkhwiỏssỏss-ci
FUTURE	halkhwikess-ỏ	halkhwikess-ci
PAST FUTURE	halkhwiỏsskess-ỏ	halkhwiỏsskess-ci
PROPOSITIVE *IMPERATIVE*	halkhwi-ỏ	halkhwi-ci

CAUSATIVE: *PASSIVE:*

HALTH.TA
to lick, to lap

핥다

FORMAL *Plain*

	INDICATIVE	RETROSPECTIVE
DECLARATIVE/ *INTERROGATIVE*		
PRESENT	halth-nún.ta/-núnya	halth-tóla/-tónya
PAST	halthass-ta	halthass-tóla
REMOTE PAST	halthassóss-ta	halthassóss-tóla
FUTURE	halthkess-ta	halthkess-tóla
PAST FUTURE	halthasskess-ta	halthasskess-tóla
PROPOSITIVE	halth-ca	
IMPERATIVE	halth-ala	

FORMAL *Polite*

	INDICATIVE	RETROSPECTIVE
DECLARATIVE/ *INTERROGATIVE*		
PRESENT	halthsúpni-ta/-kka	halthsúpti-ta/-kka
PAST	halthassúpni-ta	halthassúpti-ta
REMOTE PAST	halthassóssúpni-ta	halthassóssúpti-ta
FUTURE	halthkessúpni-ta	halthkessúpti-ta
PAST FUTURE	halthasskessúpni-ta	halthasskessúpti-ta
PROPOSITIVE	halthúpsi-ta	
IMPERATIVE	halthú(si)psi-o	

INFORMAL *Familiar*

	INDICATIVE	RETROSPECTIVE
DECLARATIVE/ *INTERROGATIVE*		
PRESENT	halth-ne/-núnka	halth-te/-tónka
PAST	halthass-ne	halthass-te
REMOTE PAST	halthassóss-ne	halthassóss-te
FUTURE	halthkess-ne	halthkess-te
PAST FUTURE	halthasskess-ne	halthasskess-te
PROPOSITIVE	halth-se	
IMPERATIVE	halth-ke	

	INFORMAL *Intimate* INDICATIVE	INFORMAL *Casual* INDICATIVE
DECLARATIVE/ *INTERROGATIVE*		
PRESENT	halth-a	halth-ci
PAST	halthass-ó	halthass-ci
REMOTE PAST	halthassóss-ó	halthassóss-ci
FUTURE	halthkess-ó	halthkess-ci
PAST FUTURE	halthasskess-ó	halthasskess-ci
PROPOSITIVE *IMPERATIVE*	halth-a	halth-ci

CAUSATIVE: *PASSIVE:*

37

FORMAL *Plain*

	INDICATIVE	RETROSPECTIVE
DECLARATIVE/ *INTERROGATIVE*		
PRESENT	hemae-n.ta/-núnya	hemae-tóla/-tónya
PAST	hemaeóss-ta	hemaeóss-tóla
REMOTE PAST	hemaeóssóss-ta	hemaeóssóss-tóla
FUTURE	hemaekess-ta	hemaekess-tóla
PAST FUTURE	hemaeósskess-ta	hemaeósskess-tóla
PROPOSITIVE	hemae-ca	
IMPERATIVE	hemae-óla	

FORMAL *Polite*

	INDICATIVE	RETROSPECTIVE
DECLARATIVE/ *INTERROGATIVE*		
PRESENT	hemaepni-ta/-kka	hamaepti-ta/-kka
PAST	hemaeóssúpni-ta	hemaeóssúpti-ta
REMOTE PAST	hemaeóssóssúpni-ta	hemaeóssóssúpti-ta
FUTURE	hemaekessúpni-ta	hemaekessúpti-ta
PAST FUTURE	hemaeósskessúpni-ta	hemaeósskessúpti-ta
PROPOSITIVE	hemaepsi-ta	
IMPERATIVE	hemae(si)psi-o	

INFORMAL *Familiar*

	INDICATIVE	RETROSPECTIVE
DECLARATIVE/ *INTERROGATIVE*		
PRESENT	hemae-ne/-núnka	hemae-te/-tónka
PAST	hemaeóss-ne	hemaeóss-te
REMOTE PAST	hemaeóssóss-ne	hemaeóssóss-te
FUTURE	hemaekess-ne	hemaekess-te
PAST FUTURE	hemaeósskess-ne	hemaeósskess-te
PROPOSITIVE	hemae-se	
IMPERATIVE	hemae-ke	

	INFORMAL *Intimate* INDICATIVE	INFORMAL *Casual* INDICATIVE
DECLARATIVE/ *INTERROGATIVE*		
PRESENT	hemae-ó	hemae-ci
PAST	hemaeóss-ó	hemaeóss-ci
REMOTE PAST	hemaeóssóss-ó	hemaeóssóss-ci
FUTURE	hemaekess-ó	hemaekess-ci
PAST FUTURE	hemaeósskess-ó	hemaeósskess-ci
PROPOSITIVE *IMPERATIVE*	hemae-ó	hemae-ci

CAUSATIVE: *PASSIVE:*

HEPHÚ.TA   헤프다
to wear out easily, to go fast   DESCRIPTIVE

FORMAL *Plain*

	INDICATIVE	RETROSPECTIVE

DECLARATIVE/
INTERROGATIVE

PRESENT	hephú-ta/-nya	hephú-tóla/-tónya
PAST	hephóss-ta/-núnya	hephóss-tóla
REMOTE PAST	hephóssóss-ta	hephóssóss-tóla
FUTURE	hephúkess-ta	hephúkess-tóla
PAST FUTURE	hephósskess-ta	hephósskess-tóla

PROPOSITIVE
IMPERATIVE

FORMAL *Polite*

	INDICATIVE	RETROSPECTIVE

DECLARATIVE/
INTERROGATIVE

PRESENT	hephúpni-ta/-kka	hephúpti-ta/-kka
PAST	hephóssúpni-ta	hephóssúpti-ta
REMOTE PAST	hephóssóssúpni-ta	hephóssóssúpti-ta
FUTURE	hephúkessúpni-ta	hephúkessúpti-ta
PAST FUTURE	hephósskessúpni-ta	hephósskessúpti-ta

PROPOSITIVE
IMPERATIVE

INFORMAL *Familiar*

	INDICATIVE	RETROSPECTIVE

DECLARATIVE/
INTERROGATIVE

PRESENT	hephú-ne/-nka	hephú-te/-tónka
PAST	hephóss-ne/-núnka	hephóss-te
REMOTE PAST	hephóssóss-ne	hephóssóss-te
FUTURE	hephúkess-ne	hephúkess-te
PAST FUTURE	hephósskess-ne	hephósskess-te

PROPOSITIVE
IMPERATIVE

	INFORMAL *Intimate* INDICATIVE	INFORMAL *Casual* INDICATIVE

DECLARATIVE/
INTERROGATIVE

PRESENT	heph-ó	hephú-ci
PAST	hephóss-ó	hephóss-ci
REMOTE PAST	hephóssóss-ó	hephóssóss-ci
FUTURE	hephúkess-ó	hephúkess-ci
PAST FUTURE	hephósskess-ó	hephósskess-ci

PROPOSITIVE
IMPERATIVE

CAUSATIVE: *PASSIVE:*

to be possessed, to be bewitched   INTRANSITIVE

FORMAL *Plain*

	INDICATIVE	RETROSPECTIVE
DECLARATIVE/ *INTERROGATIVE*		
PRESENT	holli-n.ta/-núnya	halli-tóla/-tónya
PAST	hollyóss-ta	hollyóss-tóla
REMOTE PAST	hollyóssóss-ta	hollyóssóss-tóla
FUTURE	hollikess-ta	hollikess-tóla
PAST FUTURE	hollyósskess-ta	hollyósskess-tóla

PROPOSITIVE
IMPERATIVE

FORMAL *Polite*

	INDICATIVE	RETROSPECTIVE
DECLARATIVE/ *INTERROGATIVE*		
PRESENT	hollipni-ta/-kka	hollipti-ta/-kka
PAST	hollyóssúpni-ta	hollyóssúpti-ta
REMOTE PAST	hollyóssóssúpni-ta	hollyóssóssúpti-ta
FUTURE	hollikessúpni-ta	hollikessúpti-ta
PAST FUTURE	hollyósskessúpni-ta	hollyósskessúpti-ta

PROPOSITIVE
IMPERATIVE

INFORMAL *Familiar*

	INDICATIVE	RETROSPECTIVE
DECLARATIVE/ *INTERROGATIVE*		
PRESENT	holli-ni/-núnka	holli-te/-tónka
PAST	hollyóss-ne	hollyóss-te
REMOTE PAST	hollyóssóss-ne	hollyóssóss-te
FUTURE	hollikess-ne	hollikess-te
PAST FUTURE	hollyósskess-ne	hollyósskess-te

PROPOSITIVE
IMPERATIVE

	INFORMAL *Intimate* INDICATIVE	INFORMAL *Casual* INDICATIVE
DECLARATIVE/ *INTERROGATIVE*		
PRESENT	hol.ly-ó	holli-ci
PAST	hollyóss-ó	hollyóss-ci
REMOTE PAST	hollyóssóss-ó	hollyóssóss-ci
FUTURE	holikess-ó	hollikess-ci
PAST FUTURE	hollyósskess-ó	hollyósskess-ci

PROPOSITIVE
IMPERATIVE

CAUSATIVE: *PASSIVE:*

HOMUL.TA 허물다
to destroy, to demolish

FORMAL Plain

	INDICATIVE	RETROSPECTIVE
DECLARATIVE/ *INTERROGATIVE*		
PRESENT	hómu-n.ta/-núnya	hómul-tóla/-tónya
PAST	hómulóss-ta	hómulóss-tóla
REMOTE PAST	hómulóssóss-ta	hómulóssóss-tóla
FUTURE	hómulkess-ta	hómulkess-tóla
PAST FUTURE	hómulósskess-ta	hómulósskess-tóla
PROPOSITIVE	hómul-ca	
IMPERATIVE	hómul-óla	

FORMAL Polite

	INDICATIVE	RETROSPECTIVE
DECLARATIVE/ *INTERROGATIVE*		
PRESENT	hómupni-ta/-kka	hómupti-ta/-kka
PAST	hómulóssúpni-ta	hómulóssúpti-ta
REMOTE PAST	hómulóssóssúpni-ta	hómulóssóssúpti-ta
FUTURE	hómulkessúpni-ta	hómulkessúpti-ta
PAST FUTURE	hómulósskessúpni-ta	hómulósskessúpti-ta
PROPOSITIVE	hómupsi-ta	
IMPERATIVE	hómu(si)psi-o	

INFORMAL Familiar

	INDICATIVE	RETROSPECTIVE
DECLARATIVE/ *INTERROGATIVE*		
PRESENT	hómu-ne-/-núnka	hómul-te/-tónka
PAST	hómulóss-ne	hómulóss-te
REMOTE PAST	hómulóssóss-ne	hómulóssóss-te
FUTURE	hómulkess-ne	hómulkess-te
PAST FUTURE	hómulósskess-ne	hómulósskess-te
PROPOSITIVE	hómu-se	
IMPERATIVE	hómul-ke	

	INFORMAL <i>Intimate</i> INDICATIVE	INFORMAL <i>Casual</i> INDICATIVE
DECLARATIVE/ *INTERROGATIVE*		
PRESENT	hómul-ó	hómul-ci
PAST	hómulóss-ó	hómulóss-ci
REMOTE PAST	hómulóssóss-ó	hómulóssóss-ci
FUTURE	hómulkess-ó	hómulkess-ci
PAST FUTURE	hómulósskess-ó	hómulósskess-ci
PROPOSITIVE *IMPERATIVE*	hómul-ó	hómul-ci

CAUSATIVE:　　　　　　　　　　*PASSIVE:*

FORMAL *Plain*

DECLARATIVE/ INTERROGATIVE	INDICATIVE	RETROSPECTIVE
PRESENT	hó-n.ta/-núnya	hól-tóla/-tónya
PAST	hólóss-ta	hólóss-tóla
REMOTE PAST	hólóssóss-ta	hólóssóss-tóla
FUTURE	hólkess-ta	hólkess-tóla
PAST FUTURE	hólósskess-ta	hólósskess-tóla
PROPOSITIVE	hól-ca	
IMPERATIVE	hól-óla	

FORMAL *Polite*

DECLARATIVE/ INTERROGATIVE	INDICATIVE	RETROSPECTIVE
PRESENT	hópni-ta/-kka	hópti-ta/-kka
PAST	hólóssúpni-ta	hólóssúpti-ta
REMOTE PAST	hólóssóssúpni-ta	hólóssóssúpti-ta
FUTURE	hólkessúpni-ta	hólkessúpti-ta
PAST FUTURE	hólósskessúpni-ta	hólósskessúpti-ta
PROPOSITIVE	hópsi-ta	
IMPERATIVE	hó(si)psi-o	

INFORMAL *Familiar*

DECLARATIVE/ INTERROGATIVE	INDICATIVE	RETROSPECTIVE
PRESENT	hó-ne/-núnka	hól-te/-tónka
PAST	hólóss-ne	hólóss-te
REMOTE PAST	hólóssóss-ne	hólóssóss-te
FUTURE	hólkess-ne	hólkess-te
PAST FUTURE	hólósskess-ne	hólósskess-te
PROPOSITIVE	hó-se	
IMPERATIVE	hól-ke	

DECLARATIVE/ INTERROGATIVE	INFORMAL *Intimate* INDICATIVE	INFORMAL *Casual* INDICATIVE
PRESENT	hól-ó	hól-ci
PAST	hólóss-ó	hólóss-ci
REMOTE PAST	hólóssóss-ó	hólóssóss-ci
FUTURE	hólkess-ó	hólkess-ci
PAST FUTURE	hólósskess-ó	hólósskess-ci
PROPOSITIVE IMPERATIVE	hól-ó	hól-ci

CAUSATIVE: *PASSIVE:* HOLLI.TA
                                                to get pulled down

FORMAL *Plain*

	INDICATIVE	RETROSPECTIVE
DECLARATIVE/ *INTERROGATIVE*		
PRESENT	hulth-nùn.ta/-nùnya	hulth-tóla/-tónya
PAST	hulthóss-ta	hulthóss-tóla
REMOTE PAST	hulthóssóss-ta	hulthóssóss-tóla
FUTURE	hulthkess-ta	hulthkess-tóla
PAST FUTURE	hulthósskess-ta	hulthósskess-tóla
PROPOSITIVE	hulth-ca	
IMPERATIVE	hulth-óla	

FORMAL *Polite*

	INDICATIVE	RETROSPECTIVE
DECLARATIVE/ *INTERROGATIVE*		
PRESENT	hulthsùpni-ta/-kka	hulthsùpti-ta/-kka
PAST	hulthóssùpni-ta	hulthóssùpti-ta
REMOTE PAST	hulthóssóssùpni-ta	hulthóssóssùpti-ta
FUTURE	hulthkessùpni-ta	hulthkessùpti-ta
PAST FUTURE	hulthósskessùpni-ta	hulthósskessùpti-ta
PROPOSITIVE	hulthùpsi-ta	
IMPERATIVE	hulthù(si)psi-o	

INFORMAL *Familiar*

	INDICATIVE	RETROSPECTIVE
DECLARATIVE/ *INTERROGATIVE*		
PRESENT	hulth-ne/-nùnka	hulth-te/-tónka
PAST	hulthóss-ne	hulthóss-te
REMOTE PAST	hulthóssóss-ne	hulthóssóss-te
FUTURE	hulthkess-ne	hulthkess-te
PAST FUTURE	hulthósskess-ne	hulthósskess-te
PROPOSITIVE	hulth-se	
IMPERATIVE	hulth-ke	

	INFORMAL *Intimate* INDICATIVE	INFORMAL *Casual* INDICATIVE
DECLARATIVE/ *INTERROGATIVE*		
PRESENT	hulth-ó	hulth-ci
PAST	hulthóss-ó	hulthóss-ci
REMOTE PAST	hulthóssóss-ó	hulthóssóss-ci
FUTURE	hulthkess-ó	hulthkess-ci
PAST FUTURE	hulthósskess-ó	hulthósskess-ci
PROPOSITIVE *IMPERATIVE*	hulth-ó	hulth-ci

CAUSATIVE: *PASSIVE:*

HUMCHI-TA   홈치다
1) to steal, to pilfer   2) to wipe (off)

FORMAL *Plain*

	INDICATIVE	RETROSPECTIVE
DECLARATIVE/ INTERROGATIVE		
PRESENT	humchi-n.ta/-núnya	humchi-tóla/-tónya
PAST	humchyóss-ta	humchyóss-tóla
REMOTE PAST	humchyóssóss-ta	humchyóssóss-tóla
FUTURE	humchikess-ta	humchikess-tóla
PAST FUTURE	humchyósskess-ta	humchyósskess-tóla
PROPOSITIVE	humchi-ca	
IMPERATIVE	humchy-ó.la	

FORMAL *Polite*

	INDICATIVE	RETROSPECTIVE
DECLARATIVE/ INTERROGATIVE		
PRESENT	humchipni-ta/-kka	humchipti-ta/-kka
PAST	humchyóssúpni-ta	humchyóssúpti-ta
REMOTE PAST	humchyóssóssúpni-ta	humchyóssóssúpti-ta
FUTURE	humchikessúpni-ta	humchikessúpti-ta
PAST FUTURE	humchyósskessúpni-ta	humchyósskessúpti-ta
PROPOSITIVE	humchipsi-ta	
IMPERATIVE	humchi(si)psi-o	

INFORMAL *Familiar*

	INDICATIVE	RETROSPECTIVE
DECLARATIVE/ INTERROGATIVE		
PRESENT	humchi-ne/-núnka	humchi-te/-tónka
PAST	humchyóss-ne	humchyóss-te
REMOTE PAST	humchyóssóss-ne	humchyóssóss-te
FUTURE	humchikess-ne	humchikess-te
PAST FUTURE	humchyósskess-ne	humchyósskess-te
PROPOSITIVE	humchi-se	
IMPERATIVE	humchi-ke	

	INFORMAL *Intimate* INDICATIVE	INFORMAL *Casual* INDICATIVE
DECLARATIVE/ INTERROGATIVE		
PRESENT	hum.chy-ó	humchi-ci
PAST	humchyóss-ó	humchyóss-ci
REMOTE PAST	humchyóssóss-ó	humchyóssóss-ci
FUTURE	humchikess-ó	humchikess-ci
PAST FUTURE	humchyósskess-ó	humchyósskess-ci
PROPOSITIVE *IMPERATIVE*	hum.chy-ó	humchi-ci

CAUSATIVE: *PASSIVE:*

to be white, to be gray   DESCRIPTIVE

FORMAL *Plain*

	INDICATIVE	RETROSPECTIVE
DECLARATIVE/ *INTERROGATIVE*		
PRESENT	húi-ta/-nya	húi-tóla/-tónya
PAST	húióss-ta/-núnya	húióss-tóla
REMOTE PAST	húióssóss-ta	húióssóss-tóla
FUTURE	húikess-ta	húikess-tóla
PAST FUTURE	húiósskess-ta	húiósskess-tóla

PROPOSITIVE
IMPERATIVE

FORMAL *Polite*

	INDICATIVE	RETROSPECTIVE
DECLARATIVE/ *INTERROGATIVE*		
PRESENT	húipni-ta/-kka	húipti-ta/-kka
PAST	húióssúpni-ta	húióssúpti-ta
REMOTE PAST	húióssóssúpni-ta	húióssóssúpti-ta
FUTURE	húikessúpni-ta	húikessúpti-ta
PAST FUTURE	húiósskessúpni-ta	húiósskessúpti-ta

PROPOSITIVE
IMPERATIVE

INFORMAL *Familiar*

	INDICATIVE	RETROSPECTIVE
DECLARATIVE/ *INTERROGATIVE*		
PRESENT	húi-ne/-nka	húi-te/-tónka
PAST	húióss-ne/-núnka	húióss-te
REMOTE PAST	húióssóss-ne	húióssóss-te
FUTURE	húikess-ne	húikess-te
PAST FUTURE	húiósskess-ne	húiósskess-te

PROPOSITIVE
IMPERATIVE

	INFORMAL *Intimate* INDICATIVE	INFORMAL *Casual* INDICATIVE
DECLARATIVE/ *INTERROGATIVE*		
PRESENT	húi-ó	húi-ci
PAST	húióss-ó	húióss-ci
REMOTE PAST	húióssóss-ó	húióssóss-ci
FUTURE	húikess-ó	húikess-ci
PAST FUTURE	húiósskess-ó	húiósskess-ci

PROPOSITIVE
IMPERATIVE

CAUSATIVE: *PASSIVE:*

HULI.TA
to be cloudy, to be dim, to be muddy   DESCRIPTIVE

FORMAL *Plain*

	INDICATIVE	RETROSPECTIVE
DECLARATIVE/		
INTERROGATIVE		
PRESENT	hùli-ta/-nya	hùli-tòla/-tònya
PAST	hùlyòss-ta/-nùnya	hùlyòss-tòla
REMOTE PAST	hùlyòssòss-ta	hùlyòssòss-tòla
FUTURE	hùlikess-ta	hùlikess-tòla
PAST FUTURE	hùlyòsskess-ta	hùlyòsskess-tòla

PROPOSITIVE
IMPERATIVE

FORMAL *Polite*

	INDICATIVE	RETROSPECTIVE
DECLARATIVE/		
INTERROGATIVE		
PRESENT	hùlipni-ta/-kka	hùlipti/-kka
PAST	hùlyòssùpni-ta	hùlyòssùpti-ta
REMOTE PAST	hùlyòssòssùpni-ta	hùlyòssòssùpti-ta
FUTURE	hùlikessùpni-ta	hùlikessùpti-ta
PAST FUTURE	hùlyòsskessùpni-ta	hùlyòsskessùpti-ta

PROPOSITIVE
IMPERATIVE

INFORMAL *Familiar*

	INDICATIVE	RETROSPECTIVE
DECLARATIVE/		
INTERROGATIVE		
PRESENT	hùli-ne/-nka	hùli-te/tònka
PAST	hùlyòss-ne/-nùnka	hùlyòss-te
REMOTE PAST	hùlyòssòss-ne	hùlyòssòss-te
FUTURE	hùlikess-ne	hùlikess-te
PAST FUTURE	hùlyòsskess-ne	hùlyòsskess-te

PROPOSITIVE
IMPERATIVE

	INFORMAL *Intimate*	INFORMAL *Casual*
	INDICATIVE	INDICATIVE
DECLARATIVE/		
INTERROGATIVE		
PRESENT	hù.ly-ò	hùli-ci
PAST	hùlyòss-ò	hùlyòss-ci
REMOTE PAST	hùlyòssòss-ò	hùlyòssòss-ci
FUTURE	hùlikess-ò	hùlikess-ci
PAST FUTURE	hùlyòsskess-ò	hùlyòsskess-ci

PROPOSITIVE
IMPERATIVE

CAUSATIVE:	*PASSIVE:*

FORMAL *Plain*

	INDICATIVE	RETROSPECTIVE
DECLARATIVE/ INTERROGATIVE		
PRESENT	húlú-n.ta/-núnya	húlú-tóla/-tónya
PAST	húllóss-ta	hullóss-tóla
REMOTE PAST	húllóssóss-ta	húllóssóss-tóla
FUTURE	húlúkess-ta	húlúkess-tóla
PAST FUTURE	húllósskess-ta	húllósskess-tóla

PROPOSITIVE
IMPERATIVE

FORMAL *Polite*

	INDICATIVE	RETROSPECTIVE
DECLARATIVE/ INTERROGATIVE		
PRESENT	húlúpni-ta/-kka	húlúpti-ta/-kka
PAST	húllóssúpni-ta	húllóssúpti-ta
REMOTE PAST	húllóssóssúpni-ta	húllóssóssúpti-ta
FUTURE	húlúkessúpni-ta	húlúkessúpti-ta
PAST FUTURE	húllósskessúpni-ta	húllósskessúpti-ta

PROPOSITIVE
IMPERATIVE

INFORMAL *Familiar*

	INDICATIVE	RETROSPECTIVE
DECLARATIVE/ INTERROGATIVE		
PRESENT	húlú-ne/-núnka	húlú-te/-tónka
PAST	húllóss-ne	húllóss-te
REMOTE PAST	húllóssóss-ne	húllóssóss-te
FUTURE	húlúkess-ne	húlúkess-te
PAST FUTURE	húllósskess-ne	húllósskess-te

PROPOSITIVE
IMPERATIVE

	INFORMAL *Intimate* INDICATIVE	INFORMAL *Casual* INDICATIVE
DECLARATIVE/ INTERROGATIVE		
PRESENT	húll-ó	húlú-ci
PAST	húllóss-ó	húllóss-ci
REMOTE PAST	húllóssóss-ó	húllóssóss-ci
FUTURE	húlúkess-ó	húlúkess-ci
PAST FUTURE	húllósskess-ó	húllósskess-ci

PROPOSITIVE
IMPERATIVE

CAUSATIVE: *PASSIVE:*

FORMAL *Plain*

	INDICATIVE	RETROSPECTIVE
DECLARATIVE/ *INTERROGATIVE*		
PRESENT	húntú-n.ta/-núnya	húntúl-tóla/-tónya
PAST	húntúlóss-ta	húntúlóss-tóla
REMOTE PAST	húntúlóssóss-ta	húntúlóssóss-tóla
FUTURE	húntúlkess-ta	húntúlkess-tóla
PAST FUTURE	húntúlósskess-ta	húntúlósskess-tóla
PROPOSITIVE	húntúl-ca	
IMPERATIVE	húntúl-óla	

FORMAL *Polite*

	INDICATIVE	RETROSPECTIVE
DECLARATIVE/ *INTERROGATIVE*		
PRESENT	húntúpni-ta/-kka	húntúpti-ta/-kka
PAST	húntúlóssúpni-ta	húntúlóssúpti-ta
REMOTE PAST	húntúlóssóssúpni-ta	húntúlóssóssúpti-ta
FUTURE	húntúlkessúpni-ta	húntúlkessúpti-ta
PAST FUTURE	húntúlósskessúpni-ta	húntúlósskessúpti-ta
PROPOSITIVE	húntúpsi-ta	
IMPERATIVE	húntú(si)psi-o	

INFORMAL *Familiar*

	INDICATIVE	RETROSPECTIVE
DECLARATIVE/ *INTERROGATIVE*		
PRESENT	húntú-ne/-núnka	húntúl-te/-tónka
PAST	húntúlóss-ne	húntúlóss-te
REMOTE PAST	húntúlóssóss-ne	húntúlóssóss-te
FUTURE	húntúlkess-ne	húntúlkess-te
PAST FUTURE	húntúlósskess-ne	húntúlósskess-te
PROPOSITIVE	húntú-se	
IMPERATIVE	húntúl-ke	

	INFORMAL *Intimate* INDICATIVE	INFORMAL *Casual* INDICATIVE
DECLARATIVE/ *INTERROGATIVE*		
PRESENT	húntúl-ó	húntúl-ci
PAST	húntúlóss-ó	húntúlóss-ci
REMOTE PAST	húntúlóssóss-ó	húntúlóssóss-ci
FUTURE	húntúlkess-ó	húntúlkess-ci
PAST FUTURE	húntúlósskess-ó	húntúlósskess-ci
PROPOSITIVE *IMPERATIVE*	húntúl-ó	

CAUSATIVE:

PASSIVE: HUNTULLI.TA
to be swayed,
to be shakey

I.TA
to be, to equal   COPULA   이다

FORMAL *Plain*

	INDICATIVE	RETROSPECTIVE
DECLARATIVE/		
INTERROGATIVE		
PRESENT	i-ta/-nya	i-tóla/-tónya
PAST	ióss-ta/-núnya	ióss-tóla
REMOTE PAST	ióssóss-ta	ióssóss-tóla
FUTURE	ikess-ta	ikess-tóla
PAST FUTURE	iósskess-ta	iósskess-tóla

PROPOSITIVE
IMPERATIVE

FORMAL *Polite*

	INDICATIVE	RETROSPECTIVE
DECLARATIVE/		
INTERROGATIVE		
PRESENT	ipni-ta/-kka	ipti-ta/-kka
PAST	ióssúpni-ta	ióssúpti-ta
REMOTE PAST	ióssóssúpni-ta	ióssóssúpti-ta
FUTURE	ikessúpni-ta	ikessúpti-ta
PAST FUTURE	iósskessúpni-ta	iósskessúpti-ta

PROPOSITIVE
IMPERATIVE

INFORMAL *Familiar*

	INDICATIVE	RETROSPECTIVE
DECLARATIVE/		
INTERROGATIVE		
PRESENT	i-ne/-nka	i-te/-tónka
PAST	ióss-ne/-núnka	ióss-te
REMOTE PAST	ióssóss-ne	ióssóss-te
FUTURE	ikess-ne	ikess-te
PAST FUTURE	iósskess-ne	iósskess-te

PROPOSITIVE
IMPERATIVE

	INFORMAL *Intimate*	INFORMAL *Casual*
	INDICATIVE	INDICATIVE
DECLARATIVE/		
INTERROGATIVE		
PRESENT	i-ya	i-ci
PAST	ióss-ó	ióss-ci
REMOTE PAST	ióssóss-ó	ióssóss-ci
FUTURE	ikess-ó	ikess-ci
PAST FUTURE	iósskess-ó	iósskess-ci

PROPOSITIVE
IMPERATIVE

CAUSATIVE: *PASSIVE:*

FORMAL *Plain*

	INDICATIVE	RETROSPECTIVE
DECLARATIVE/ *INTERROGATIVE*		
PRESENT	ic-nùn.ta/-núnya	ic-tóla/-tònya
PAST	icóss-ta	icóss-tóla
REMOTE PAST	icóssóss-ta	icóssóss-tóla
FUTURE	ickess-ta	ickess-tóla
PAST FUTURE	icósskess-ta	icósskess-tóla
PROPOSITIVE	ic-ca	
IMPERATIVE	ic-óla	

FORMAL *Polite*

	INDICATIVE	RETROSPECTIVE
DECLARATIVE/ *INTERROGATIVE*		
PRESENT	icsùpni-ta/-kka	icsùpti-ta/-kka
PAST	icóssùpni-ta	icóssùpti-ta
REMOTE PAST	icóssóssùpni-ta	icóssóssùpti-ta
FUTURE	ickessùpni-ta	ickessùpti-ta
PAST FUTURE	icósskessùpni-ta	icósskessùpti-ta
PROPOSITIVE	icùpsi-ta	
IMPERATIVE	icù(si)psi-ó	

INFORMAL *Familiar*

	INDICATIVE	RETROSPECTIVE
DECLARATIVE/ *INTERROGATIVE*		
PRESENT	ic-ne/-núnka	ic-te/-tónka
PAST	icóss-ne	icóss-te
REMOTE PAST	icóssóss-ne	icóssóss-te
FUTURE	ickess-ne	ickess-te
PAST FUTURE	icósskess-ne	icósskess-te
PROPOSITIVE	ic-se	
IMPERATIVE	ic-ke	

	INFORMAL *Intimate* INDICATIVE	INFORMAL *Casual* INDICATIVE
DECLARATIVE/ *INTERROGATIVE*		
PRESENT	ic-ó	ic-ci
PAST	icóss-ó	icóss-ci
REMOTE PAST	icóssóss-ó	icóssóss-ci
FUTURE	ickess-ó	ickess-ci
PAST FUTURE	icósskess-ó	icósskess-ci
PROPOSITIVE *IMPERATIVE*	ic-ó	ic-ci

CAUSATIVE: *PASSIVE:*

FORMAL *Plain*

	INDICATIVE	RETROSPECTIVE
DECLARATIVE/ *INTERROGATIVE*		
PRESENT	ilh-nún.ta/-núnya	ilh-tóla/-tònya
PAST	ilhóss-ta	ilhòss-tòla
REMOTE PAST	ilhóssóss-ta	ilhòssóss-tòla
FUTURE	ilhkess-ta	ilhkess-tòla
PAST FUTURE	ilhósskess-ta	ilhòsskess-tòla
PROPOSITIVE	ilh-ca	
IMPERATIVE	ilh-óla	

FORMAL *Polite*

	INDICATIVE	RETROSPECTIVE
DECLARATIVE/ *INTERROGATIVE*		
PRESENT	ilhsúpni-ta/-kka	ilhsúpti-ta/-kka
PAST	ilhòssúpni-ta	ilhóssúpti-ta
REMOTE PAST	ilhóssóssúpni-ta	ilhòssóssúpti-ta
FUTURE	ilhkessúpni-ta	ilhkessúpti-ta
PAST FUTURE	ilhósskessúpni-ta	ilhósskessúpti-ta
PROPOSITIVE	ilhúpsi-ta	
IMPERATIVE	ilhú(si)psi-o	

INFORMAL *Familiar*

	INDICATIVE	RETROSPECTIVE
DECLARATIVE/ *INTERROGATIVE*		
PRESENT	ilh-ne/-núnka	ilh-te/-tónka
PAST	ilhóss-ne	ilhóss-te
REMOTE PAST	ilhóssóss-ne	ilhòssóss-te
FUTURE	ilhkess-ne	ilhkess-te
PAST FUTURE	ilhósskess-ne	ilhòsskess-te
PROPOSITIVE	ilh-se	
IMPERATIVE	ilh-ke	

	INFORMAL *Intimate* INDICATIVE	INFORMAL *Casual* INDICATIVE
DECLARATIVE/ *INTERROGATIVE*		
PRESENT	ilh-ó	ilh-ci
PAST	ilhóss-ó	ilhóss-ci
REMOTE PAST	ilhóssóss-ó	ilhòssóss-ci
FUTURE	ilhkess-ó	ilhkess-ci
PAST FUTURE	ilhósskess-ó	ilhósskess-ci
PROPOSITIVE		
IMPERATIVE		

CAUSATIVE: *PASSIVE:*

FORMAL *Plain*

DECLARATIVE/ INTERROGATIVE	INDICATIVE	RETROSPECTIVE
PRESENT	ilk-nún.ta/-núnya	ilk-tóla/-tónya
PAST	ilkóss-ta	ilkóss-tóla
REMOTE PAST	ilkóssóss-ta	ilkóssóss-tóla
FUTURE	ilkkess-ta	ilkkess-tóla
PAST FUTURE	ilkósskess-ta	ilkósskess-tóla
PROPOSITIVE	ilk-ca	
IMPERATIVE	ilk-óla	

FORMAL *Polite*

DECLARATIVE/ INTERROGATIVE	INDICATIVE	RETROSPECTIVE
PRESENT	ilksúpni-ta/-kka	ilksúpti-ta/-kka
PAST	ilkóssúpni-ta	ilkóssúpti-ta
REMOTE PAST	ilkóssóssúpni-ta	ilkóssóssúpti-ta
FUTURE	ilkkessúpni-ta	ilkkessúpti-ta
PAST FUTURE	ilkósskessúpni-ta	ilkósskessúpti-ta
PROPOSITIVE	ilkupsita	
IMPERATIVE	ilku(si)psi-o	

INFORMAL *Familiar*

DECLARATIVE/ INTERROGATIVE	INDICATIVE	RETROSPECTIVE
PRESENT	ilk-ne/-núnka	ilk-te/-tónka
PAST	ilkóss-ne	ilkóss-te
REMOTE PAST	ilkóssóss-ne	ilkóssóss-te
FUTURE	ilkkess-ne	ilkkess-te
PAST FUTURE	ilkósskess-ne	ilkósskess-te
PROPOSITIVE	ilk-se	
IMPERATIVE	ilk-ke	

DECLARATIVE/ INTERROGATIVE	INFORMAL *Intimate* INDICATIVE	INFORMAL *Casual* INDICATIVE
PRESENT	ilk-ó	ilk-ci
PAST	ilkóss-ó	ilkóss-ci
REMOTE PAST	ilkóssóss-ó	ilkóssóss-ci
FUTURE	ilkkess-ó	ilkkess-ci
PAST FUTURE	ilkósskess-ó	ilkósskess-ci
PROPOSITIVE IMPERATIVE	ilk-ó	ilk-ci

CAUSATIVE:	ILKHI.TA to make someone read	PASSIVE:	ILKH.TA to be read

FORMAL *Plain*

	INDICATIVE	RETROSPECTIVE
DECLARATIVE/ *INTERROGATIVE*		
PRESENT	ilô-h.ta/-nya	ilôh-tôla/-tônya
PAST	ilaess-ta/-nûnya	ilaess-tôla
REMOTE PAST	ilaessôss-ta	ilaessôss-tôla
FUTURE	ilôhkess-ta	ilôhkess-tôla
PAST FUTURE	ilaesskess-ta	ilaesskess-tôla

PROPOSITIVE
IMPERATIVE

FORMAL *Polite*

	INDICATIVE	RETROSPECTIVE
DECLARATIVE/ *INTERROGATIVE*		
PRESENT	ilôhsûpni-ta/-kka	ilôhsûpti-ta/-kka
PAST	ilaessûpni-ta	ilaessûpti-ta
REMOTE PAST	ilaessôssûpni-ta	ilaessôssûpti-ta
FUTURE	ilôhkessûpni-ta	ilôhkessûpti-ta
PAST FUTURE	ilaesskessûpni-ta	ilaesskessûpti-ta

PROPOSITIVE
IMPERATIVE

INFORMAL *Familiar*

	INDICATIVE	RETROSPECTIVE
DECLARATIVE/ *INTERROGATIVE*		
PRESENT	ilô-h.ne/-nka	ilôh-te/-tônka
PAST	ilaess-ne/-nûnka	ilaess-te
REMOTE PAST	ilaessôss-ne	ilaessôss-te
FUTURE	ilôhkess-ne	ilôhkess-te
PAST FUTURE	ilaesskess-ne	ilaesskess-te

PROPOSITIVE
IMPERATIVE

	INFORMAL *Intimate* INDICATIVE	INFORMAL *Casual* INDICATIVE
DECLARATIVE/ *INTERROGATIVE*		
PRESENT	ilae	iloh-ci
PAST	ilaess-ô	ilaess-ci
REMOTE PAST	ilaessôss-ô	ilaessôss-ci
FUTURE	ilohkess-ô	ilôhkess-ci
PAST FUTURE	ilaesskess-ô	ilaesskess-ci

PROPOSITIVE
IMPERATIVE

CAUSATIVE:	*PASSIVE:*

to be early, to be premature   DESCRIPTIVE

FORMAL *Plain*

	INDICATIVE	RETROSPECTIVE
DECLARATIVE/ INTERROGATIVE		
PRESENT	ilú-ta/-nya	ilú-tóla/-tónya
PAST	illóss-ta/-núnya	illóss-tóla
REMOTE PAST	illóssóss-ta	illóssóss-tóla
FUTURE	ilúkess-ta	ilúkess-tóla
PAST FUTURE	illósskess-ta	illósskess-tóla

PROPOSITIVE
IMPERATIVE

FORMAL *Polite*

	INDICATIVE	RETROSPECTIVE
DECLARATIVE/ INTERROGATIVE		
PRESENT	ilúpni-ta/-kka	ilúpti-ta/-kka
PAST	illóssúpni-ta	illóssúpti-ta
REMOTE PAST	illóssóssúpni-ta	illóssóssúpti-ta
FUTURE	ilúkessúpni-ta	ilúkessúpti-ta
PAST FUTURE	illósskessúpni-ta	illósskessúpti-ta

PROPOSITIVE
IMPERATIVE

INFORMAL *Familiar*

	INDICATIVE	RETROSPECTIVE
DECLARATIVE/ INTERROGATIVE		
PRESENT	ilú-ne/-nka	ilú-te/-tónka
PAST	illóss-ne/-núnka	illóss-te
REMOTE PAST	illóssóss-ne	illóssóss-te
FUTURE	ilúkess-ne	ilúkess-te
PAST FUTURE	illósskess-ne	illósskess-te

PROPOSITIVE
IMPERATIVE

	INFORMAL *Intimate* INDICATIVE	INFORMAL *Casual* INDICATIVE
DECLARATIVE/ INTERROGATIVE		
PRESENT	ill-ó	ilú-ci
PAST	illóss-ó	illóss-ci
REMOTE PAST	illóssóss-ó	illóssóss-ci
FUTURE	ilúkess-ó	ilúkess-ci
PAST FUTURE	illósskess-ó	illósskess-ci

PROPOSITIVE
IMPERATIVE

CAUSATIVE: *PASSIVE:*

ILU.TA 이르다
to arrive, to lead to   INTRANSITIVE

FORMAL *Plain*

	INDICATIVE	RETROSPECTIVE
DECLARATIVE/ *INTERROGATIVE*		
PRESENT	ilú-n.ta/-núnya	ilú-tóla/-tónya
PAST	ilúlóss-ta	ilúlóss-tóla
REMOTE PAST	ilúlóssóss-ta	ilúlóssóss-tóla
FUTURE	ilúkess-ta	ilúkess-tóla
PAST FUTURE	ilúlósskess-ta	ilúlósskess-tóla

PROPOSITIVE
IMPERATIVE

FORMAL *Polite*

	INDICATIVE	RETROSPECTIVE
DECLARATIVE/ *INTERROGATIVE*		
PRESENT	ilúpni-ta/-kka	ilúpti-ta/-kka
PAST	ilúlóssúpni-ta	ilúlóssúpti-ta
REMOTE PAST	ilúlóssóssúpni-ta	ilúlóssóssúpti-ta
FUTURE	ilúkessúpni-ta	ilúkessúpti-ta
PAST FUTURE	ilúlósskessúpni-ta	ilúlósskessúpti-ta

PROPOSITIVE
IMPERATIVE

INFORMAL *Familiar*

	INDICATIVE	RETROSPECTIVE
DECLARATIVE/ *INTERROGATIVE*		
PRESENT	ilú-ne/-núnka	ilú-te/-tónka
PAST	ilúlóss-ne	ilúlóss-te
REMOTE PAST	ilúlóssóss-ne	ilúlóssóss-te
FUTURE	ilúkess-ne	ilúkess-te
PAST FUTURE	ilúlósskess-ne	ilúlósskess-te

PROPOSITIVE
IMPERATIVE

	INFORMAL *Intimate* INDICATIVE	INFORMAL *Casual* INDICATIVE
DECLARATIVE/ *INTERROGATIVE*		
PRESENT	ilúli-ó	ilú-ci
PAST	ilúlóss-ó	ilúlóss-ci
REMOTE PAST	ilúlóssóss-ó	ilúlóssóss-ci
FUTURE	ilúkess-ó	ilúkess-ci
PAST FUTURE	ilúkósskess-ó	ilúlósskess-ci

PROPOSITIVE
IMPERATIVE

CAUSATIVE: *PASSIVE:*

잇다

FORMAL *Plain*

DECLARATIVE/ INTERROGATIVE	INDICATIVE	RETROSPECTIVE
PRESENT	is-ta/-nŭnya	is-tóla/-tónka
PAST	ióss-ta	ióss-tóla
REMOTE PAST	ióssóss-ta	ióssóss-tóla
FUTURE	iskess-ta	iskess-tóla
PAST FUTURE	iósskess-ta	iósskess-tóla
PROPOSITIVE	is-ca	
IMPERATIVE	i-óla	

FORMAL *Polite*

DECLARATIVE/ INTERROGATIVE	INDICATIVE	RETROSPECTIVE
PRESENT	issŭpni-ta/-kka	issŭpti-ta/-kka
PAST	ióssŭpni-ta	ióssŭpti-ta
REMOTE PAST	ióssóssŭpni-ta	ióssóssŭpti-ta
FUTURE	iskessŭpni-ta	iskessŭpti-ta
PAST FUTURE	iósskessŭpni-ta	iósskessŭpti-ta
PROPOSITIVE	iŭpsi-ta	
IMPERATIVE	iŭ(si)psi-o	

INFORMAL *Familiar*

DECLARATIVE/ INTERROGATIVE	INDICATIVE	RETROSPECTIVE
PRESENT	is-ne/-nŭnka	is-te/-tónka
PAST	ióss-ne	ióss-te
REMOTE PAST	ióssóss-ne	ióssóss-te
FUTURE	iskess-ne	iskess-te
PAST FUTURE	iósskess-ne	iósskess-te
PROPOSITIVE	is-se	
IMPERATIVE	is-ke	

DECLARATIVE/ INTERROGATIVE	INFORMAL *Intimate* INDICATIVE	INFORMAL *Casual* INDICATIVE
PRESENT	i-ó	is-ci
PAST	ióss-ó	ióss-ci
REMOTE PAST	ióssóss-ó	ióssóss-ci
FUTURE	iskess-ó	iskess-ci
PAST FUTURE	iósskess-ó	iósskess-ci
PROPOSITIVE IMPERATIVE	i-ó	is-ci

CAUSATIVE: *PASSIVE:*

```
ISS.TA                                                                          있다
to be, to exist       EXISTENTIAL
```

FORMAL *Plain*

	INDICATIVE	RETROSPECTIVE
DECLARATIVE/ *INTERROGATIVE*		
PRESENT	iss-ta/-núnya	iss-tóla/-tónya
PAST	issóss-ta	issóss-tóla
REMOTE PAST	issóssó-ta	issóssóss-tóla
FUTURE	isskess-ta	isskess-tóla
PAST FUTURE	issósskess-ta	issósskess-tóla
PROPOSITIVE	iss-ca	
IMPERATIVE	iss-óla ~ iss-kóla	

FORMAL *Polite*

	INDICATIVE	RETROSPECTIVE
DECLARATIVE/ *INTERROGATIVE*		
PRESENT	issúpni-ta/-kka	issúpti-ta/-kka
PAST	issóssúpni-ta	issóssúpti-ta
REMOTE PAST	issóssóssúpni-ta	issóssóssúpti-ta
FUTURE	isskessúpni-ta	isskessúpti-ta
PAST FUTURE	issósskessúpni-ta	issósskessúpti-ta
PROPOSITIVE	issúpsi-ta	
IMPERATIVE	issú(si)psi-o	

INFORMAL *Familiar*

	INDICATIVE	RETROSPECTIVE
DECLARATIVE/ *INTERROGATIVE*		
PRESENT	iss-ne/-núnka	iss-te/-tónka
PAST	issóss-ne	issóss-te
REMOTE PAST	issóssóss-ne	issóssóss-te
FUTURE	isskess-ne	isskess-te
PAST FUTURE	issósskess-ne	issósskess-te
PROPOSITIVE	iss-se	
IMPERATIVE	iss-ke	

	INFORMAL *Intimate* INDICATIVE	INFORMAL *Casual* INDICATIVE
DECLARATIVE/ *INTERROGATIVE*		
PRESENT	iss-ó	iss-ci
PAST	issóss-ó	issóss-ci
REMOTE PAST	issóssóss-ó	issóssóss-ci
FUTURE	isskess-ó	isskess-ci
PAST FUTURE	issósskess-ó	issósskess-ci
PROPOSITIVE *IMPERATIVE*	iss-ó	iss-ci

CAUSATIVE:	*PASSIVE:*

FORMAL *Plain*

	INDICATIVE	RETROSPECTIVE
DECLARATIVE/ *INTERROGATIVE*		
PRESENT	ka-n.ta-/núnya	ka-tóla/-tónya
PAST	kass-ta	kass-tóla
REMOTE PAST	kassóss-ta	kassóss-tóla
FUTURE	kakess-ta	kakess-tóla
PAST FUTURE	kasskess-ta	kasskess-tóla
PROPOSITIVE	ka-ca	
IMPERATIVE	ka-la~ka-kóla	

FORMAL *Polite*

	INDICATIVE	RETROSPECTIVE
DECLARATIVE/ *INTERROGATIVE*		
PRESENT	kapni-ta/-kka	kapti-ta/-kka
PAST	kassúpni-ta	kassúpti-ta
REMOTE PAST	kassóssúpni-ta	kassóssúpti-ta
FUTURE	kakessúpni-ta	kakessúpti-ta
PAST FUTURE	kasskessúpni-ta	kasskessúpti-ta
PROPOSITIVE	kapsi-ta	
IMPERATIVE	ka(si)psi-o	

INFORMAL *Familiar*

	INDICATIVE	RETROSPECTIVE
DECLARATIVE/ *INTERROGATIVE*		
PRESENT	ka-ne/-núnka	ka-te/-tónka
PAST	kass-ne	kass-te
REMOTE PAST	kassóss-ne	kassóss-te
FUTURE	kakess-ne	kakess-te
PAST FUTURE	kasskess-ne	kasskess-te
PROPOSITIVE	ka-se	
IMPERATIVE	ka-ke	

	INFORMAL *Intimate* INDICATIVE	INFORMAL *Casual* INDICATIVE
DECLARATIVE/ *INTERROGATIVE*		
PRESENT	ka	ka-ci
PAST	kass-ó	kass-ci
REMOTE PAST	kassóss-ó	kassóss-ci
FUTURE	kakess-ó	kakess-ci
PAST FUTURE	kasskess-o	kasskess-ci
PROPOSITIVE *IMPERATIVE*	ka	ka-ci

CAUSATIVE:	*PASSIVE:*

KAKKAP.TA
to be near, to be close by   DESCRIPTIVE

가깝다

FORMAL *Plain*

	INDICATIVE	RETROSPECTIVE
DECLARATIVE/ *INTERROGATIVE*		
PRESENT	kakka-p.ta/-unya	kakkap-tóla/-tónya
PAST	kakkawass-ta/-núnya	kakkawass-tóla
REMOTE PAST	kakkawassóss-ta	kakkawassóss-tóla
FUTURE	kakkapkess-ta	kakkapkess-tóla
PAST FUTURE	kakkawasskess-ta	kakkawasskess-tóla

PROPOSITIVE
IMPERATIVE

FORMAL *Polite*

	INDICATIVE	RETROSPECTIVE
DECLARATIVE/ *INTERROGATIVE*		
PRESENT	kakkapsúpni-ta/-kka	kakkapsúpti-ta/-kka
PAST	kakkaswassúpni-ta	kakkawassúpti-ta
REMOTE PAST	kakkawassóssúpni-ta	kakkawassóssúpti-ta
FUTURE	kakkapkessúpni-ta	kakkapkessúpti-ta
PAST FUTURE	kakkawasskessúpni-ta	kakkawasskessúpti-ta

PROPOSITIVE
IMPERATIVE

INFORMAL *Familiar*

	INDICATIVE	RETROSPECTIVE
DECLARATIVE/ *INTERROGATIVE*		
PRESENT	kakka-p.ne/-únka	kakkap-te/-tónka
PAST	kakkawass-ne/-núnka	kakkawass-te
REMOTE PAST	kakkawassóss-ne	kakkawassóss-te
FUTURE	kakkapkess-ne	kakkapkess-te
PAST FUTURE	kakkawasskess-ne	kakkawasskess-te

PROPOSITIVE
IMPERATIVE

	INFORMAL *Intimate* INDICATIVE	INFORMAL *Casual* INDICATIVE
DECLARATIVE/ *INTERROGATIVE*		
PRESENT	kakka.w-a	kakkap-ci
PAST	kakkawass-ó	kakkawass-ci
REMOTE PAST	kakkawassóss-ó	kakkawassóss-ci
FUTURE	kakkapkess-ó	kakkapkess-ci
PAST FUTURE	kakkawasskess-ó	kakkawasskess-ci

PROPOSITIVE
IMPERATIVE

CAUSATIVE: *PASSIVE:*

KAM.TA
to wash, to bathe

감다

FORMAL *Plain*

	INDICATIVE	RETROSPECTIVE
DECLARATIVE/ *INTERROGATIVE*		
PRESENT	kam-nún.ta/-núnya	kam-tóla/-tónya
PAST	kamass-ta	kamass-tóla
REMOTE PAST	kamassóss-ta	kamassóss-tóla
FUTURE	kamkess-ta	kamkess-tóla
PAST FUTURE	kamasskess-ta	kamasskess-tóla
PROPOSITIVE	kam-ca	
IMPERATIVE	kam-ala	

FORMAL *Polite*

	INDICATIVE	RETROSPECTIVE
DECLARATIVE/ *INTERROGATIVE*		
PRESENT	kamsúpni-ta/-kka	kamsúpti-ta/-kka
PAST	kamassúpni-ta	kamassúpti-ta
REMOTE PAST	kamassóssúpni-ta	kamassóssúpti-ta
FUTURE	kamkessúpni-ta	kamkessúpti-ta
PAST FUTURE	kamasskessúpni-ta	kamasskessúpti-ta
PROPOSITIVE	kamúpsi-ta	
IMPERATIVE	kamú(si)psi-o	

INFORMAL *Familiar*

	INDICATIVE	RETROSPECTIVE
DECLARATIVE/ *INTERROGATIVE*		
PRESENT	kam-ne/-núnka	kam-te/-tónka
PAST	kamass-ne	kamass-te
REMOTE PAST	kamassóss-ne	kamassóss-te
FUTURE	kamkess-ne	kamkess-te
PAST FUTURE	kamasskess-ne	kamasskess-te
PROPOSITIVE	kam-se	
IMPERATIVE	kam-ke	

	INFORMAL *Intimate* INDICATIVE	INFORMAL *Casual* INDICATIVE
DECLARATIVE/ *INTERROGATIVE*		
PRESENT	kam-a	kam-ci
PAST	kamass-ó	kamass-ci
REMOTE PAST	kamassóss-ó	kamassóss-ci
FUTURE	kamkess-ó	kamkess-ci
PAST FUTURE	kamasskess-ó	kamasskess-ci
PROPOSITIVE *IMPERATIVE*	kam-a	kam-ci

CAUSATIVE: KAMKI.TA   *PASSIVE:*
to wash (a person)
to bathe (a person)

to pay, to settle one's account, to repay

FORMAL *Plain*

	INDICATIVE	RETROSPECTIVE
DECLARATIVE/ *INTERROGATIVE*		
PRESENT	kaph-nún.ta/-núnya	kaph-tóla/-tónya
PAST	kaphass-ta	kaphass-tóla
REMOTE PAST	kaphassóss-ta	kaphassóss-tóla
FUTURE	kaphkess-ta	kaphkess-tóla
PAST FUTURE	kaphasskess-ta	kaphasskess-tóla
PROPOSITIVE	kaph-ca	
IMPERATIVE	kaph-ala	

FORMAL *Polite*

	INDICATIVE	RETROSPECTIVE
DECLARATIVE/ *INTERROGATIVE*		
PRESENT	kaphsúpni-ta/-kka	kaphsúpti-ta/-kka
PAST	kaphassúpni-ta	kaphassúpti-ta
REMOTE PAST	kaphassóssúpni-ta	kaphassóssúpti-ta
FUTURE	kaphkessúpni-ta	kaphkessúpti-ta
PAST FUTURE	kaphasskessúpni-ta	kaphasskessúpti-ta
PROPOSITIVE	kaphúpsi-ta	
IMPERATIVE	kaphú(si)psi-o	

INFORMAL *Familiar*

	INDICATIVE	RETROSPECTIVE
DECLARATIVE/ *INTERROGATIVE*		
PRESENT	kaph-ne/-núnka	kaph-te/-tónka
PAST	kaphass-ne	kaphass-te
REMOTE PAST	kaphassóss-ne	kaphassóss-te
FUTURE	kaphkess-ne	kaphkess-te
PAST FUTURE	kaphasskess-ne	kaphasskess-te
PROPOSITIVE	kaph-se	
IMPERATIVE	kaph-ke	

	INFORMAL *Intimate* INDICATIVE	INFORMAL *Casual* INDICATIVE
DECLARATIVE/ *INTERROGATIVE*		
PRESENT	kaph-a	kaph-ci
PAST	kaphass-ó	kaphass-ci
REMOTE PAST	kaphassóss-ó	kaphassóss-ci
FUTURE	kaphkess-ó	kaphkess-ci
PAST FUTURE	kaphasskess-ó	kaphasskess-ci
PROPOSITIVE *IMPERATIVE*	kaph-a	kaph-ci

CAUSATIVE: *PASSIVE:*

FORMAL *Plain*

	INDICATIVE	RETROSPECTIVE
DECLARATIVE/ *INTERROGATIVE*		
PRESENT	kath-ta/-únya	kath-tóla/-tónya
PAST	kathass-ta/-núnya	kathass-tóla
REMOTE PAST	kathassóss-ta	kathassóss-tóla
FUTURE	kathkess-ta	kathkess-tóla
PAST FUTURE	kathasskess-ta	kathasskess-tóla
PROPOSITIVE		
IMPERATIVE		

FORMAL *Polite*

	INDICATIVE	RETROSPECTIVE
DECLARATIVE/ *INTERROGATIVE*		
PRESENT	kathsúpni-ta/-kka	kathsúpti-ta/-kka
PAST	kathassúpni-ta	kathassúpti-ta
REMOTE PAST	kathassóssúpni-ta	kathassóssúpti-ta
FUTURE	kathkessúpni-ta	kathkessúpti-ta
PAST FUTURE	kathasskessúpni-ta	kathasskessúpti-ta
PROPOSITIVE		
IMPERATIVE		

INFORMAL *Familiar*

	INDICATIVE	RETROSPECTIVE
DECLARATIVE/ *INTERROGATIVE*		
PRESENT	kath-ne/-únka	kath-te/-tónka
PAST	kathass-ne/-núnka	kathass-te
REMOTE PAST	kathassóss-ne	kathassóss-te
FUTURE	kathkess-ne	kathkess-te
PAST FUTURE	kathasskess-ne	kathasskess-te
PROPOSITIVE		
IMPERATIVE		

	INFORMAL *Intimate* INDICATIVE	INFORMAL *Casual* INDICATIVE
DECLARATIVE/ *INTERROGATIVE*		
PRESENT	kath-a	kath-ci
PAST	kathass-ó	kathass-ci
REMOTE PAST	kathassóss-ó	kathassóss-ci
FUTURE	kathkess-ó	kathkess-ci
PAST FUTURE	kathasskess-ó	kathasskess-ci
PROPOSITIVE		
IMPERATIVE		

CAUSATIVE: *PASSIVE:*

KEÚLÚ.TA 게 으르다
to be lazy, to be slothful   DESCRIPTIVE

FORMAL *Plain*

	INDICATIVE	RETROSPECTIVE
DECLARATIVE/ *INTERROGATIVE*		
PRESENT	keúlú-ta/-nya	keúlú-tóla-/tónya
PAST	keúllóss-ta/-núnya	keúllóss-tóla
REMOTE PAST	keúllóssóss-ta	keúllóssóss-tóla
FUTURE	keúlúkess-ta	keúlúkess-tóla
PAST FUTURE	keúllósskess-ta	keúllósskess-tóla

PROPOSITIVE
IMPERATIVE

FORMAL *Polite*

	INDICATIVE	RETROSPECTIVE
DECLARATIVE/ *INTERROGATIVE*		
PRESENT	keúlúpni-ta/-kka	keúlúpti-ta/-kka
PAST	keúllóssúpni-ta	keúllóssúpti-ta
REMOTE PAST	keúllóssóssúpni-ta	keúllóssóssúpti-ta
FUTURE	keúlúlkessúpni-ta	keúlúkessúpti-ta
PAST FUTURE	keúllósskessúpni-ta	keúllósskessúpti-ta

PROPOSITIVE
IMPERATIVE

INFORMAL *Familiar*

	INDICATIVE	RETROSPECTIVE
DECLARATIVE/ *INTERROGATIVE*		
PRESENT	keúlú-ne/-nka	keúlú-te/-tónka
PAST	keúllóss-ne/-núnka	keúllóss-te
REMOTE PAST	keúllóssóss-ne	keúllóssóss-te
FUTURE	keúlúkess-ne	keúlúkess-te
PAST FUTURE	keúllósskess-ne	keúllósskess-te

PROPOSITIVE
IMPERATIVE

	INFORMAL *Intimate* INDICATIVE	INFORMAL *Casual* INDICATIVE
DECLARATIVE/ *INTERROGATIVE*		
PRESENT	keúll-ó	keúlú-ci
PAST	keúllóss-ó	keúllóss-ci
REMOTE PAST	keúllóssóss-ó	keúllóssóss-ci
FUTURE	keúlúkess-ó	keúlúkess-ci
PAST FUTURE	keúllósskess-ó	keúllósskess-ci

PROPOSITIVE
IMPERATIVE

CAUSATIVE: *PASSIVE:*

FORMAL *Plain*

DECLARATIVE/ INTERROGATIVE	INDICATIVE	RETROSPECTIVE
PRESENT	kip-nûn.ta/-nûnya	kip-tóla/-tónya
PAST	kiwóss-ta	kiwóss-tóla
REMOTE PAST	kiwóssóss-ta	kiwóssóss-tóla
FUTURE	kipkess-ta	kipkess-tóla
PAST FUTURE	kiwósskess-ta	kiwósskess-tóla
PROPOSITIVE	kip-ca	
IMPERATIVE	kiw-ó.la	

FORMAL *Polite*

DECLARATIVE/ INTERROGATIVE	INDICATIVE	RETROSPECTIVE
PRESENT	kipsúpni-ta/-kka	kipsúpti-ta/-kka
PAST	kiwóssúpni-ta	kiwóssúpti-ta
REMOTE PAST	kiwóssóssúpni-ta	kiwóssóssúpti-ta
FUTURE	kipkessúpni-ta	kipkessúpti-ta
PAST FUTURE	kiwósskessúpni-ta	kiwósskessúpti-ta
PROPOSITIVE	kiupsi-ta	
IMPERATIVE	kiu(si)psi-o	

INFORMAL *Familiar*

DECLARATIVE/ INTERROGATIVE	INDICATIVE	RETROSPECTIVE
PRESENT	kip-ne/-nûnka	kip-te/-tònka
PAST	kiwóss-ne	kiwóss-te
REMOTE PAST	kiwóssóss-ne	kiwóssóss-te
FUTURE	kipkess-ne	kipkess-te
PAST FUTURE	kiwósskess-ne	kiwósskess-te
PROPOSITIVE	kip-se	
IMPERATIVE	kip-ke	

DECLARATIVE/ INTERROGATIVE	INFORMAL *Intimate* INDICATIVE	INFORMAL *Casual* INDICATIVE
PRESENT	ki.w-ó	kip-ci
PAST	kiwóss-ó	kiwóss-ci
REMOTE PAST	kiwóssóss-ó	kiwóssóss-ci
FUTURE	kipkess-ó	kipkess-ci
PAST FUTURE	kiwósskess-ó	kiwósskess-ci
PROPOSITIVE *IMPERATIVE*	ki.w-ó	

CAUSATIVE: *PASSIVE:*

to be distressing, to be trying, to be ill at ease   DESCRIPTIVE

FORMAL *Plain*

	INDICATIVE	RETROSPECTIVE
DECLARATIVE/ *INTERROGATIVE*		
PRESENT	koilo-p.ta/-unya	kiolop-tóla/-tónya
PAST	koilowass-ta/-núnya	koilowass-tóla
REMOTE PAST	koilowassóss-ta	koilowassóss-tóla
FUTURE	koilopkess-ta	koilopkess-tóla
PAST FUTURE	koilowasskess-ta	koilowasskess-tóla
PROPOSITIVE		
IMPERATIVE		

FORMAL *Polite*

	INDICATIVE	RETROSPECTIVE
DECLARATIVE/ *INTERROGATIVE*		
PRESENT	koilopsúpni-ta/-kka	koilopsúpti-ta/-kka
PAST	koilowassúpni-ta	koilowassúpti-ta
REMOTE PAST	koilowassóssúpni-ta	koilowassóssúpti-ta
FUTURE	koilopkessúpni-ta	koilopkessúpti-ta
PAST FUTURE	koilowasskessúpni-ta	koilowasskessúpti-ta
PROPOSITIVE		
IMPERATIVE		

INFORMAL *Familiar*

	INDICATIVE	RETROSPECTIVE
DECLARATIVE/ *INTERROGATIVE*		
PRESENT	koilo-p.ne/-unka	koilop-te/-tónka
PAST	koilowass-ne/-núnka	koilowass-te
REMOTE PAST	koilowassóss-ne	koilowassóss-te
FUTURE	koilopkess-ne	koilopkess-te
PAST FUTURE	koilowasskess-ne	koilowasskess-te
PROPOSITIVE		
IMPERATIVE		

	INFORMAL *Intimate* INDICATIVE	INFORMAL *Casual* INDICATIVE
DECLARATIVE/ *INTERROGATIVE*		
PRESENT	koilo.w-a	koilop-ci
PAST	koilowass-ó	koilowass-ci
REMOTE PAST	koilowassóss-ó	koilowassóss-ci
FUTURE	koilopkess-ó	koilopkess-ci
PAST FUTURE	koilowasskess-ó	koilowasskess-ci
PROPOSITIVE		
IMPERATIVE		

CAUSATIVE: *PASSIVE:*

FORMAL *Plain*

	INDICATIVE	RETROSPECTIVE
DECLARATIVE/ *INTERROGATIVE*		
PRESENT	kŏt-nŭn.ta/-nŭnya	kŏt-tóla/-tónya
PAST	kŏlŏss-ta	kŏlŏss-tóla
REMOTE PAST	kŏlŏssŏss-ta	kŏlŏssŏss-tóla
FUTURE	kŏtkess-ta	kŏtkess-tóla
PAST FUTURE	kŏlŏsskess-ta	kŏlŏsskess-tóla
PROPOSITIVE	kŏt-ca	
IMPERATIVE	kŏl-óla	

FORMAL *Polite*

	INDICATIVE	RETROSPECTIVE
DECLARATIVE/ *INTERROGATIVE*		
PRESENT	kŏtsŭpni-ta/-kka	kŏtsŭpti-ta/-kka
PAST	kŏlŏssŭpni-ta	kŏlŏssŭpti-ta
REMOTE PAST	kŏlŏssŏssŭpni-ta	kŏlŏssŏssŭpti-ta
FUTURE	kŏtkessŭpni-ta	kŏtkessŭpti-ta
PAST FUTURE	kŏlŏsskessŭpni-ta	kŏlŏsskessŭpti-ta
PROPOSITIVE	kŏlŭpsi-ta	
IMPERATIVE	kŏlŭ(si)psi-o	

INFORMAL *Familiar*

	INDICATIVE	RETROSPECTIVE
DECLARATIVE/ *INTERROGATIVE*		
PRESENT	kŏt-ne/-nŭnka	kŏt-te/-tónka
PAST	kŏlŏss-ne	kŏlŏss-te
REMOTE PAST	kŏlŏssŏss-ne	kŏlŏssŏss-te
FUTURE	kŏtkess-ne	kŏtkess-te
PAST FUTURE	kŏlŏsskess-ne	kŏlŏsskess-te
PROPOSITIVE	kŏt-se	
IMPERATIVE	kŏt-ke	

	INFORMAL *Intimate* INDICATIVE	INFORMAL *Casual* INDICATIVE
DECLARATIVE/ *INTERROGATIVE*		
PRESENT	kŏl-ó	kŏt-ci
PAST	kŏlŏss-ó	kŏlŏss-ci
REMOTE PAST	kŏlŏssŏss-ó	kŏlŏssŏss-ci
FUTURE	kŏtkess-ó	kŏtkess-ci
PAST FUTURE	kŏlŏsskess-ó	kŏlŏsskess-ci
PROPOSITIVE	kŏl-ó	
IMPERATIVE		

CAUSATIVE: *PASSIVE:*

KŎT.TA   걷다
to gather up, to fold up, to roll up

	FORMAL *Plain*	
	INDICATIVE	RETROSPECTIVE
DECLARATIVE/ *INTERROGATIVE*		
PRESENT	kŏt-nŭn.ta/-nŭnya	kŏt-tóla/-tónya
PAST	kótóss-ta	kótóss-tóla
REMOTE PAST	kótóssóss-ta	kótóssóss-tóla
FUTURE	kótkess-ta	kótkess-tóla
PAST FUTURE	kótósskess-ta	kótósskess-tóla
PROPOSITIVE	kót-ca	
IMPERATIVE	kót-óla	

	FORMAL *Polite*	
	INDICATIVE	RETROSPECTIVE
DECLARATIVE/ *INTERROGATIVE*		
PRESENT	kótsŭpni-ta/-kka	kótsŭpti-ta/-kka
PAST	kótóssŭpni-ta	kótóssŭpti-ta
REMOTE PAST	kótóssóssŭpni-ta	kótóssóssŭpti-ta
FUTURE	kótkessŭpni-ta	kótkessŭpti-ta
PAST FUTURE	kótósskesssŭpni-ta	kótósskessŭpti-ta
PROPOSITIVE	kótŭpsi-ta	
IMPERATIVE	kótŭ(si)psi-o	

	INFORMAL *Familiar*	
	INDICATIVE	RETROSPECTIVE
DECLARATIVE/ *INTERROGATIVE*		
PRESENT	kót-ne/-nŭnka	kót-te/-tónka
PAST	kótóss-ne	kótóss-te
REMOTE PAST	kótóssóss-ne	kótóssóss-te
FUTURE	kótkess-ne	kótkess-te
PAST FUTURE	kótósskess-ne	kótósskess-te
PROPOSITIVE	kót-se	
IMPERATIVE	kót-ke	

	INFORMAL *Intimate*	INFORMAL *Casual*
	INDICATIVE	INDICATIVE
DECLARATIVE/ *INTERROGATIVE*		
PRESENT	kót-ó	kót-ci
PAST	kótóss-ó	kótóss-ci
REMOTE PAST	kótóssóss-ó	kótóssóss-ci
FUTURE	kótkess-ó	kótkess-ci
PAST FUTURE	kótósskess-ó	kótósskess-ci
PROPOSITIVE *IMPERATIVE*	kót-ó	kót-ci

CAUSATIVE: *PASSIVE:*

KULÙ.TA   구르다
1) to roll INTRANSITIVE 2) to stamp one's feet, to tread noisily TRANSITIVE

FORMAL *Plain*

	INDICATIVE	RETROSPECTIVE
DECLARATIVE/ *INTERROGATIVE*		
PRESENT	kulù-n.ta/-nùnya	kulù-tóla/-tónya
PAST	kullóss-ta	kullóss-tóla
REMOTE PAST	kullóssóss-ta	kullóssóss-tóla
FUTURE	kulùkess-ta	kulùkess-tóla
PAST FUTURE	kullósskess-ta	kullósskess-tóla
PROPOSITIVE	kulù-ca	
IMPERATIVE	kull-óla	

FORMAL *Polite*

	INDICATIVE	RETROSPECTIVE
DECLARATIVE/ *INTERROGATIVE*		
PRESENT	kulùpní-ta/-kka	kulùpti-ta/-kka
PAST	kullóssùpni-ta	kullóssùpti-ta
REMOTE PAST	kullóssóssùpni-ta	kullóssóssùpti-ta
FUTURE	kulùkessùpni-ta	kulùkessùpti-ta
PAST FUTURE	kullósskessùpni-ta	kullósskessùpti-ta
PROPOSITIVE	kulùpsi-ta	
IMPERATIVE	kulù(si)psi-o	

INFORMAL *Familiar*

	INDICATIVE	RETROSPECTIVE
DECLARATIVE/ *INTERROGATIVE*		
PRESENT	kulù-ne/-nùnka	kulù-te/-tónka
PAST	kullóss-ne	kullóss-te
REMOTE PAST	kullóssóss-ne	kullóssóss-te
FUTURE	kulùkess-ne	kulùkess-te
PAST FUTURE	kullósskess-ne	kullósskess-te
PROPOSITIVE	kulù-se	
IMPERATIVE	kulù-ke	

	INFORMAL *Intimate* INDICATIVE	INFORMAL *Casual* INDICATIVE
DECLARATIVE/ *INTERROGATIVE*		
PRESENT	kull-ó	kulù-ci
PAST	kullóss-ó	kullóss-ci
REMOTE PAST	kullóssóss-ó	kullóssóss-ci
FUTURE	kulùkess-ó	kulùkess-ci
PAST FUTURE	kullósskess-ó	kullósskess-ci
PROPOSITIVE *IMPERATIVE*	kull-ó	kulù-ci

CAUSATIVE: *PASSIVE:*

KUP.TA
to roast, to broil, to bake

굽다

FORMAL *Plain*

	INDICATIVE	RETROSPECTIVE
DECLARATIVE/ *INTERROGATIVE*		
PRESENT	kup-nún.ta/-núnya	kup-tóla/-tónya
PAST	kuwóss-ta	kuwóss-tóla
REMOTE PAST	kuwóssóss-ta	kuwóssóss-tóla
FUTURE	kupkess-ta	kupkess-tóla
PAST FUTURE	kuwósskess-ta	kuwósskess-tóla
PROPOSITIVE	kup-ca	
IMPERATIVE	kuwó-la	

FORMAL *Polite*

	INDICATIVE	RETROSPECTIVE
DECLARATIVE/ *INTERROGATIVE*		
PRESENT	kupsúpni-ta/-kka	kupsúpti-ta/-kka
PAST	kuwóssúpni-ta	kuwóssúpti-ta
REMOTE PAST	kuwóssóssúpti-ta	kuwóssóssúpti-ta
FUTURE	kupkessúpni-ta	kupkessúpti-ta
PAST FUTURE	kupwósskessúpni-ta	kuwósskessúpti-ta
PROPOSITIVE	kupsi-ta	
IMPERATIVE	ku(si)psi-o	

INFORMAL *Familiar*

	INDICATIVE	RETROSPECTIVE
DECLARATIVE/ *INTERROGATIVE*		
PRESENT	kup-ne/-núnka	kup-te/-tónka
PAST	kuwóss-ne	kuwóss-te
REMOTE PAST	kuwóssóss-ne	kuwóssóss-te
FUTURE	kupkess-ne	kupkess-te
PAST FUTURE	kuwósskess-ne	kuwósskess-te
PROPOSITIVE	kup-se	
IMPERATIVE	kup-ke	

	INFORMAL *Intimate* INDICATIVE	INFORMAL *Casual* INDICATIVE
DECLARATIVE/ *INTERROGATIVE*		
PRESENT	ku-wó	kup-ci
PAST	kuwóss-ó	kuwóss-ci
REMOTE PAST	kuwóssóss-ó	kuwóssóss-ci
FUTURE	kupkess-ó	kupkess-ci
PAST FUTURE	·kuwósskess-ó	kuwósskess-ci
PROPOSITIVE *IMPERATIVE*	ku-wó	kup-ci

CAUSATIVE: *PASSIVE:* KUPHI.TA
                                                       to be roasted

KULK.TA   굵다
to be thick, to be burly   DESCRIPTIVE

FORMAL *Plain*

	INDICATIVE	RETROSPECTIVE

DECLARATIVE/
INTERROGATIVE

PRESENT	kulk-ta/-únya	kulk-tóla/-tónya
PAST	kulkóss-ta/-núnya	kulkóss-tóla
REMOTE PAST	kulkóssóss-ta	kulkóssóss-tóla
FUTURE	kulkkess-ta	kulkkess-tóla
PAST FUTURE	kulkósskess-ta	kulkósskess-tóla

PROPOSITIVE
IMPERATIVE

FORMAL *Polite*

	INDICATIVE	RETROSPECTIVE

DECLARATIVE/
INTERROGATIVE

PRESENT	kulksúpni-ta/-kka	kulksúpti-ta/-kka
PAST	kulkóssúpni-ta	kulkóssúpti-ta
REMOTE PAST	kulkóssóssúpni-ta	kulkóssóssúpti-ta
FUTURE	kulkkessúpni-ta	kulkkessúpti-ta
PAST FUTURE	kulkósskessúpni-ta	kulkósskessúpti-ta

PROPOSITIVE
IMPERATIVE

INFORMAL *Familiar*

	INDICATIVE	RETROSPECTIVE

DECLARATIVE/
INTERROGATIVE

PRESENT	kulk-ne/-únka	kulk-te/-tónka
PAST	kulkóss-ne/-núnka	kulkóss-te
REMOTE PAST	kulkóssóss-ne	kulkóssóss-te
FUTURE	kulkkess-ne	kulkkess-te
PAST FUTURE	kulkósskess-ne	kulkósskess-te

PROPOSITIVE
IMPERATIVE

	INFORMAL *Intimate*	INFORMAL *Casual*
	INDICATIVE	INDICATIVE

DECLARATIVE/
INTERROGATIVE

PRESENT	kulk-ó	kulk-ci
PAST	kulkóss-ó	kulkóss-ci
REMOTE PAST	kulkóssóss-ó	kulkóssóss-ci
FUTURE	kulkkess-ó	kulkkess-ci
PAST FUTURE	kulkósskess-ó	kulkósskess-ci

PROPOSITIVE
IMPERATIVE

CAUSATIVE: *PASSIVE:*

to draw, to mark

FORMAL *Plain*

	INDICATIVE	RETROSPECTIVE
DECLARATIVE/ *INTERROGATIVE*		
PRESENT	kùs-nùn.ta/-nùnya	kùs-tóla/-tònya
PAST	kùóss-ta	kùóss-tóla
REMOTE PAST	kùóssóss-ta	kùóssóss-tóla
FUTURE	kùskess-ta	kùskess-tóla
PAST FUTURE	kùósskess-ta.	kùósskess-tóla
PROPOSITIVE	kùs-ca	
IMPERATIVE	kù-óla	

FORMAL *Polite*

	INDICATIVE	RETROSPECTIVE
DECLARATIVE/ *INTERROGATIVE*		
PRESENT	kùssùpni-ta/-kka	kùssùpti-ta/-kka
PAST	kùóssùpni-ta	kùóssùpti-ta
REMOTE PAST	kùóssóssùpni-ta	kùóssóssùpti-ta
FUTURE	kùskessùpni-ta	kùskessùpti-ta
PAST FUTURE	kùósskessùpni-ta	kùósskessùpti-ta
PROPOSITIVE	kùpsi-ta	
IMPERATIVE	kù(si)psi-o	

INFORMAL *Familiar*

	INDICATIVE	RETROSPECTIVE
DECLARATIVE/ *INTERROGATIVE*		
PRESENT	kùs-ne/-nùnka	kùs-te/-tònka
PAST	kùóss-ne	kùóss-te
REMOTE PAST	kùóssóss-ne	kùóssóss-te
FUTURE	kùskess-ne	kùskess-te
PAST FUTURE	kùósskess-ne	kùósskess-te
PROPOSITIVE	kùs-se	
IMPERATIVE	kùs-ke	

	INFORMAL *Intimate* INDICATIVE	INFORMAL *Casual* INDICATIVE
DECLARATIVE/ *INTERROGATIVE*		
PRESENT	kù-ó	kùs-ci
PAST	kùóss-ó	kùóss-ci
REMOTE PAST	kùóssóss-ó	kùóssóss-ci
FUTURE	kùskess-ó	kùskess-ci
PAST FUTURE	kùósskess-ó	kùósskess-ci
PROPOSITIVE *IMPERATIVE*	kù-ó	kùs-ci

CAUSATIVE: *PASSIVE:*

to be troublesome, to be irksome   DESCRIPTIVE

FORMAL *Plain*

	INDICATIVE	RETROSPECTIVE
DECLARATIVE/ *INTERROGATIVE*		
PRESENT	kwichanh-ta/-ὐnya	kwichanh-tóla/-tónya
PAST	kwichanhass-ta/-nὐnya	kwishanhass-tóla
REMOTE PAST	kwichanhassóss-ta	kwichanhassóss-tóla
FUTURE	kwichanhkess-ta	kwishanhkess-tóla
PAST FUTURE	kwichanhasskess-ta	kwichanhasskess-tóla
PROPOSITIVE		
IMPERATIVE		

FORMAL *Polite*

	INDICATIVE	RETROSPECTIVE
DECLARATIVE/ *INTERROGATIVE*		
PRESENT	kwichanhsὐpni-ta/-kka	kwichanhsὐpti-ta/-kka
PAST	kwichanhassὐpni-ta	kwichanhassὐpti-ta ·
REMOTE PAST	kwichanhassóssὐpni-ta	kwichanhassóssὐpti-ta
FUTURE	kwichanhkessὐpni-ta	kwichanhkessὐpti-ta
PAST FUTURE	kwichanhasskessὐpni-ta	kwishanhasskessὐpti-ta
PROPOSITIVE		
IMPERATIVE		

INFORMAL *Familiar*

	INDICATIVE	RETROSPECTIVE
DECLARATIVE/ *INTERROGATIVE*		
PRESENT	kwichanh-ne/-ὐnya	kwichanh-te/-tónya
PAST	kwichanhass-ne/-nὐnya	kwichanhass-te
REMOTE PAST	kwichanhassóss-ne	kwichanhassóss-te
FUTURE	kwichanhkess-ne	kwichanhkess-te
PAST FUTURE	kwichanhasskess-ne	kwichanhasskess-te
PROPOSITIVE		
IMPERATIVE		

	INFORMAL *Intimate* INDICATIVE	INFORMAL *Casual* INDICATIVE
DECLARATIVE/ *INTERROGATIVE*		
PRESENT	kwichanh-a	kwichanh-ci
PAST	kwichanhass-ó	kwichanhass-ci
REMOTE PAST	kwichanhassóss-ó	kwichanhassóss-ci
FUTURE	kwichanhkess-ó	kwichanhkess-ci
PAST FUTURE	kwichanhasskess-ó	kwichanhasskess-ci
PROPOSITIVE		
IMPERATIVE		

CAUSATIVE: *PASSIVE:*

KHAE.TA
to dig up, to unearth

캐다

FORMAL *Plain*

	INDICATIVE	RETROSPECTIVE
DECLARATIVE/ *INTERROGATIVE*		
PRESENT	khae-n.ta/-núnya	khae-tóla/-tónya
PAST	khaeóss-ta	khaeóss-tóla
REMOTE PAST	khaeóssóss-ta	khaeóssóss-tóla
FUTURE	khaekess-ta	khaekess-tóla
PAST FUTURE	khaeósskess-ta	khaeósskess-tóla
PROPOSITIVE	khae-ca	
IMPERATIVE	khae-óla	

FORMAL *Polite*

	INDICATIVE	RETROSPECTIVE
DECLARATIVE/ *INTERROGATIVE*		
PRESENT	khaepni-ta/-kka	khaesúpti-ta/-kka
PAST	khaeóssúpni-ta	khaeóssúpti-ta
REMOTE PAST	khaeóssóssúpni-ta	khaeóssóssúpti-ta
FUTURE	khaekessúpni-ta	khaekessúpti-ta
PAST FUTURE	khaeósskessúpni-ta	khaeósskessúpti-ta
PROPOSITIVE	khaepsi-ta	
IMPERATIVE	khae(si)psi-o	

INFORMAL *Familiar*

	INDICATIVE	RETROSPECTIVE
DECLARATIVE/ *INTERROGATIVE*		
PRESENT	khae-ne/-núnka	khae-te/-tónka
PAST	khaeóss-ne	khaeóss-te
REMOTE PAST	khaeóssóss-ne	khaeóssóss-te
FUTURE	khaekess-ne	khaekess-te
PAST FUTURE	khaeósskess-ne	khaeósskess-te
PROPOSITIVE	khae-se	
IMPERATIVE	khae-ke	

	INFORMAL *Intimate* INDICATIVE	INFORMAL *Casual* INDICATIVE
DECLARATIVE/ *INTERROGATIVE*		
PRESENT	khae-ó	khae-ci
PAST	khaeóss-ó	khaeóss-ci
REMOTE PAST	khaeóssóss-ó	khaeóssóss-ci
FUTURE	khaekess-ó	khaekess-ci
PAST FUTURE	khaeósskess-ó	khaeósskess-ci
PROPOSITIVE *IMPERATIVE*	khae-ó	

CAUSATIVE: *PASSIVE:*

FORMAL *Plain*

	INDICATIVE	RETROSPECTIVE
DECLARATIVE/ INTERROGATIVE		
PRESENT	khengki-n.ta/-nùnya	khengki-tóla/-tónya
PAST	khengkyóss-ta	khengkyóss-tóla
REMOTE PAST	khengkyóssóss-ta	khengkyóssóss-tóla
FUTURE	khengkikess-ta	khengkikess-tóla
PAST FUTURE	khengkyósskess-ta	khengkyósskess-tóla

PROPOSITIVE
IMPERATIVE

FORMAL *Polite*

	INDICATIVE	RETROSPECTIVE
DECLARATIVE/ INTERROGATIVE		
PRESENT	khengkipni-ta/-kka	khengkipti-ta/-kka
PAST	khengkyóssùpni-ta	khengkyóssùpti-ta
REMOTE PAST	khenghyóssóssùpni-ta	khenghkyóssóssùpti-ta
FUTURE	khengkikessùpni-ta	khengkikessùpti-ta
PAST FUTURE	khenghyósskessùpni-ta	khengkyósskessùpti-ta

PROPOSITIVE
IMPERATIVE

INFORMAL *Familiar*

	INDICATIVE	RETROSPECTIVE
DECLARATIVE/ INTERROGATIVE		
PRESENT	khengki-ne/-nùnka	khengki-te/-tónka
PAST	khengkyóss-ne	khengkyóss-te
REMOTE PAST	khengkyóssóss-ne	khengkyóssóss-te
FUTURE	khengkikess-ne	khengkikess-te
PAST FUTURE	khengkyósskess-ne	khenghyósskess-te

PROPOSITIVE
IMPERATIVE

	INFORMAL *Intimate* INDICATIVE	INFORMAL *Casual* INDICATIVE
DECLARATIVE/ INTERROGATIVE		
PRESENT	kheng.ky-ò	khengki-ci
PAST	khengkyóss-ò	khengkyóss-ci
REMOTE PAST	khengkyóssóss-ò	khengkyóssóss-ci
FUTURE	khengkikess-ò	khengkikess-ci
PAST FUTURE	khengkyósskess-ò	khengkyósskess-ci

PROPOSITIVE
IMPERATIVE

CAUSATIVE:	*PASSIVE:*

1) to light 2) to saw 3) to play (a violin)

FORMAL *Plain*

	INDICATIVE	RETROSPECTIVE
DECLARATIVE/ *INTERROGATIVE*		
PRESENT	khi-n.ta/-núnya	khi-tóla/-tónya
PAST	khyóss-ta	khyóss-tóla
REMOTE PAST	khyóssóss-ta	khyóssóss-tóla
FUTURE	khikess-ta	khikess-tóla
PAST FUTURE	khyósskess-ta	khyósskess-tóla
PROPOSITIVE	khi-ca	
IMPERATIVE	khy-ò.la	

FORMAL *Polite*

	INDICATIVE	RETROSPECTIVE
DECLARATIVE/ *INTERROGATIVE*		
PRESENT	khipni-ta/-kka	khipti-ta/-kka
PAST	khyóssúpni-ta	khyóssúpti-ta
REMOTE PAST	khyóssóssúpni-ta	khyóssóssúpti-ta
FUTURE	khikessúpni-ta	khikessúpti-ta
PAST FUTURE	khyósskessúpni-ta	khyósskessúpti-ta
PROPOSITIVE	khipsi-ta	
IMPERATIVE	khi(si)psi-o	

INFORMAL *Familiar*

	INDICATIVE	RETROSPECTIVE
DECLARATIVE/ *INTERROGATIVE*		
PRESENT	khi-ne/-núnka	khi-te/-tónka
PAST	khyóss-ne	khyóss-te
REMOTE PAST	khyóssóss-ne	khyóssóss-te
FUTURE	khikess-ne	khikess-te
PAST FUTURE	khyósskess-ne	khyósskess-te
PROPOSITIVE	khi-se	
IMPERATIVE	khi-ke	

	INFORMAL *Intimate* INDICATIVE	INFORMAL *Casual* INDICATIVE
DECLARATIVE/ *INTERROGATIVE*		
PRESENT	khy-ò	khi-ci
PAST	khyóss-ò	khyóss-ci
REMOTE PAST	khyóssóss-ò	khyóssóss-ci
FUTURE	khikess-ò	khikess-ci
PAST FUTURE	khyósskess-ò	khyósskess-ci
PROPOSITIVE	khy-ò	khi-ci
IMPERATIVE		

CAUSATIVE:　　　　　　　　　　　　　*PASSIVE:*

FORMAL *Plain*

	INDICATIVE	RETROSPECTIVE
DECLARATIVE/ *INTERROGATIVE*		
PRESENT	khiu-n.ta/-nŭnya	khiu-tóla/-tónya
PAST	khiwóss-ta	khiwóss-tóla
REMOTE PAST	khiwóssóss-ta	khiwóssóss-tóla
FUTURE	khiukess-ta	khiukess-tóla
PAST FUTURE	khiwósskess-ta	khiwósskess-tóla
PROPOSITIVE	khiu-ca	
IMPERATIVE	khiw-ó.la	

FORMAL *Polite*

	INDICATIVE	RETROSPECTIVE
DECLARATIVE/ *INTERROGATIVE*		
PRESENT	khiupni-ta/-kka	khiupti-ta/-kka
PAST	khiwóssŭpni-ta	khiwóssŭpti-ta
REMOTE PAST	khiwóssóssŭpni-ta	khiwóssóssŭpti-ta
FUTURE	khiukessŭpni-ta	khiukessŭpti-ta
PAST FUTURE	khiwósskessŭpni-ta	khiwósskessŭpti-ta
PROPOSITIVE	khiupsi-ta	
IMPERATIVE	khiu(si)psi-o	

INFORMAL *Familiar*

	INDICATIVE	RETROSPECTIVE
DECLARATIVE/ *INTERROGATIVE*		
PRESENT	khiu-ne/-nŭnka	khiu-te/-tónka
PAST	khiwóss-ne	khiwóss-te
REMOTE PAST	khiwóssóss-ne	khiwóssóss-te
FUTURE	khiukess-ne	khiukess-te
PAST FUTURE	khiwósskess-ne	khiwósskess-te
PROPOSITIVE	khiu-se	
IMPERATIVE	khiu-ke	

	INFORMAL *Intimate* INDICATIVE	INFORMAL *Casual* INDICATIVE
DECLARATIVE/ *INTERROGATIVE*		
PRESENT	khi.w-ó	khiu-ci
PAST	khiwóss-ó	khiwóss-ci
REMOTE PAST	khiwóssóss-ó	khiwóssóss-ci
FUTURE	khiukess-ó	khiukess-ci
PAST FUTURE	khiwósskess-ó	khiwósskess-ci
PROPOSITIVE *IMPERATIVE*	khi.w-ó	

CAUSATIVE:　　　　　　　　　　　*PASSIVE:*

FORMAL *Plain*

	INDICATIVE	RETROSPECTIVE
DECLARATIVE/ *INTERROGATIVE*		
PRESENT	khótala-h.ta/-nya	khótalah-tóla/-tónya
PAST	khótalaess-ta/-núnya	khótalaess-tóla
REMOTE PAST	khótalaessóss-ta	khótalaessóss-tóla
FUTURE	khótalahkess-ta	khótalahkess-tóla
PAST FUTURE	khótalaesskess-ta	khótalaesskess-tóla
PROPOSITIVE		
IMPERATIVE		

FORMAL *Polite*

	INDICATIVE	RETROSPECTIVE
DECLARATIVE/ *INTERROGATIVE*		
PRESENT	khótalahsúpni-ta/-kka	khótalahsúpti-ta/-kka
PAST	khótalaessúpni-ta	khótalaessúpti-ta
REMOTE PAST	khótalaessóssúpni-ta	khótalaessóssúpti-ta
FUTURE	khótalahkessúpni-ta	khótalahkessúpti-ta
PAST FUTURE	khótalaesskessúpni-ta	khótalaesskessúpti-ta
PROPOSITIVE		
IMPERATIVE		

INFORMAL *Familiar*

	INDICATIVE	RETROSPECTIVE
DECLARATIVE/ *INTERROGATIVE*		
PRESENT	khótala-h.ne/-nka	khótalah-te/-tónka
PAST	khótalaess-ne/-núnka	khótalaess-te
REMOTE PAST	khótalaessóss-ne	khótalaessóss-te
FUTURE	khótalahkess-ne	khótalahkess-te
PAST FUTURE	khótalaesskess-ne	khótalaesskess-te
PROPOSITIVE		
IMPERATIVE		

	INFORMAL *Intimate* INDICATIVE	INFORMAL *Casual* INDICATIVE
DECLARATIVE/ *INTERROGATIVE*		
PRESENT	khótalae	khótalah-ci
PAST	khótalaess-ó	khótalaess-ci
REMOTE PAST	khótalaessóss-ó	khótalaessóss-ci
FUTURE	khótalahkess-ó	khótalahkess-ci
PAST FUTURE	khótalaesskess-ó	khótalaesskess-ci
PROPOSITIVE		
IMPERATIVE		

CAUSATIVE: *PASSIVE:*

77

to be big, to be large, to be great   DESCRIPTIVE

FORMAL *Plain*

	INDICATIVE	RETROSPECTIVE
DECLARATIVE/ *INTERROGATIVE*		
PRESENT	khú-ta/-nya	khú-tóla/-tónya
PAST	khóss-ta/-núnya	khóss-tóla
REMOTE PAST	khóssóss-ta	khóssóss-tóla
FUTURE	khúkess-ta	khúkess-tóla
PAST FUTURE	khósskess-ta	khósskess-tóla

PROPOSITIVE
IMPERATIVE

FORMAL *Polite*

	INDICATIVE	RETROSPECTIVE
DECLARATIVE/ *INTERROGATIVE*		
PRESENT	khúpni-ta/-kka	khúpti-ta/-kka
PAST	khóssúpni-ta	khóssúpti-ta
REMOTE PAST	khóssóssúpni-ta	khóssóssúpti-ta
FUTURE	khúkessúpni-ta	khúkessúpti-ta
PAST FUTURE	khósskessúpni-ta	khósskessúpti-ta

PROPOSITIVE
IMPERATIVE

INFORMAL *Familiar*

	INDICATIVE	RETROSPECTIVE
DECLARATIVE/ *INTERROGATIVE*		
PRESENT	khú-ne/-nka	khú-te/-tónka
PAST	khóss-ne/-núnka	khóss-te
REMOTE PAST	khóssóss-ne	khóssóss-te
FUTURE	khúkess-ne	khúkess-te
PAST FUTURE	khósskess-ne	khósskess-te

PROPOSITIVE
IMPERATIVE

	INFORMAL *Intimate* INDICATIVE	INFORMAL *Casual* INDICATIVE
DECLARATIVE/ *INTERROGATIVE*		
PRESENT	khó	khú-ci
PAST	khóss-ó	khóss-ci
REMOTE PAST	khóssóss-ó	khóssóss-ci
FUTURE	khúkess-ó	khúkess-ci
PAST FUTURE	khósskess-ó	khósskess-ci

PROPOSITIVE
IMPERATIVE

CAUSATIVE:	*PASSIVE:*

KHU.TA   크다
to grow, to become big   INTRANSITIVE

FORMAL *Plain*

	INDICATIVE	RETROSPECTIVE
DECLARATIVE/ *INTERROGATIVE*		
PRESENT	khu̇-n.ta/-nu̇nya	khu̇-tȯla/tȯnya
PAST	khȯss-ta	khȯss-tȯla
REMOTE PAST	khȯssȯss-ta	khȯssȯss-tȯla
FUTURE	khu̇kess-ta	khu̇kess-tȯla
PAST FUTURE	khȯsskess-te	khȯsskess-tȯla
PROPOSITIVE	khu̇-ca	
IMPERATIVE	khȯ-la	

FORMAL *Polite*

	INDICATIVE	RETROSPECTIVE
DECLARATIVE/ *INTERROGATIVE*		
PRESENT	ku̇pni-ta/-kka	ku̇pti-ta/-kka
PAST	khȯssu̇pni-ta	khȯssu̇pti-ta
REMOTE PAST	khȯssȯssu̇pni-ta	khȯssȯssu̇pti-ta
FUTURE	khu̇kessu̇pni-ta	khu̇kessu̇pti-ta
PAST FUTURE	khȯsskessu̇pni-ta	khȯsskessu̇pti-ta
PROPOSITIVE	khu̇psi-ta	
IMPERATIVE	khu̇(si)psi-o	

INFORMAL *Familiar*

	INDICATIVE	RETROSPECTIVE
DECLARATIVE/ *INTERROGATIVE*		
PRESENT	khu̇-ne/-nu̇nka	khu̇-te/-tȯnka
PAST	khȯss-ne	khȯss-te
REMOTE PAST	khȯssȯss-ne	khȯssȯss-te
FUTURE	khu̇kess-ne	khu̇kess-te
PAST FUTURE	khȯsskess-ne	khȯsskess-te
PROPOSITIVE	khu̇-se	
IMPERATIVE	khu̇-ke	

	INFORMAL *Intimate* INDICATIVE	INFORMAL *Casual* INDICATIVE
DECLARATIVE/ *INTERROGATIVE*		
PRESENT	khȯ	khu̇-ci
PAST	khȯss-ȯ	khȯss-ci
REMOTE PAST	khȯssȯss-ȯ	khȯssȯss-ci
FUTURE	khu̇kess-ȯ	khu̇kess-ci
PAST FUTURE	khȯsskess-ȯ	khȯsskess-ci
PROPOSITIVE *IMPERATIVE*	khȯ	khu̇-ci

CAUSATIVE: *PASSIVE:*

FORMAL *Plain*

	INDICATIVE	RETROSPECTIVE
DECLARATIVE/ *INTERROGATIVE*		
PRESENT	kkama-h.ta/-nya	kkamah-tóla/-tónya
PAST	kkamaess-ta/-núnya	kkamaess-tóla
REMOTE PAST	kkamaessóss-ta	kkamaessóss-tóla
FUTURE	kkamahkess-ta	kkamahkess-tóla
PAST FUTURE	kkamaesskess-ta	kkamaesskess-tóla

PROPOSITIVE
IMPERATIVE

FORMAL *Polite*

	INDICATIVE	RETROSPECTIVE
DECLARATIVE/ *INTERROGATIVE*		
PRESENT	kkamahsúpni-ta/-kka	kkamahsúpti-ta/-kka
PAST	kkamaessúpni-ta	kkamaessúpti-ta
REMOTE PAST	kkamaessóssúpni-ta	kkamaessóssúpti-ta
FUTURE	kkamahkessúpni-ta	kkamahkessúpti-ta
PAST FUTURE	kkamaesskessúpni-ta	kkamaesskessúpti-ta

PROPOSITIVE
IMPERATIVE

INFORMAL *Familiar*

	INDICATIVE	RETROSPECTIVE
DECLARATIVE/ *INTERROGATIVE*		
PRESENT	kkama-h.ne/-nka	kkamah-te/-tónka
PAST	kkamaess-ne/-núnka	kkamaess-te
REMOTE PAST	kkamaessóss-ne	kkamaessóss-te
FUTURE	kkamahkess-ne	kkamahkess-te
PAST FUTURE	kkamaesskess-ne	kkamaesskess-te

PROPOSITIVE
IMPERATIVE

	INFORMAL *Intimate* INDICATIVE	INFORMAL *Casual* INDICATIVE
DECLARATIVE/ *INTERROGATIVE*		
PRESENT	kkamae	kkamah-ci
PAST	kkamaess-ó	kkamaess-ci
REMOTE PAST	kkamaessóss-ó	kkamaessóss-ci
FUTURE	kkamahkess-ó	kkamahkess-ci
PAST FUTURE	kkamaesskess-ó	kkamaesskess-ci

PROPOSITIVE
IMPERATIVE

CAUSATIVE: *PASSIVE:*

to apprehend, to perceive, to wake up to

FORMAL *Plain*

	INDICATIVE	RETROSPECTIVE
DECLARATIVE/ *INTERROGATIVE*		
PRESENT	kkaetat-núnta/-núnya	kkaetat-tóla/-tónya
PAST	kkaetalass-ta	kkaetalass-tóla
REMOTE PAST	kkaetalassóss-ta	kkaetalassóss-tóla
FUTURE	kkaetatkess-ta	kkaetatkess-tóla
PAST FUTURE	kkaetalasskess-ta	kkaetalasskess-tóla
PROPOSITIVE	kkaetat-ca	
IMPERATIVE	kkaetal-ala	

FORMAL *Polite*

	INDICATIVE	RETROSPECTIVE
DECLARATIVE/ *INTERROGATIVE*		
PRESENT	kkaetatsúpni-ta/-kka	kkaetatsúpti-ta/-kka
PAST	kkaetalassúpni-ta	kkaetalassúpti-ta
REMOTE PAST	kkaetalassóssúpni-ta	kkaetalassóssúpti-ta
FUTURE	kkatatkessúpni-ta	kkaetatkessúpti-ta
PAST FUTURE	kkaetalasskessúpni-ta	kkaetalasskessúpti-ta
PROPOSITIVE	kkaetalúpsi-ta	
IMPERATIVE	kkaetalú(si)psi-o	

INFORMAL *Familiar*

	INDICATIVE	RETROSPECTIVE
DECLARATIVE/ *INTERROGATIVE*		
PRESENT	kkaetat-ne/-núnka	kkaetat-te/-tónka
PAST	kkaetalass-ne	kkaetalass-te
REMOTE PAST	kkaetalassóss-ne	kkaetalassóss-te
FUTURE	kkaetatkess-ne	kkaetatkess-te
PAST FUTURE	kkaetalasskess-ne	kkaetalasskess-te
PROPOSITIVE	kkaetat-se	
IMPERATIVE	kkaetat-ke	

	INFORMAL *Intimate* INDICATIVE	INFORMAL *Casual* INDICATIVE
DECLARATIVE/ *INTERROGATIVE*		
PRESENT	kkaetal-a	kkaetat-ci
PAST	kkaetaláss-ó	kkaetalass-ci
REMOTE PAST	kkaetalássóss-ó	kkaetalassóss-ci
FUTURE	kkaetatkess-ó	kkaetatkess-ci
PAST FUTURE	kkaetalasskess-ó	kkaetalasskess-ci
PROPOSITIVE *IMPERATIVE*	kkaetal-a	kkaetat-ci

CAUSATIVE: *PASSIVE:*

to put out, to extinguish

FORMAL *Plain*

	INDICATIVE	RETROSPECTIVE
DECLARATIVE/ INTERROGATIVE		
PRESENT	kkú-n.ta/-núnya	kkú-tóla/-tónya
PAST	kkòss-ta	kkòss-tóla
REMOTE PAST	kkòssóss-ta	kkòssóss-tóla
FUTURE	kkúkess-ta	kkúkess-tóla
PAST FUTURE	kkòsskess-ta	kkòsskess-tóla
PROPOSITIVE	kkú-ca	
IMPERATIVE	kkò-la	

FORMAL *Polite*

	INDICATIVE	RETROSPECTIVE
DECLARATIVE/ INTERROGATIVE		
PRESENT	kkúpni-ta/-kka	kkúpti-ta/-kka
PAST	kkòssúpni-ta	kkòssúpti-ta
REMOTE PAST	kkòssóssúpni-ta	kkòssóssúpti-ta
FUTURE	kkúkessúpni-ta	kkúkessúpti-ta
PAST FUTURE	kkòsskessúpni-ta	kkòsskessúpti-ta
PROPOSITIVE	kkúpsi-ta	
IMPERATIVE	kkú(si)psi-o	

INFORMAL *Familiar*

	INDICATIVE	RETROSPECTIVE
DECLARATIVE/ INTERROGATIVE		
PRESENT	kkú-ne/-núnka	kkú-te/-tónka
PAST	kkòss-ne	kkòss-te
REMOTE PAST	kkòssóss-ne	kkòssóss-te
FUTURE	kkúkess-ne	kkúkess-te
PAST FUTURE	kkòsskess-ne	kkòsskess-te
PROPOSITIVE	kkú-se	
IMPERATIVE	kkú-ke	

	INFORMAL *Intimate* INDICATIVE	INFORMAL *Casual* INDICATIVE
DECLARATIVE/ INTERROGATIVE		
PRESENT	kkò	kkú-ci
PAST	kkòss-ò	kkòss-ci
REMOTE PAST	kkòssóss-ò	kkòssóss-ci
FUTURE	kkúkess-ò	kkúkess-ci
PAST FUTURE	kkòsskess-ò	kkòsskess-ci
PROPOSITIVE IMPERATIVE	kkò	kkú-ci

CAUSATIVE: *PASSIVE:*

KKÚLH.TA
to boil, to bubble up, to seethe   INTRANSITIVE

FORMAL *Plain*

	INDICATIVE	RETROSPECTIVE
DECLARATIVE/ *INTERROGATIVE*		
PRESENT	kkúlh-nún.ta/-núnya	kkúlh-tóla/-tónya
PAST	kkúlhóss-ta	kkúlhóss-tóla
REMOTE PAST	kkúlhóssóss-ta	kkúlhóssóss-tóla
FUTURE	kkúlhkess-ta	kkúlhkess-tóla
PAST FUTURE	kkúlhósskess-ta	kkúlhósskess-tóla

PROPOSITIVE
IMPERATIVE

FORMAL *Polite*

	INDICATIVE	RETROSPECTIVE
DECLARATIVE/ *INTERROGATIVE*		
PRESENT	kkúlhsúpni-ta/-kka	kkúlhsúpti-ta/-kka
PAST	kkúlhóssúpni-ta	kkúlhóssúpti-ta
REMOTE PAST	kkúlhóssóssúpni-ta	kkúlhóssóssúpti-ta
FUTURE	kkúlhkessúpni-ta	kkúlhkessúpti-ta
PAST FUTURE	kkúlhósskessúpni-ta	kkúlhósskessúpti-ta

PROPOSITIVE
IMPERATIVE

INFORMAL *Familiar*

	INDICATIVE	RETROSPECTIVE
DECLARATIVE/ *INTERROGATIVE*		
PRESENT	kkúlh-ne/-núnka	kkúlh-te/-tónka
PAST	kkúlhóss-ne	kkúlhóss-te
REMOTE PAST	kkúlhóssóss-ne	kkúlhóssóss-te
FUTURE	kkúlhkess-ne	kkúlhkess-te
PAST FUTURE	kkúlhósskess-ne	kkúlhósskess-te

PROPOSITIVE
IMPERATIVE

	INFORMAL *Intimate* INDICATIVE	INFORMAL *Casual* INDICATIVE
DECLARATIVE/ *INTERROGATIVE*		
PRESENT	kkúlh-ó	kkúlh-ci
PAST	kkúlhóss-ó	kkúlhóss-ci
REMOTE PAST	kkúlhóssóss-ó	kkúlhóssóss-ci
FUTURE	kkúlhkess-ó	kkúlhkess-ci
PAST FUTURE	kkúlhósskess-ó	kkúlhósskess-ci

PROPOSITIVE
IMPERATIVE

CAUSATIVE: KKÚLHI.TA   *PASSIVE:*
to boil it, to heat it

FORMAL *Plain*

	INDICATIVE	RETROSPECTIVE
DECLARATIVE/ **INTERROGATIVE**		
PRESENT	kkúlú-n.ta/-núnya	kkúlú-tóla/-tónya
PAST	kkúllóss-ta	kkúllóss-tóla
REMOTE PAST	kkúllóssóss-ta	kkúllóssóss-tóla
FUTURE	kkúlúkess-ta	kkúlúkess-tóla
PAST FUTURE	kkúllósskess-ta	kkúllósskess-tóla
PROPOSITIVE	kkúlú-ca	
IMPERATIVE	kúll-óla	

FORMAL *Polite*

	INDICATIVE	RETROSPECTIVE
DECLARATIVE/ **INTERROGATIVE**		
PRESENT	kkúlúpni-ta/-kka	kkúlúpti-ta/-kka
PAST	kkúllóssúpni-ta	kkúllóssúpti-ta
REMOTE PAST	kkúllóssóssúpni-ta	kkúllóssóssúpti-ta
FUTURE	kkúlúkessúpni-ta	kkúlúkessúpti-ta
PAST FUTURE	kkúllósskessúpni-ta	kkúllósskessúpti-ta
PROPOSITIVE	kkúlúpsi-ta	
IMPERATIVE	kkúlú(si)psi-o	

INFORMAL *Familiar*

	INDICATIVE	RETROSPECTIVE
DECLARATIVE/ **INTERROGATIVE**		
PRESENT	kkúlú-ne/-núnka	kkúlú-te/-tónka
PAST	kkúllóss-ne	kkúllóss-te
REMOTE PAST	kkúllóssóss-ne	kkúllóssóss-te
FUTURE	kkúlúkess-ne	kkúlúkess-te
PAST FUTURE	kkúllósskess-ne	kkúllósskess-te
PROPOSITIVE	kkúlú-se	
IMPERATIVE	kkúlú-ke	

	INFORMAL *Intimate* INDICATIVE	INFORMAL *Casual* INDICATIVE
DECLARATIVE/ **INTERROGATIVE**		
PRESENT	kkúll-ó	kkúlú-ci
PAST	kkúllóss-ó	kkúllóss-ci
REMOTE PAST	kkúllóssóss-ó	kkúllóssóss-ci
FUTURE	kkúlúkess-ó	kkúlúkess-ci
PAST FUTURE	kkúllósskess-ó	kkúllósskess-ci
PROPOSITIVE **IMPERATIVE**	kkúll-ó	kkúlú-ci

CAUSATIVE: *PASSIVE:*

KKÙNH.TA   끊다
to cut, to snap

FORMAL *Plain*

	INDICATIVE	RETROSPECTIVE
DECLARATIVE/ *INTERROGATIVE*		
PRESENT	kkùnh-nùn.ta/-nùnya	kkùnh-tóla/-tónya
PAST	kkùnhòss-ta	kkùnhòss-tóla
REMOTE PAST	kkùnhòssòss-ta	kkùnhòssòss-tóla
FUTURE	kkùnhkess-ta	kkùnhkess-tóla
PAST FUTURE	kkùnhòsskess-ta	kkùnhòsskess-tóla
PROPOSITIVE	kkùnh-ca	
IMPERATIVE	kkùnh-óla	

FORMAL *Polite*

	INDICATIVE	RETROSPECTIVE
DECLARATIVE/ *INTERROGATIVE*		
PRESENT	kkùnhsùpni-ta/-kka	kkùnhsùpti-ta/-kka
PAST	kkùnhòssùpni-ta	kkùnhòssùpti-ta
REMOTE PAST	kkùnhòssòssùpni-ta	kkùnhòssòssùpti-ta
FUTURE	kkùnhkessùpni-ta	kkùnhkessùpti-ta
PAST FUTURE	kkùnhòsskessùpni-ta	kkùnhòsskessùpti-ta
PROPOSITIVE	kkùnhùpsi-ta	
IMPERATIVE	kkùnhù(si)psi-o	

INFORMAL *Familiar*

	INDICATIVE	RETROSPECTIVE
DECLARATIVE/ *INTERROGATIVE*		
PRESENT	kkùnh-ne/-nùnka	kkùnh-te/-tónka
PAST	kkùnhòss-ne	kkùnhòss-te
REMOTE PAST	kkùnhòssòss-ne	kkùnhòssòss-te
FUTURE	kkùnhkess-ne	kkùnhkess-te
PAST FUTURE	kkùnhòsskess-ne	kkùnhòsskess-te
PROPOSITIVE	kkùnh-se	
IMPERATIVE	kkùnh-ke	

	INFORMAL *Intimate* INDICATIVE	INFORMAL *Casual* INDICATIVE
DECLARATIVE/ *INTERROGATIVE*		
PRESENT	kkùnh-ó	kkùnh-ci
PAST	kkùnhòss-ó	kkùnhòss-ci
REMOTE PAST	kkùnhòssòss-ó	kkùnhòssòss-ci
FUTURE	kkùnhkess-ó	kkùnhkess-ci
PAST FUTURE	kkùnhòsskess-ó	kkùnhòsskess-ci
PROPOSITIVE *IMPERATIVE*	kkùnh-o	kkùnh-ci

CAUSATIVE: *PASSIVE:*

85

FORMAL *Plain*

DECLARATIVE/ INTERROGATIVE	INDICATIVE	RETROSPECTIVE
PRESENT	mac-ta/-núnya	mac-tóla/-tónya
PAST	macass-ta	macass-tóla
REMOTE PAST	macassóss-ta	macassóss-tóla
FUTURE	mackess-te	mackess-tóla
PAST FUTURE	macasskess-ta	macasskess-tóla

PROPOSITIVE
IMPERATIVE

FORMAL *Polite*

DECLARATIVE/ INTERROGATIVE	INDICATIVE	RETROSPECTIVE
PRESENT	macsúpni-ta/-kka	macsúpti-ta/-kka
PAST	macassúpni-ta	macassúpti-ta
REMOTE PAST	macassóssúpni-ta	macassóssúpti-ta
FUTURE	mackessúpni-ta	mackessúpti-ta
PAST FUTURE	macasskessúpni-ta	macasskessúpti-ta

PROPOSITIVE
IMPERATIVE

INFORMAL *Familiar*

DECLARATIVE/ INTERROGATIVE	INDICATIVE	RETROSPECTIVE
PRESENT	mac-ne/-núnka	mac-te/-tónka
PAST	macass-ne	macass-te
REMOTE PAST	macassóss-ne	macassóss-te
FUTURE	mackess-ne	mackess-te
PAST FUTURE	macasskess-ne	macasskess-te

PROPOSITIVE
IMPERATIVE

DECLARATIVE/ INTERROGATIVE	INFORMAL *Intimate* INDICATIVE	INFORMAL *Casual* INDICATIVE
PRESENT	mac-a	mac-ci
PAST	macass-ó	macass-ci
REMOTE PAST	macassóss-ó	macassóss-ci
FUTURE	mackess-ó	mackess-ci
PAST FUTURE	màcasskess-ó	macasskess-ci

PROPOSITIVE
IMPERATIVE

CAUSATIVE: *PASSIVE:*

1) to meet, to receive TRANSITIVE
2) to fit together, to agree with 3) to hit, to be exposed to(rain)   INTRANSITIVE

FORMAL *Plain*

	INDICATIVE	RETROSPECTIVE
DECLARATIVE/ *INTERROGATIVE*		
PRESENT	mac-nún.ta/-núnya	mac-tóla/-tónya
PAST	macass-ta	macass-tóla
REMOTE PAST	macassóss-ta	macassóss-tóla
FUTURE	mackess-ta	mackess-tóla
PAST FUTURE	macasskess-ta	macasskess-tóla
PROPOSITIVE	mac-ca	
IMPERATIVE	mac-ala	

FORMAL *Polite*

	INDICATIVE	RETROSPECTIVE
DECLARATIVE/ *INTERROGATIVE*		
PRESENT	macsúpni-ta/-kka	macsúpti-ta/-kka
PAST	macassúpni-ta	macassúpti-ta
REMOTE PAST	macassóssúpni-ta	macassóssúpti-ta
FUTURE	mackessúpni-ta	mackessúpti-ta
PAST FUTURE	macasskessúpni-ta	macasskessúpti-ta
PROPOSITIVE	macúpsi-ta	
IMPERATIVE	macú(si)psi-o	

INFORMAL *Familiar*

	INDICATIVE	RETROSPECTIVE
DECLARATIVE/ *INTERROGATIVE*		
PRESENT	mac-ne/-núnka	mac-te/-tónka
PAST	macass-ne	macass-te
REMOTE PAST	macassóss-ne	macassoss-te
FUTURE	mackess-ne	mackess-te
PAST FUTURE	macasskess-ne	macasskess-te
PROPOSITIVE	mac-se	
IMPERATIVE	mac-ke	

	INFORMAL *Intimate* INDICATIVE	INFORMAL *Casual* INDICATIVE
DECLARATIVE/ *INTERROGATIVE*		
PRESENT	mac-a	mac-ci
PAST	macass-ó	macass-ci
REMOTE PAST	macassóss-ó	macassóss-ci
FUTURE	mackess-ó	mackess-ci
PAST FUTURE	macasskess-ó	macasskess-ci
PROPOSITIVE *IMPERATIVE*	mac-a	mac-ci

CAUSATIVE: MAC.CHU.TA   *PASSIVE:*
to fix (fit) into, to assemble
MACHI.TA
to make to hit the mark,
to expose to (rain, snow or wind)

to be hot, to be pungent   DESCRIPTIVE

FORMAL *Plain*

	INDICATIVE	RETROSPECTIVE
DECLARATIVE/ *INTERROGATIVE*		
PRESENT	mae-p.ta/-unya	maep-tóla/-tónya
PAST	maewóss-ta/-núnya	maewóss-tóla
REMOTE PAST	maewóssóss-ta	maewóssóss-tóla
FUTURE	maepkess-ta	maepkess-tóla
PAST FUTURE	maewósskess-ta	maewósskess-tóla

PROPOSITIVE
IMPERATIVE

FORMAL *Polite*

	INDICATIVE	RETROSPECTIVE
DECLARATIVE/ *INTERROGATIVE*		
PRESENT	maepsúpni-ta/-kka	maepsúpti-ta/-kka
PAST	maewóssúpni-ta	maewóssúpti-ta
REMOTE PAST	maewóssóssúpni-ta	maewóssóssúpti-ta
FUTURE	maepkessúpni-ta	maepkessúpti-ta
PAST FUTURE	maewósskessúpni-ta	maewósskessúpti-ta

PROPOSITIVE
IMPERATIVE

INFORMAL *Familiar*

	INDICATIVE	RETROSPECTIVE
DECLARATIVE/ *INTERROGATIVE*		
PRESENT	mae-p.ne/-unka	maep-te/-tónka
PAST	maewóss-ne/-núnka	maewóss-te
REMOTE PAST	maewóssóss-ne	maewóssóss-te
FUTURE	maepkess-ne	maepkess-te
PAST FUTURE	maewósskess-ne	maewósskess-te

PROPOSITIVE
IMPERATIVE

	INFORMAL *Intimate* INDICATIVE	INFORMAL *Casual* INDICATIVE
DECLARATIVE/ *INTERROGATIVE*		
PRESENT	mae.w-ó	maep-ci
PAST	maewóss-ó	maewóss-ci
REMOTE PAST	maewóssóss-ó	maewóssóss-ci
FUTURE	·maepkess-ó	maepkess-ci
PAST FUTURE	maewósskess-ó	maewósskess-ci

PROPOSITIVE
IMPERATIVE

CAUSATIVE: *PASSIVE:*

MAK.TA
to stop it up, to ward it off, to prevent   막다

FORMAL *Plain*

	INDICATIVE	RETROSPECTIVE
DECLARATIVE/ *INTERROGATIVE*		
PRESENT	mak-nŭn.ta/-nŭnya	mak-tŏla/-tŏnya
PAST	makass-ta	makass-tŏla
REMOTE PAST	makassŏss-ta	makassŏss-tŏla
FUTURE	makkess-ta	makkess-tŏla
PAST FUTURE	makasskess-ta	makasskess-tŏla
PROPOSITIVE	mak-ca	
IMPERATIVE	mak-ala	

FORMAL *Polite*

	INDICATIVE	RETROSPECTIVE
DECLARATIVE/ *INTERROGATIVE*		
PRESENT	maksŭpni-ta/-kka	maksŭpti-ta/-kka
PAST	makassŭpni-ta	makassŭpti-ta
REMOTE PAST	makassŏssŭpni-ta	makassŏssŭpti-ta
FUTURE	makessŭpni-ta	makkessŭpti-ta
PAST FUTURE	makasskessŭpni-ta	makasskessŭpti-ta
PROPOSITIVE	makŭpsi-ta	
IMPERATIVE	makŭ(si)psi-o	

INFORMAL *Familiar*

	INDICATIVE	RETROSPECTIVE
DECLARATIVE/ *INTERROGATIVE*		
PRESENT	mak-ne/-nŭnka	mak-te/-tŏnka
PAST	makass-ne	makass-te
REMOTE PAST	makassŏss-ne	makassŏss-te
FUTURE	makkess-ne	makkess-te
PAST FUTURE	makasskess-ne	makasskess-te
PROPOSITIVE	mak-se	
IMPERATIVE	mak-ke	

	INFORMAL *Intimate* INDICATIVE	INFORMAL *Casual* INDICATIVE
DECLARATIVE/ *INTERROGATIVE*		
PRESENT	mak-a	mak-ci
PAST	makass-ŏ	makass-ci
REMOTE PAST	makassŏss-ŏ	makassŏss-ci
FUTURE	makkess-ŏ	makkess-ci
PAST FUTURE	makasskess-ŏ	makasskess-ci
PROPOSITIVE *IMPERATIVE*	mak-a	mak-ci

CAUSATIVE: *PASSIVE:* MAKHI.TA
                                                          to be stopped up

MAL.TA

말다

1) to roll (up) 2) to put (solid food) into soup 3) to stop, to cease

---

FORMAL *Plain*

	INDICATIVE	RETROSPECTIVE
DECLARATIVE/ *INTERROGATIVE*		
PRESENT	ma-n.ta/-núnya	mal-tóla/-tónya
PAST	malass-ta	malass-tóla
REMOTE PAST	malassóss-te	malassóss-tóla
FUTURE	malkess-ta	malkess-tóla
PAST FUTURE	malasskess-ta	malasskess-tóla
PROPOSITIVE	mal-ca	
IMPERATIVE	mal-ala	

FORMAL *Polite*

	INDICATIVE	RETROSPECTIVE
DECLARATIVE/ *INTERROGATIVE*		
PRESENT	mapni-ta/-kka	mapti-ta/-kka
PAST	malassúpni-ta	malassúpti-ta
REMOTE PAST	malassóssúpni-ta	malassóssúpti-ta
FUTURE	malkessúpni-ta	malkessúpti-ta
PAST FUTURE	malasskessúpni-ta	malasskessúpti-ta
PROPOSITIVE	mapsi-ta	
IMPERATIVE	ma(si)psi-o	

INFORMAL *Familiar*

	INDICATIVE	RETROSPECTIVE
DECLARATIVE/ *INTERROGATIVE*		
PRESENT	ma-ne/-núnka	mal-te/-tónka
PAST	malass-ne	malass-te
REMOTE PAST	malassóss-ne	malassóss-te
FUTURE	malkess-ne	malkess-te
PAST FUTURE	malasskess-ne	malasskess-te
PROPOSITIVE	ma-se	
IMPERATIVE	mal-ke	

	INFORMAL *Intimate* INDICATIVE	INFORMAL *Casual* INDICATIVE
DECLARATIVE/ *INTERROGATIVE*		
PRESENT	mal-a	mal-ci
PAST	malass-ó	malass-ci
REMOTE PAST	malassóss-ó	malassóss-ci
FUTURE	malkess-ó	malkess-ci
PAST FUTURE	malasskess-ó	malasskess-ci
PROPOSITIVE *IMPERATIVE*	mal-a	mal-ci

CAUSATIVE: MALLI.TA
   to stop, to dissuade

PASSIVE: MALLI.TA
   to be rolled up

MALK.TA
to be clear, to be limpid   DESCRIPTIVE   맑다

FORMAL *Plain*

	INDICATIVE	RETROSPECTIVE
DECLARATIVE/ *INTERROGATIVE*		
PRESENT	malk-ta/-únya	malk-tóla/-tónya
PAST	malkass-ta/-núnya	malkass-tóla
REMOTE PAST	malkassóss-ta	malkassóss-tóla
FUTURE	malkkess-ta	malkkess-tóla
PAST FUTURE	malkasskess-ta	malkasskess-tóla

PROPOSITIVE
IMPERATIVE

FORMAL *Polite*

	INDICATIVE	RETROSPECTIVE
DECLARATIVE/ *INTERROGATIVE*		
PRESENT	malksúpni-ta/-kka	malksúpti-ta/-kka
PAST	malkassúpni-ta	malkassúpti-ta
REMOTE PAST	malkassóssúpni-ta	malkassóssúpti-ta
FUTURE	malkkessúpni-ta	malkkesúpti-ta
PAST FUTURE	malkasskessúpni-ta	malkasskessúpti-ta

PROPOSITIVE
IMPERATIVE

INFORMAL *Familiar*

	INDICATIVE	RETROSPECTIVE
DECLARATIVE/ *INTERROGATIVE*		
PRESENT	malk-ne/-únka	malk-te/-tónka
PAST	malkass-ne/-núnka	malkass-te
REMOTE PAST	malkassóss-ne	malkassóss-te
FUTURE	malkkess-ne	malkkess-te
PAST FUTURE	malkasskess-ne	malkasskess-te

PROPOSITIVE
IMPERATIVE

	INFORMAL *Intimate* INDICATIVE	INFORMAL *Casual* INDICATIVE
DECLARATIVE/ *INTERROGATIVE*		
PRESENT	malk-a	malk-ci
PAST	malkass-ó	malkass-ci
REMOTE PAST	malkassóss-ó	malkassóss-ci
FUTURE	malkkess-ó	malkkess-ci
PAST FUTURE	malkasskess-ó	malkasskess-ci

PROPOSITIVE
IMPERATIVE

CAUSATIVE: *PASSIVE:*

91

to be clear, to be clean   DESCRIPTIVE   말갛다

FORMAL *Plain*

	INDICATIVE	RETROSPECTIVE
DECLARATIVE/ *INTERROGATIVE*		
PRESENT	malka-h.ta/-nya	malkah-tóla/-tónya
PAST	malkaess-ta/-nùnya	malkaess-tóla
REMOTE PAST	malkaessóss-ta	malkaessóss-tóla
FUTURE	malkahkess-ta	malkahkess-tóla
PAST FUTURE	malkaesskess-ta	malkaesskess-tóla
PROPOSITIVE *IMPERATIVE*		

FORMAL *Polite*

	INDICATIVE	RETROSPECTIVE
DECLARATIVE/ *INTERROGATIVE*		
PRESENT	malkahsùpni-ta/-kka	malkahsùpti-ta/-kka
PAST	malkaessùpni-ta	malkaessùpti-ta
REMOTE PAST	malkaessóssùpni-ta	malkaessóssùpti-ta
FUTURE	malkahkessùpni-ta	malkahkessùpti-ta
PAST FUTURE	malkaesskessùpni-ta	malkaesskessùpti-ta
PROPOSITIVE *IMPERATIVE*		

INFORMAL *Familiar*

	INDICATIVE	RETROSPECTIVE
DECLARATIVE/ *INTERROGATIVE*		
PRESENT	malka-h.ne/-nka	malkah-te/-tónka
PAST	malkaess-ne/-nùnka	malkaess-te
REMOTE PAST	malkaessóss-ne	malkaessóss-te
FUTURE	malkahkess-ne	malkahkess-te
PAST FUTURE	malkaesskess-ne	malkaesskess-te
PROPOSITIVE *IMPERATIVE*		

	INFORMAL *Intimate* INDICATIVE	INFORMAL *Casual* INDICATIVE
DECLARATIVE/ *INTERROGATIVE*		
PRESENT	malkae	malkah-ci
PAST	malkaess-ó	malkaess-ci
REMOTE PAST	malkaessóss-ó	malkaessóss-ci
FUTURE	malkahkess-ó	malkahkess-ci
PAST FUTURE	malkaesskess-ó	malkaesskess-ci
PROPOSITIVE *IMPERATIVE*		

CAUSATIVE: *PASSIVE:*

MALÚ.TA   마르다
to dry, to dry up   INTRANSITIVE

FORMAL *Plain*

	INDICATIVE	RETROSPECTIVE
DECLARATIVE/ *INTERROGATIVE*		
PRESENT	malú-n.ta/-núnya	malú-tóla/-tónya
PAST	mallass-ta	mallass-tóla
REMOTE PAST	mallassóss-ta	mallassóss-tóla
FUTURE	malúkess-ta	malúkess-tóla
PAST FUTURE	mallasskess-ta	mallasskess-tóla

PROPOSITIVE
IMPERATIVE

FORMAL *Polite*

	INDICATIVE	RETROSPECTIVE
DECLARATIVE/ *INTERROGATIVE*		
PRESENT	malúpni-ta/-kka	malúpti-ta/-kka
PAST	mallassúpni-ta	mallassúpti-ta
REMOTE PAST	mallassóssúpni-ta	mallassóssúpti-ta
FUTURE	malúkessúpni-ta	malúkessúpti-ta
PAST FUTURE	mallasskessúpni-ta	mallasskessúpti-ta

PROPOSITIVE
IMPERATIVE

INFORMAL *Familiar*

	INDICATIVE	RETROSPECTIVE
DECLARATIVE/ *INTERROGATIVE*		
PRESENT	malú-ne/-núnka	malú-te/-tónka
PAST	mallass-ne	mallass-te
REMOTE PAST	mallassóss-ne	mallassóss-te
FUTURE	malúkess-ne	malúkess-te
PAST FUTURE	mallasskess-ne	mallasskess-te

PROPOSITIVE
IMPERATIVE

	INFORMAL *Intimate* INDICATIVE	INFORMAL *Casual* INDICATIVE
DECLARATIVE/ *INTERROGATIVE*		
PRESENT	mall-a	malú-ci
PAST	mallass-ó	mallass-ci
REMOTE PAST	mallassóss-ó	mallassóss-ci
FUTURE	malúkess-ó	malúkess-ci
PAST FUTURE	mallasskess-ó	mallasskess-ci

PROPOSITIVE
IMPERATIVE

CAUSATIVE: MALLI.TA   *PASSIVE:*
          to make dry, to dry

FORMAL *Plain*

	INDICATIVE	RETROSPECTIVE
DECLARATIVE/ *INTERROGATIVE*		
PRESENT	manh-ta/-ŭnya	manh-tóla/-tónya
PAST	manhass-ta/-núnya	manhass-tóla
REMOTE PAST	manhassóss-ta	manhassóss-tóla
FUTURE	manhkess-ta	manhkess-tóla
PAST FUTURE	manhasskess-ta	

PROPOSITIVE
IMPERATIVE

FORMAL *Polite*

	INDICATIVE	RETROSPECTIVE
DECLARATIVE/ *INTERROGATIVE*		
PRESENT	manhsúpni-ta/-kka	manhsúpti-ta/-kka
PAST	manhassúpni-ta	manhassúpti-ta
REMOTE PAST	manhassóssúpni-ta	manhassóssúpti-ta
FUTURE	manhkessúpni-ta	manhkessúpti-ta
PAST FUTURE	manhasskessúpni-ta	manhasskessúpti-ta

PROPOSITIVE
IMPERATIVE

INFORMAL *Familiar*

	INDICATIVE	RETROSPECTIVE
DECLARATIVE/ *INTERROGATIVE*		
PRESENT	manh-ne/-únka	manh-te/-tónka
PAST	manhass-ne/-núnka	manhass-te
REMOTE PAST	manhassóss-ne	manhassóss-te
FUTURE	manhkess-ne	manhkess-te
PAST FUTURE	manhasskess-ne	manhasskess-te

PROPOSITIVE
IMPERATIVE

	INFORMAL *Intimate* INDICATIVE	INFORMAL *Casual* INDICATIVE
DECLARATIVE/ *INTERROGATIVE*		
PRESENT	manh-a	manh-ci
PAST	manhass-ó	manhass-ci
REMOTE PAST	manhassóss-ó	manhassóss-ci
FUTURE	manhkess-ó	manhkess-ci
PAST FUTURE	manhasskess-ó	manhasskess-ci

PROPOSITIVE
IMPERATIVE

CAUSATIVE: *PASSIVE:*

MATH.TA   맡다
1) to take charge of, to be entrusted with 2) to smell

FORMAL Plain

	INDICATIVE	RETROSPECTIVE
DECLARATIVE/ *INTERROGATIVE*		
PRESENT	math-nún.ta/-núnya	math-tóla/-tónya
PAST	mathass-ta	mathass-tóla
REMOTE PAST	mathassóss-ta	mathassóss-tóla
FUTURE	mathkess-ta	mathkess-tóla
PAST FUTURE	mathasskess-ta	mathasskess-tóla
PROPOSITIVE	math-ca	
IMPERATIVE	math-ala	

FORMAL Polite

	INDICATIVE	RETROSPECTIVE
DECLARATIVE/ *INTERROGATIVE*		
PRESENT	mathsúpni-ta/-kka	mathsúpti-ta/-kka
PAST	mathassúpni-ta	mathassúpti-ta
REMOTE PAST	mathassóssúpni-ta	mathassóssúpti-ta
FUTURE	mathkessúpni-ta	mathkessúpti-ta
PAST FUTURE	mathasskessúpni-ta	mathasskessúpti-ta
PROPOSITIVE	mathúpsi-ta	
IMPERATIVE	mathú(si)psi-o	

INFORMAL Familiar

	INDICATIVE	RETROSPECTIVE
DECLARATIVE/ *INTERROGATIVE*		
PRESENT	math-ne/-núnk	math-te/-tónka
PAST	mathass-ne	mathass-te
REMOTE PAST	mathassóss-ne	mathassóss-te
FUTURE	mathkess-ne	mathkess-te
PAST FUTURE	mathasskess-ne	mathasskess-te
PROPOSITIVE	math-se	
IMPERATIVE	math-ke	

	INFORMAL Intimate INDICATIVE	INFORMAL Casual INDICATIVE
DECLARATIVE/ *INTERROGATIVE*		
PRESENT	math-a	math-ci
PAST	mathass-ó	mathass-ci
REMOTE PAST	mathassóss-ó	mathassóss-ci
FUTURE	mathkess-ó	mathkess-ci
PAST FUTURE	mathasskess-ó	mathasskess-ci
PROPOSITIVE *IMPERATIVE*	math-a	math-ci

CAUSATIVE: MATHKI.TA   *PASSIVE:*
        to entrust (a matter) to

FORMAL *Plain*

	INDICATIVE	RETROSPECTIVE
DECLARATIVE/ *INTERROGATIVE*		
PRESENT	mi-p.ta/unya	mip-tóla/-tónya
PAST	miwóss-ta/núnya	miwóss-tóla
REMOTE PAST	miwóssóss-ta	miwóssóss-tóla
FUTURE	mipkess-ta	mipkess-tóla
PAST FUTURE	miwósskess-ta	miwósskess-tóla

PROPOSITIVE
IMPERATIVE

FORMAL *Polite*

	INDICATIVE	RETROSPECTIVE
DECLARATIVE/ *INTERROGATIVE*		
PRESENT	mipsúpni-ta/-kka	mipsúpti-ta/-kka
PAST	miwóssúpni-ta	miwóssúpti-ta
REMOTE PAST	miwóssóssúpni-ta	miwóssóssúpti-ta
FUTURE	mipkessúpni-ta	mipkessúpti-ta
PAST FUTURE	miwósskessúpni-ta	miwósskessúpti-ta

PROPOSITIVE
IMPERATIVE

INFORMAL *Familiar*

	INDICATIVE	RETROSPECTIVE
DECLARATIVE/ *INTERROGATIVE*		
PRESENT	mip-ne/-unka	mip-te/-tónka
PAST	miwóss-ne/-nánka	miwóss-te
REMOTE PAST	miwóssóss-ne	miwóssóss-te
FUTURE	mipkess-ne	mipkess-te
PAST FUTURE	miwósskess-ne	miwósskess-te

PROPOSITIVE
IMPERATIVE

	INFORMAL *Intimate* INDICATIVE	INFORMAL *Casual* INDICATIVE
DECLARATIVE/ *INTERROGATIVE*		
PRESENT	mi.w-ó	mip-ci
PAST	miwóss-ó	miwóss-ci
REMOTE PAST	miwóssóss-ó	miwóssóss-ci
FUTURE	mipkess-ó	mipkess-ci
PAST FUTURE	miwósskess-ó	miwósskess-ci

PROPOSITIVE
IMPERATIVE

CAUSATIVE:	*PASSIVE:*

MOLÙ.TA 모르다
to be ignorant of, to be unaware, to be unaquainted with

FORMAL *Plain*

	INDICATIVE	RETROSPECTIVE
DECLARATIVE/		
INTERROGATIVE		
PRESENT	molù-n.ta/-nùnya	molù-tóla/-tónya
PAST	mollass-ta	mollass-tóla
REMOTE PAST	mollassóss-ta	mollassóss-tóla
FUTURE	molùkess-ta	molùkess-tóla
PAST FUTURE	mollasskess-ta	mollasskess-tóla

PROPOSITIVE
IMPERATIVE

FORMAL *Polite*

	INDICATIVE	RETROSPECTIVE
DECLARATIVE/		
INTERROGATIVE		
PRESENT	molùpni-ta/-kka	molùpti-ta/-kka
PAST	mollassùpni-ta	mollassùpti-ta
REMOTE PAST	mollassóssùpni-ta	mollassóssùpti-ta
FUTURE	molùkessùpni-ta	molùkessùpti-ta
PAST FUTURE	mollasskessùpni-ta	mollasskessùpti-ta

PROPOSITIVE
IMPERATIVE

INFORMAL *Familiar*

	INDICATIVE	RETROSPECTIVE
DECLARATIVE/		
INTERROGATIVE		
PRESENT	molù-ne/-nùnka	molù-te/-tónka
PAST	mollass-ne	mollass-te
REMOTE PAST	mollassóss-ne	mollassóss-te
FUTURE	molùkess-ne	molùkess-te
PAST FUTURE	mollasskess-ne	mollasskess-te

PROPOSITIVE
IMPERATIVE

	INFORMAL *Intimate*	INFORMAL *Casual*
	INDICATIVE	INDICATIVE
DECLARATIVE/		
INTERROGATIVE		
PRESENT	moll-a	molù-ci
PAST	mollass-ó	mollass-ci
REMOTE PAST	mollassóss-ó	mollassóss-ci
FUTURE	molùkess-ó	molùkess-ci
PAST FUTURE	mollasskess-ó	mollasskess-ci

PROPOSITIVE
IMPERATIVE

CAUSATIVE: *PASSIVE:*

FORMAL *Plain*

DECLARATIVE/ INTERROGATIVE	INDICATIVE	RETROSPECTIVE
PRESENT	moú-n.ta/-núnya	moú-tóla/-tónya
PAST	moass-ta	moass-tóla
REMOTE PAST	moassóss-ta	moassóss-tóla
FUTURE	moúkess-ta	moúkess-tóla
PAST FUTURE	moasskess-ta	moasskess-tóla
PROPOSITIVE	moú-ca	
IMPERATIVE	mo-ala	

FORMAL *Polite*

DECLARATIVE/ INTERROGATIVE	INDICATIVE	RETROSPECTIVE
PRESENT	moúpni-ta/-kka	moúpti-ta/-kka
PAST	moassúpni-ta	moassúpti-ta
REMOTE PAST	moassóssúpni-ta	moassóssúpti-ta
FUTURE	moúkessúpni-ta	moúkessúpti-ta
PAST FUTURE	moasskessúpni-ta	moasskessúpti-ta
PROPOSITIVE	moúpsi-ta	
IMPERATIVE	moú(si)psi-o	

INFORMAL *Familiar*

DECLARATIVE/ INTERROGATIVE	INDICATIVE	RETROSPECTIVE
PRESENT	moú-ne/-núnka	moú-te/-tónka
PAST	moass-ne	moass-te
REMOTE PAST	moassóss-ne	moassóss-te
FUTURE	moúkess-ne	moúkess-te
PAST FUTURE	moasskess-ne	moasskess-te
PROPOSITIVE	moú-se	
IMPERATIVE	moú-ke	

DECLARATIVE/ INTERROGATIVE	INFORMAL *Intimate* INDICATIVE	INFORMAL *Casual* INDICATIVE
PRESENT	mo-a	moú-ci
PAST	moass-ó	moass-ci
REMOTE PAST	moassóss-ó	moassóss-ci
FUTURE	moúkess-o	moúkess-ci
PAST FUTURE	moasskess-ó	moasskess-ci
PROPOSITIVE *IMPERATIVE*	mo-a	moú-ci

CAUSATIVE:

PASSIVE: MOI.TA
to gather, to swarm

FORMAL *Plain*

	INDICATIVE	RETROSPECTIVE
DECLARATIVE/ *INTERROGATIVE*		
PRESENT	mók-nún.ta/-núnya	mók-tóla/-tónya
PAST	mókóss-ta	mókóss-tóla
REMOTE PAST	mókóssóss-ta	mókóssóss-tóla
FUTURE	mókkess-ta	mókkess-tóla
PAST FUTURE	mókósskess-ta	mókósskess-tóla
PROPOSITIVE	mók-ca	
IMPERATIVE	mók-óla	

FORMAL *Polite*

	INDICATIVE	RETROSPECTIVE
DECLARATIVE/ *INTERROGATIVE*		
PRESENT	móksúpni-ta/-kka	móksúpti-ta/-kka
PAST	mókóssúpni-ta	mókóssúpti-ta
REMOTE PAST	mókóssóssúpni-ta	mókóssóssúpti-ta
FUTURE	mókkessúpni-ta	mókkessúpti-ta
PAST FUTURE	mókósskessúpni-ta	mókósskessúpti-ta
PROPOSITIVE	mókúpsi-ta	
IMPERATIVE	mókú(si)psi-o	

INFORMAL *Familiar*

	INDICATIVE	RETROSPECTIVE
DECLARATIVE/ *INTERROGATIVE*		
PRESENT	mók-ne/-núnka	mók-te/-tónka
PAST	mókóss-ne	mókóss-te
REMOTE PAST	mókóssóss-ne	mókóssóss-te
FUTURE	mókkess-ne	mókkess-te
PAST FUTURE	mókósskess-ne	mókósskess-te
PROPOSITIVE	mók-se	
IMPERATIVE	mók-ke	

	INFORMAL *Intimate* INDICATIVE	INFORMAL *Casual* INDICATIVE
DECLARATIVE/ *INTERROGATIVE*		
PRESENT	mók-ó	mók-ci
PAST	mókóss-ó	mókóss-ci
REMOTE PAST	mókóssóss-ó	mókóssóss-ci
FUTURE	mókkess-ó	mókkess-ci
PAST FUTURE	mókósskess-ó	mókósskess-ci
PROPOSITIVE *IMPERATIVE*	mók-ó	mók-ci

CAUSATIVE: MÓKI.TA to let someone eat, to feed	*PASSIVE:* MÓKHI.TA to get eaten, to be swallowed up

to be soft, to be tender   DESCRIPTIVE

FORMAL *Plain*

	INDICATIVE	RETROSPECTIVE
DECLARATIVE/
INTERROGATIVE		
PRESENT	mulù-ta/-nya	mulù-tóla/-tónya
PAST	mullóss-ta/-nùnya	mullóss-tóla
REMOTE PAST	mullóssóss-ta	mullóssóss-tóla
FUTURE	mulùkess-ta	mulùkess-tóla
PAST FUTURE	mullósskess-ta	mullósskess-tóla

PROPOSITIVE
IMPERATIVE

FORMAL *Polite*

	INDICATIVE	RETROSPECTIVE
DECLARATIVE/
INTERROGATIVE		
PRESENT	mulùpni-ta/-kka	mulùpti-ta/-kka
PAST	mullóssùpni-ta	mullóssùpti-ta
REMOTE PAST	mullóssóssùpni-ta	mullóssóssùpti-ta
FUTURE	mulùkessùpni-ta	mulùkessùpti-ta
PAST FUTURE	mullósskessùpni-ta	mullósskessùpti-ta

PROPOSITIVE
IMPERATIVE

INFORMAL *Familiar*

	INDICATIVE	RETROSPECTIVE
DECLARATIVE/
INTERROGATIVE		
PRESENT	mulù-ne/-nka	mulù-te/-tónka
PAST	mullóss-ne/-nùnka	mullóss-te
REMOTE PAST	mullóssóss-ne	mullóssóss-te
FUTURE	mulùkess-ne	mulùkess-te
PAST FUTURE	mullósskess-ne	mullósskess-te

PROPOSITIVE
IMPERATIVE

| | INFORMAL *Intimate*
INDICATIVE | INFORMAL *Casual*
INDICATIVE |
|---|---|---|
| *DECLARATIVE/*
INTERROGATIVE | | |
| PRESENT | mull-ó | mulù-ci |
| PAST | mullóss-ó | mullóss-ci |
| REMOTE PAST | mullóssóss-ó | mullóssóss-ci |
| FUTURE | mulùkess-ó | mulùkess-ci |
| PAST FUTURE | mullósskess-ó | mullósskess-ci |

PROPOSITIVE
IMPERATIVE

CAUSATIVE: *PASSIVE:*

MULU.TA   무르다
1) to (ripen and) get soft, to become tender
2) to redeem money cancelling a purchase

FORMAL *Plain*

	INDICATIVE	RETROSPECTIVE
DECLARATIVE/ *INTERROGATIVE*		
PRESENT	mulú-n.ta/-núnya	mulú-tóla/-tónya
PAST	mullóss-ta	mullóss-tóla
REMOTE PAST	mullóssóss-ta	mullóssóss-tóla
FUTURE	mulúkess-ta	mulúkess-tóla
PAST FUTURE	mullósskess-ta	mullósskess-tóla
PROPOSITIVE	mulú-ca (2)	
IMPERATIVE	mull-óla (2)	

FORMAL *Polite*

	INDICATIVE	RETROSPECTIVE
DECLARATIVE/ *INTERROGATIVE*		
PRESENT	mulúpni-ta/-kka	mulúpti-ta/-kka
PAST	mullóssúpni-ta	mullóssúpti-ta
REMOTE PAST	mullóssóssúpni-ta	mullóssóssúpti-ta
FUTURE	mulúkessúpni-ta	mulúkessúpti-ta
PAST FUTURE	mullósskessúpni-ta	mullósskessúpti-ta
PROPOSITIVE	mulúpsi-ta (2)	
IMPERATIVE	mulú(si)psi-o (2)	

INFORMAL *Familiar*

	INDICATIVE	RETROSPECTIVE
DECLARATIVE/ *INTERROGATIVE*		
PRESENT	mulú-ne/-núnka	mulú-te/-tónka
PAST	mullóss-ne	mullóss-te
REMOTE PAST	mullóssóss-ne	mullóssóss-te
FUTURE	mulúkess-ne	mulúkess-te
PAST FUTURE	mullósskess-ne	mullósskess-te
PROPOSITIVE	mulú-se (2)	
IMPERATIVE	mulú-ke (2)	

	INFORMAL *Intimate* INDICATIVE	INFORMAL *Casual* INDICATIVE
DECLARATIVE/ *INTERROGATIVE*		
PRESENT	mull-ó	mulú-ci
PAST	mullóss-ó	mullóss-ci
REMOTE PAST	mullóssóss-ó	mullóssóss-ci
FUTURE	mulúkess-ó	mulúkess-ci
PAST FUTURE	mullósskess-ó	mullósskess-ci
PROPOSITIVE *IMPERATIVE*	mull-ó (2)	mulú-ci (2)

CAUSATIVE: *PASSIVE:*

101

to be fearful, to be dreadful   DESCRIPTIVE

FORMAL *Plain*

	INDICATIVE	RETROSPECTIVE
DECLARATIVE/ *INTERROGATIVE*		
PRESENT	musó-p.ta/-unya	musóp-tóla/-tónya
PAST	musówòss-ta/-nùnya	musówòss-tóla
REMOTE PAST	musówòssóss-ta	musówòssóss-tóla
FUTURE	musópkess-ta	musópkess-tóla
PAST FUTURE	musówòsskess-ta	musówòsskess-tóla

PROPOSITIVE
IMPERATIVE

FORMAL *Polite*

	INDICATIVE	RETROSPECTIVE
DECLARATIVE/ *INTERROGATIVE*		
PRESENT	musópsùpni-ta/-kka	musópsùpti-ta/-kka
PAST	musówòssùpni-ta	musówòssùpti-ta
REMOTE PAST	musówòssóssùpni-ta	musówòssóssùpti-ta
FUTURE	musópkessùpni-ta	musópkessùpti-ta
PAST FUTURE	musówòssóssùpni-ta	musówòsskessùpti-ta

PROPOSITIVE
IMPERATIVE

INFORMAL *Familiar*

	INDICATIVE	RETROSPECTIVE
DECLARATIVE/ *INTERROGATIVE*		
PRESENT	musó-p.ne/-unka	musóp-te/-tónka
PAST	musówòss-ne/-nùnka	musówòss-te
REMOTE PAST	musówòssóss-ne	musówòssóss-te
FUTURE	musópkess-ne	musópkess-te
PAST FUTURE	musówòsskess-ne	musówòsskess-te

PROPOSITIVE
IMPERATIVE

	INFORMAL *Intimate* INDICATIVE	INFORMAL *Casual* INDICATIVE
DECLARATIVE/ *INTERROGATIVE*		
PRESENT	musó.w-o	musóp-ci
PAST	musówòss-ó	musówòss-ci
REMOTE PAST	musówòssóss-ó	musówòssóss-ci
FUTURE	musópkess-ó	musópkess-ci
PAST FUTURE	musówòsskess-ó	musówòsskess-ci

PROPOSITIVE
IMPERATIVE

CAUSATIVE: *PASSIVE:*

MUT.TA
to bury, to inter

문다

FORMAL *Plain*

	INDICATIVE	RETROSPECTIVE
DECLARATIVE/ *INTERROGATIVE*		
PRESENT	mut-nun.ta/-nùnya	mut-tóla/-tònya
PAST	mutóss-ta	mutóss-tóla
REMOTE PAST	mutóssóss-ta	mutóssóss-tóla
FUTURE	mutkess-ta	mutkess-tóla
PAST FUTURE	mutósskess-ta	mutósskess-tóla
PROPOSITIVE	mut-ca	
IMPERATIVE	mut-óla	

FORMAL *Polite*

	INDICATIVE	RETROSPECTIVE
DECLARATIVE/ *INTERROGATIVE*		
PRESENT	mutsùpni-ta/-kka	mutsùpti-ta/-kka
PAST	mutóssùpni-ta	mutóssùpti-ta
REMOTE PAST	mutóssóssùpni-ta	mutóssóssùpti-ta
FUTURE	mutkessùpni-ta	mutkessùpti-ta
PAST FUTURE	mutósskessùpni-ta	mutósskessùpti-ta
PROPOSITIVE	mutùpsi-ta	
IMPERATIVE	mutù(si)psi-o	

INFORMAL *Familiar*

	INDICATIVE	RETROSPECTIVE
DECLARATIVE/ *INTERROGATIVE*		
PRESENT	mut-ne/-nùnka	mut-te/-tònka
PAST	mutóss-ne	mutóss-te
REMOTE PAST	mutóssóss-ne	mutóssóss-te
FUTURE	mutkess-ne	mutkess-te
PAST FUTURE	mutósskess-ne	mutósskess-te
PROPOSITIVE	mut-se	
IMPERATIVE	mut-ke	

	INFORMAL *Intimate* INDICATIVE	INFORMAL *Casual* INDICATIVE
DECLARATIVE/ *INTERROGATIVE*		
PRESENT	mut-ó	mut-ci
PAST	mutóss-ó	mutóss-ci
REMOTE PAST	mutóssóss-ó	mutóssóss-ci
FUTURE	mutkess-ó	mutkess-ci
PAST FUTURE	mutósskess-ó	mutósskess-ci
PROPOSITIVE *IMPERATIVE*	mut-ó	mut-ci

CAUSATIVE:	*PASSIVE:* MUTHI.TA to get buried

MUT.TA
to ask (a question), to inquire   묻다

FORMAL *Plain*

	INDICATIVE	RETROSPECTIVE
DECLARATIVE/ *INTERROGATIVE*		
PRESENT	mut-nun.ta/-núnya	mut-tóla/-tónya
PAST	mulóss-ta	mulóss-tóla
REMOTE PAST	mulóssóss-ta	mulóssóss-tóla
FUTURE	mutkess-ta	mutkess-tóla
PAST FUTURE	mulósskess-ta	mulósskess-tóla
PROPOSITIVE	mut-ca	
IMPERATIVE	mul-óla	

FORMAL *Polite*

	INDICATIVE	RETROSPECTIVE
DECLARATIVE/ *INTERROGATIVE*		
PRESENT	mutsúpni-ta/-kka	mutsúpti-ta/-kka
PAST	mulóssúpni-ta	mulóssúpti-ta
REMOTE PAST	mulóssóssúpni-ta	mulóssóssúpti-ta
FUTURE	mutkessúpni-ta	mutkessúpti-ta
PAST FUTURE	mulósskessúpni-ta	mulósskessúpti-ta
PROPOSITIVE	mulúpsi-ta	
IMPERATIVE	mulú(si)psi-o	

INFORMAL *Familiar*

	INDICATIVE	RETROSPECTIVE
DECLARATIVE/ *INTERROGATIVE*		
PRESENT	mut-ne/-núnka	mut-te/-tónka
PAST	mulóss-ne	mulóss-te
REMOTE PAST	mulóssóss-ne	mulóssóss-te
FUTURE	mutkess-ne	mutkess-te
PAST FUTURE	mulósskess-ne	mulósskess-te
PROPOSITIVE	mut-se	
IMPERATIVE	mut-ke	

	INFORMAL *Intimate* INDICATIVE	INFORMAL *Casual* INDICATIVE
DECLARATIVE/ *INTERROGATIVE*		
PRESENT	mul-ó	mut-ci
PAST	mulóss-ó	mulóss-ci
REMOTE PAST	mulóssóss-ó	mulóssóss-ci
FUTURE	mutkess-ó	mutkess-ci
PAST FUTURE	mulósskess-ó	mulósskess-ci
PROPOSITIVE *IMPERATIVE*	mul-ó	mut-ci

CAUSATIVE: *PASSIVE:*

FORMAL *Plain*

	INDICATIVE	RETROSPECTIVE
DECLARATIVE/ *INTERROGATIVE*		
PRESENT	nah-nŭn.ta/-nŭnya	nah-tóla/-tónya
PAST	nahass-ta	nahass-tóla
REMOTE PAST	nahassóss-ta	nahassóss-tóla
FUTURE	nahkess-ta	nahkess-tóla
PAST FUTURE	nahasskess-ta	nahasskess-tóla
PROPOSITIVE	nah-ca	
IMPERATIVE	nah-ala	

FORMAL *Polite*

	INDICATIVE	RETROSPECTIVE
DECLARATIVE/ *INTERROGATIVE*		
PRESENT	nahsŭpni-ta/-kk	nahsŭpti-ta/-kka
PAST	nahassŭpni-ta	nahassŭpti-ta
REMOTE PAST	nahassóssŭpni-ta	nahassóssŭpti-ta
FUTURE	nahkessŭpni-ta	nahkessŭpti-ta
PAST FUTURE	nahasskessŭpni-ta	nahasskessŭpti-ta
PROPOSITIVE	nahŭpsi-ta	
IMPERATIVE	nahŭ(si)psi-o	

INFORMAL *Familiar*

	INDICATIVE	RETROSPECTIVE
DECLARATIVE/ *INTERROGATIVE*		
PRESENT	nah-ne/-nŭnka	nah-te/-tónka
PAST	nahass-ne	nahass-te
REMOTE PAST	nahassóss-ne	nahassóss-te
FUTURE	nahkess-ne	nahkess-te
PAST FUTURE	nahasskess-ne	nahasskess-te
PROPOSITIVE	nah-se	
IMPERATIVE	nah-ke	

	INFORMAL *Intimate* INDICATIVE	INFORMAL *Casual* INDICATIVE
DECLARATIVE/ *INTERROGATIVE*		
PRESENT	nah-a	nah-ci
PAST	nahass-ó	nahass-ci
REMOTE PAST	nahassóss-ó	nahassóss-ci
FUTURE	nahkess-ó	nahkess-ci
PAST FUTURE	nahasskess-ó	nahasskess-ci
PROPOSITIVE *IMPERATIVE*	nah-a	nah-ci

CAUSATIVE: *PASSIVE:*

FORMAL *Plain*

	INDICATIVE	RETROSPECTIVE
DECLARATIVE/ *INTERROGATIVE*		
PRESENT	na-n.ta/-núnya	nal-tóla/-tónya
PAST	nalass-ta	nalass-tóla
REMOTE PAST	nalassóss-ta	nalassóss-tóla
FUTURE	nalkess-ta	nalkess-tóla
PAST FUTURE	nalasskess-ta	nalasskess-tóla
PROPOSITIVE	nal-ca	
IMPERATIVE	nal-ala	

FORMAL *Polite*

	INDICATIVE	RETROSPECTIVE
DECLARATIVE/ *INTERROGATIVE*		
PRESENT	napni-ta/-kka	napti-ta/-kka
PAST	nalassúpni-ta	nalassúpti-ta
REMOTE PAST	nalassóssúpni-ta	nalassóssúpti-ta
FUTURE	nalkessúpni-ta	nalkessúpti-ta
PAST FUTURE	nalasskessúpni-ta	nalasskessúpti-ta
PROPOSITIVE	napsi-ta	
IMPERATIVE	na(si)psi-o	

INFORMAL *Familiar*

	INDICATIVE	RETROSPECTIVE
DECLARATIVE/ *INTERROGATIVE*		
PRESENT	na-ne/-núnka	nal-te/-tónka
PAST	nalass-ne	nalass-te
REMOTE PAST	nalassóss-ne	nalassóss-te
FUTURE	nalkess-ne	nalkess-te
PAST FUTURE	nalasskess-ne	nalasskess-te
PROPOSITIVE	na-se	
IMPERATIVE	nal-ke	

	INFORMAL *Intimate* INDICATIVE	INFORMAL *Casual* INDICATIVE
DECLARATIVE/ *INTERROGATIVE*		
PRESENT	nal-a	nal-ci
PAST	nalass-ó	nalass-ci
REMOTE PAST	nalassóss-ó	nalassóss-ci
FUTURE	nalkess-o	nalkess-ci
PAST FUTURE	nalasskess-ó	nalasskess-ci
PROPOSITIVE *IMPERATIVE*	nal-a	nal-ci

CAUSATIVE: NALLI.TA   *PASSIVE:*
to let it fly, to fly it

NALU.TA 나르다
to carry, to transport

FORMAL *Plain*

	INDICATIVE	RETROSPECTIVE
DECLARATIVE/ *INTERROGATIVE*		
PRESENT	nalu-n.ta/-núnya	nalu-tóla/-tónya
PAST	nallass-ta	nallass-tóla
REMOTE PAST	nallassóss-ta	nallassóss-tóla
FUTURE	nalúkess-ta	nalúkess-tóla
PAST FUTURE	nallasskess-ta	nallasskess-tóla
PROPOSITIVE	nalú-ca	
IMPERATIVE	nall-ala	

FORMAL *Polite*

	INDICATIVE	RETROSPECTIVE
DECLARATIVE/ *INTERROGATIVE*		
PRESENT	nalúpni-ta/-kka	nalúpti-ta/-kka
PAST	nallassúpni-ta	nallassúpti-ta
REMOTE PAST	nallassóssúpni-ta	nallassóssúpti-ta
FUTURE	nalúkessúpni-ta	halúkessúpti-ta
PAST FUTURE	nallasskessúpni-ta	nallasskessúpti-ta
PROPOSITIVE	nalúpsi-ta	
IMPERATIVE	nalú(si)psi-o	

INFORMAL *Familiar*

	INDICATIVE	RETROSPECTIVE
DECLARATIVE/ *INTERROGATIVE*		
PRESENT	nalú-ne/-núnka	nalú-te/-tónka
PAST	nallass-ne	nallass-te
REMOTE PAST	nallassóss-ne	nallassóss-te
FUTURE	nalúkess-ne	nalúkess-te
PAST FUTURE	nallasskess-ne	nallasskess-te
PROPOSITIVE	nalú-se	
IMPERATIVE	nalú-ke	

	INFORMAL *Intimate* INDICATIVE	INFORMAL *Casual* INDICATIVE
DECLARATIVE/ *INTERROGATIVE*		
PRESENT	nall-a	nalú-ci
PAST	nallass-ó	nallass-ci
REMOTE PAST	nallassóss-ó	nallassóss-ci
FUTURE	nalúkess-ó	nalúkess-ci
PAST FUTURE	nallasskess-ó	nallasskess-ci
PROPOSITIVE *IMPERATIVE*	nall-a	nalú-ci

CAUSATIVE: *PASSIVE:*

FORMAL *Plain*

	INDICATIVE	RETROSPECTIVE
DECLARATIVE/ *INTERROGATIVE*		
PRESENT	nanu-n.ta/-núnya	nanu-tóla/-tónya
PAST	nanuóss-ta	nanuóss-tóla
REMOTE PAST	nanuóssóss-ta	nanuóssóss-tóla
FUTURE	nanukess-ta	nanukess-tóla
PAST FUTURE	nanuósskess-ta	nanuósskess-tóla
PROPOSITIVE	nanu-ca	
IMPERATIVE	nanu-óla	

FORMAL *Polite*

	INDICATIVE	RETROSPECTIVE
DECLARATIVE/ *INTERROGATIVE*		
PRESENT	nanupni-ta/-kka	nanupti-ta/-kka
PAST	nanuóssúpni-ta	nanuóssúpti-ta
REMOTE PAST	nanuóssóssúpni-ta	nanuóssóssúpti-ta
FUTURE	nanukessúpni-ta	nanukessúpti-ta
PAST FUTURE	nanuósskessúpni-ta	nanuósskessúpti-ta
PROPOSITIVE	nanupsi-ta	
IMPERATIVE	nanu(si)psi-o	

INFORMAL *Familiar*

	INDICATIVE	RETROSPECTIVE
DECLARATIVE/ *INTERROGATIVE*		
PRESENT	nanu-ne/-núnka	nanu-te/-tónka
PAST	nanuóss-ne	nanuóss-te
REMOTE PAST	nanuóssóss-ne	nanuóssóss-te
FUTURE	nanukess-ne	nanukess-te
PAST FUTURE	nanuósskess-ne	nanuósskess-te
PROPOSITIVE	nanu-se	
IMPERATIVE	nanu-ke	

	INFORMAL *Intimate* INDICATIVE	INFORMAL *Casual* INDICATIVE
DECLARATIVE/ *INTERROGATIVE*		
PRESENT	nanu-ó	nanu-ci
PAST	nanuóss-ó	nanuóss-ci
REMOTE PAST	nanuóssóss-ó	nanuóssóss-ci
FUTURE	nanukess-ó	nanukess-ci
PAST FUTURE	nanuósskess-ó	nanuósskess-ci
PROPOSITIVE *IMPERATIVE*	nanu-ó	nanu-ci

CAUSATIVE: *PASSIVE:* NANUI.TA
to get divided,
to be separated

FORMAL *Plain*

	INDICATIVE	RETROSPECTIVE
DECLARATIVE/ INTERROGATIVE		
PRESENT	na-s.ta/-ùnya	nas-tóla/-tónya
PAST	naass-ta/-nùnya	naass-tóla
REMOTE PAST	naassóss-ta	naassóss-tóla
FUTURE	naskess-ta	naskess-tóla
PAST FUTURE	naasskess-ta	naasskess-tóla

PROPOSITIVE
IMPERATIVE

FORMAL *Polite*

	INDICATIVE	RETROSPECTIVE
DECLARATIVE/ INTERROGATIVE		
PRESENT	nas.sùpni-ta/-kka	nas.sùpti-ta/-kka
PAST	naassùpni-ta	naassùpti-ta
REMOTE PAST	naassóssùpni-ta	naassóssùpti-ta
FUTURE	naskessùpni-ta	naskessùpti-ta
PAST FUTURE	naasskessùpni-ta	naasskessùpti-ta

PROPOSITIVE
IMPERATIVE

INFORMAL *Familiar*

	INDICATIVE	RETROSPECTIVE
DECLARATIVE/ INTERROGATIVE		
PRESENT	na-s.ne/-ùnka	nas-te/-tónka
PAST	naass-ne/-nùnka	naass-te
REMOTE PAST	naassóss-ne	naassóss-te
FUTURE	naskess-ne	naskess-te
PAST FUTURE	naasskess-ne	naasskess-te

PROPOSITIVE
IMPERATIVE

	INFORMAL *Intimate* INDICATIVE	INFORMAL *Casual* INDICATIVE
DECLARATIVE/ INTERROGATIVE		
PRESENT	naa	nas-ci
PAST	naass-ó	naass-ci
REMOTE PAST	naassóss-ó	naassóss-ci
FUTURE	naskess-ó	naskess-ci
PAST FUTURE	naasskess-ó	naasskess-ci

PROPOSITIVE
IMPERATIVE

CAUSATIVE: *PASSIVE:*

FORMAL *Plain*

	INDICATIVE	RETROSPECTIVE
DECLARATIVE/		
INTERROGATIVE		
PRESENT	nas-nùn.ta/-nùnya	nas-tóla/-tónya
PAST	naass-ta	naass-tóla
REMOTE PAST	naassóss-ta	naassóss-tóla
FUTURE	naskess-ta	naskess-tóla
PAST FUTURE	naasskess-ta	naasskess-tóla
PROPOSITIVE	nas-ca	
IMPERATIVE	na-ala	

FORMAL *Polite*

	INDICATIVE	RETROSPECTIVE
DECLARATIVE/		
INTERROGATIVE		
PRESENT	nassùpni-ta/-kka	nassùpti-ta/-kka
PAST	naassùpni-ta	naassùpti-ta
REMOTE PAST	naassóssùpni-ta	naassóssùpti-ta
FUTURE	naskessùpni-ta	naskessùpti-ta
PAST FUTURE	naasskessùpni-ta	naasskessùpti-ta
PROPOSITIVE	naùpsi-ta	
IMPERATIVE	naù(si)psi-o	

INFORMAL *Familiar*

	INDICATIVE	RETROSPECTIVE
DECLARATIVE/		
INTERROGATIVE		
PRESENT	nas-ne/-nùnka	nas-te/-tónka
PAST	naass-ne	naass-te
REMOTE PAST	naassóss-ne	naassóss-te
FUTURE	naskess-ne	naskess-te
PAST FUTURE	naasskess-ne	naasskess-te
PROPOSITIVE	nas-se	
IMPERATIVE	nas-ke	

	INFORMAL *Intimate* INDICATIVE	INFORMAL *Casual* INDICATIVE
DECLARATIVE/		
INTERROGATIVE		
PRESENT	na-a	nas-ci
PAST	naass-ó	naass-ci
REMOTE PAST	naassóss-ó	naassóss-ci
FUTURE	naskess-ó	naskess-ci
PAST FUTURE	naasskess-ó	naasskess-ci
PROPOSITIVE	na-a	nas-ci
IMPERATIVE		

CAUSATIVE: *PASSIVE:*

FORMAL *Plain*

DECLARATIVE/ INTERROGATIVE	INDICATIVE	RETROSPECTIVE
PRESENT	noh-nùn.ta/-nùnya	noh-tóla/-tònya
PAST	nohass-ta	nohass-tóla
REMOTE PAST	nohassóss-ta	nohassóss-tóla
FUTURE	nohkess-ta	nohkess-tóla
PAST FUTURE	nohasskess-ta	nohasskess-tóla
PROPOSITIVE	noh-ca	
IMPERATIVE	noh-ala	

FORMAL *Polite*

DECLARATIVE/ INTERROGATIVE	INDICATIVE	RETROSPECTIVE
PRESENT	nohsúpni-ta/-kka	nohsúpti-ta/-kka
PAST	nohassúpni-ta	nohassúpti-ta
REMOTE PAST	nohassóssúpni-ta	nohassóssúpti-ta
FUTURE	nohkessúpni-ta	nohkessúpti-ta
PAST FUTURE	nohasskessúpni-ta	nohasskessúpti-ta
PROPOSITIVE	nohúpsi-ta	
IMPERATIVE	nohú(si)psi-o	

INFORMAL *Familiar*

DECLARATIVE/ INTERROGATIVE	INDICATIVE	RETROSPECTIVE
PRESENT	noh-ne/-nùnka	noh-te/-tónka
PAST	nohass-ne	nohass-te
REMOTE PAST	nohassóss-ne	nohassóss-te
FUTURE	nohkess-ne	nohkess-te
PAST FUTURE	nohasskess-ne	nohasskess-te
PROPOSITIVE	noh-se	
IMPERATIVE	noh-ke	

DECLARATIVE/ INTERROGATIVE	INFORMAL *Intimate* INDICATIVE	INFORMAL *Casual* INDICATIVE
PRESENT	noh-a	noh-ci
PAST	nohass-ó	nohass-ci
REMOTE PAST	nohassóssó	nohassóss-ci
FUTURE	nohkess-ó	nohkess-ci
PAST FUTURE	nohasskess-ó	nohasskess-ci
PROPOSITIVE	noh-a	noh-ci
IMPERATIVE		

CAUSATIVE: *PASSIVE:*

FORMAL *Plain*

	INDICATIVE	RETROSPECTIVE
DECLARATIVE/ *INTERROGATIVE*		
PRESENT	no-n.ta/-núnya	nol-tóla/tónya
PAST	nolass-ta	nolass-tóla
REMOTE PAST	nolassóss-ta	nolassóss-tóla
FUTURE	nolkess-ta	nolkess-tóla
PAST FUTURE	nolasskess-ta	nolasskess-tóla
PROPOSITIVE	nol-ca	
IMPERATIVE	nol-ala	

FORMAL *Polite*

	INDICATIVE	RETROSPECTIVE
DECLARATIVE/ *INTERROGATIVE*		
PRESENT	nopni-ta/-kka	nopti-ta/-kka
PAST	nolassúpni-ta	nolassúpti-ta
REMOTE PAST	nolassóssúpni-ta	nolassóssúpti-ta
FUTURE	nolkessúpni-ta	nolkessúpti-ta
PAST FUTURE	nolasskessúpni-ta	nolasskessúpti-ta
PROPOSITIVE	nopsi-ta	
IMPERATIVE	no(si)psi-o	

INFORMAL *Familiar*

	INDICATIVE	RETROSPECTIVE
DECLARATIVE/ *INTERROGATIVE*		
PRESENT	no-ne/-núnka	nol-te/-tónka
PAST	nolass-ne	nolass-te
REMOTE PAST	nolassóss-ne	nolassóss-te
FUTURE	nolkess-ne	nolkess-te
PAST FUTURE	nolasskess-ne	nolasskess-te
PROPOSITIVE	no-se	
IMPERATIVE	nol-ke	

	INFORMAL *Intimate* INDICATIVE	INFORMAL *Casual* INDICATIVE
DECLARATIVE/ *INTERROGATIVE*		
PRESENT	nol-a	nol-ci
PAST	nolass-ó	nolass-ci
REMOTE PAST	nolassóssó	nolassóss-ci
FUTURE	nolkess-ó	nolkess-ci
PAST FUTURE	nolasskessó	nolasskess-ci
PROPOSITIVE	nol-a	nol-ci
IMPERATIVE		

CAUSATIVE: NOLLI.TA
to let someone play,
to leave idle

PASSIVE:

NOPH.TA 높다
to be high, to be tall   DESCRIPTIVE

FORMAL *Plain*

	INDICATIVE	RETROSPECTIVE
DECLARATIVE/ *INTERROGATIVE*		
PRESENT	noph-ta/-uṅya	noph-tóla/-tónya
PAST	nophass-ta/-núnya	nophass-tóla
REMOTE PAST	nophassóss-ta	nophassóss-tóla
FUTURE	nophkess-ta	nophkess-tóla
PAST FUTURE	nophasskess-ta	nophasskess-tóla

PROPOSITIVE
IMPERATIVE

FORMAL *Polite*

	INDICATIVE	RETROSPECTIVE
DECLARATIVE/ *INTERROGATIVE*		
PRESENT	nophsúpni-ta/-kka	nophsúpti-ta/-kka
PAST	nophassúpni-ta	nophassúpti-ta
REMOTE PAST	nophassóssúpni-ta	nophassóssúpti-ta
FUTURE	nophkessúpni-ta	nophkessúpti-ta
PAST FUTURE	nophasskessúpni-ta	nophasskessúpti-ta

PROPOSITIVE
IMPERATIVE

INFORMAL *Familiar*

	INDICATIVE	RETROSPECTIVE
DECLARATIVE/ *INTERROGATIVE*		
PRESENT	noph-ne/-únka	noph-te/-tónka
PAST	nophass-ne/-núnka	nophass-te
REMOTE PAST	nophassóss-ne	nophassóss-te
FUTURE	nophkess-ne	nophkess-te
PAST FUTURE	nophasskess-ne	nophasskess-te

PROPOSITIVE
IMPERATIVE

	INFORMAL *Intimate* INDICATIVE	INFORMAL *Casual* INDICATIVE
DECLARATIVE/ *INTERROGATIVE*		
PRESENT	noph-a	noph-ci
PAST	nophass-ó	nophass-ci
REMOTE PAST	nophassóss-ó	nophassóss-ci
FUTURE	nophkess-ó	nophkess-ci
PAST FUTURE	nophasskess-ó	nophasskess-ci

PROPOSITIVE
IMPERATIVE

CAUSATIVE: NOPHI.TA   *PASSIVE:*
to make higher, to elevate

FORMAL *Plain*

	INDICATIVE	RETROSPECTIVE
DECLARATIVE/ *INTERROGATIVE*		
PRESENT	noyó-p.ta/-unya	noyóp-tóla/-tónya
PAST	noyówòss-ta/-nùnya	noyówòss-tóla
REMOTE PAST	noyówòssòss-ta	noyówòssòss-tóla
FUTURE	noyópkess-ta	noyópkess-tóla
PAST FUTURE	noyówòsskess-ta	noyówòsskess-tóla
PROPOSITIVE *IMPERATIVE*		

FORMAL *Polite*

	INDICATIVE	RETROSPECTIVE
DECLARATIVE/ *INTERROGATIVE*		
PRESENT	noyópsùpni-ta/-kka	noyópsùpti-ta/-kka
PAST	noyówòssùpni-ta	noyówòssùpti-ta
REMOTE PAST	noyówòssòssùpni-ta	noyówòssòssùpti-ta
FUTURE	noyópkessùpni-ta	noyópkessùpti-ta
PAST FUTURE	noyówòsskessùpni-ta	noyówòsskessùpti-ta
PROPOSITIVE *IMPERATIVE*		

INFORMAL *Familiar*

	INDICATIVE	RETROSPECTIVE
DECLARATIVE/ *INTERROGATIVE*		
PRESENT	noyó-p.ne/-unka	noyóp-te/-tónka
PAST	noyówòss-ne/-nùnka	noyówòss-te
REMOTE PAST	noyówòssòss-ne	noyówòssòss-te
FUTURE	noyópkess-ne	noyópkess-te
PAST FUTURE	noyówòsskess-ne	noyówòsskess-te
PROPOSITIVE *IMPERATIVE*		

	INFORMAL *Intimate* INDICATIVE	INFORMAL *Casual* INDICATIVE
DECLARATIVE/ *INTERROGATIVE*		
PRESENT	noyó.w-ó	noyóp-ci
PAST	noyówòss-ó	noyówòss-ci
REMOTE PAST	noyówòssòss-ó	noyówòssòss-ci
FUTURE	noyópkess-ó	noyópkess-ci
PAST FUTURE	noyówòsskess-ó	noyówòsskess-ci
PROPOSITIVE *IMPERATIVE*		

CAUSATIVE: *PASSIVE:*

FORMAL *Plain*

	INDICATIVE	RETROSPECTIVE
DECLARATIVE/ *INTERROGATIVE*		
PRESENT	nòh-nùnta/-nùnya	nòh-tòla/-tònya
PAST	nòhòss-ta	nòhòss-tòla
REMOTE PAST	nòhòssòss-ta	nòhòssòss-tòla
FUTURE	nòhkess-ta	nòhkess-tòla
PAST FUTURE	nòhòsskess-ta	nòhòsskess-tòla
PROPOSITIVE	nòh-ca	
IMPERATIVE	nòh-òla	

FORMAL *Polite*

	INDICATIVE	RETROSPECTIVE
DECLARATIVE/ *INTERROGATIVE*		
PRESENT	nòhsùpni-ta/-kka	nòhsùpti-ta/-kka
PAST	nòhòssùpni-ta	nòhòssùpti-ta
REMOTE PAST	nòhòssòssùpni-ta	nòhòssòssùpti-ta
FUTURE	nòhkessùpni-ta	nòhkessùpti-ta
PAST FUTURE	nòhòsskessùpni-ta	nòhòsskessùpti-ta
PROPOSITIVE	nòhùpsi-ta	
IMPERATIVE	nòhù(si)psi-o	

INFORMAL *Familiar*

	INDICATIVE	RETROSPECTIVE
DECLARATIVE/ *INTERROGATIVE*		
PRESENT	nòh-ne/-nùnka	nòh-te/-tònka
PAST	nòhòss-ne	nòhòss-te
REMOTE PAST	nòhòssòss-ne	nòhòssòss-te
FUTURE	nòhkess-ne	nòhkess-te
PAST FUTURE	nòhòsskess-ne	nòhòsskess-te
PROPOSITIVE	nòh-se	
IMPERATIVE	nòh-ke	

	INFORMAL *Intimate* INDICATIVE	INFORMAL *Casual* INDICATIVE
DECLARATIVE/ *INTERROGATIVE*		
PRESENT	nòh-ò	nòh-ci
PAST	nòhòss-ò	nòhòss-ci
REMOTE PAST	nòhòssòss-ò	nòhòssòss-ci
FUTURE	nòhkessò	nòhkess-ci
PAST FUTURE	nòhòsskess-ò	nòhòsskess-ci
PROPOSITIVE *IMPERATIVE*	nòh-ò	nòh-ci

CAUSATIVE: *PASSIVE:*

FORMAL *Plain*

	INDICATIVE	RETROSPECTIVE
DECLARATIVE/ INTERROGATIVE		
PRESENT	nòlp-ta/-únya	nòlp-tóla/-tónya
PAST	nòlpòss-ta/-núnya	nòlpòss-tóla
REMOTE PAST	nòlpòssòss-ta	nòlpòssòss-tóla
FUTURE	nòlpkess-ta	nòlpkess-tóla
PAST FUTURE	nòlpòsskess-ta	nòlpòsskess-tóla

PROPOSITIVE
IMPERATIVE

FORMAL *Polite*

	INDICATIVE	RETROSPECTIVE
DECLARATIVE/ INTERROGATIVE		
PRESENT	nòlpsúpni-ta/-kka	nòlpsúpti-ta/-kka
PAST	nòlpòssúpni-ta	nòlpòssúpti-ta
REMOTE PAST	nòlpòssòssúpni-ta	nòlpòssòssúpti-ta
FUTURE	nòlpkessúpni-ta	nòlpkessúpti-ta
PAST FUTURE	nòlpòsskessúpni-ta	nòlpòsskessúpti-ta

PROPOSITIVE
IMPERATIVE

INFORMAL *Familiar*

	INDICATIVE	RETROSPECTIVE
DECLARATIVE/ INTERROGATIVE		
PRESENT	nòlp-ne/-únka	nòlp-te/-tónka
PAST	nòlpòss-ne/-núnka	nòlpòss-te
REMOTE PAST	nòlpòssòss-ne	nòlpòssòss-te
FUTURE	nòlpkess-ne	nòlpkess-te
PAST FUTURE	nòlpòsskess-ne	nòlpòsskess-te

PROPOSITIVE
IMPERATIVE

	INFORMAL *Intimate* INDICATIVE	INFORMAL *Casual* INDICATIVE
DECLARATIVE/ INTERROGATIVE		
PRESENT	nòlp-ó	nòlp-ci
PAST	nòlpòss-ó	nòlpòss-ci
REMOTE PAST	nòlpòssòss-ó	nòlpòssòss-ci
FUTURE	nòlpkess-ó	nòlpkess-ci
PAST FUTURE	nòlpòsskess-ó	nòlpòsskess-ci

PROPOSITIVE
IMPERATIVE

CAUSATIVE: NÒLPHI.TA   *PASSIVE:*
              to widen

to be yellow, to be golden   DESCRIPTIVE

FORMAL *Plain*

	INDICATIVE	RETROSPECTIVE
DECLARATIVE/		
INTERROGATIVE		
PRESENT	nulù-ta/-nya	nulù-tóla/-tónya
PAST	nulúlóss-ta/-núnya	nulúlóss-tóla
REMOTE PAST	nulúlóssóss-ta	nulúlóssóss-tóla
FUTURE	nulúkess-ta	nulúkess-tóla
PAST FUTURE	nulúlósskess-ta	nulúlósskess-tóla

PROPOSITIVE
IMPERATIVE

FORMAL *Polite*

	INDICATIVE	RETROSPECTIVE
DECLARATIVE/		
INTERROGATIVE		
PRESENT	nulúpni-ta/-kka	nulúpti-ta/-kka
PAST	nulúlóssúpni-ta	nulúlóssúpti-ta
REMOTE PAST	nulúlóssóssúpni-ta	nulúlóssóssúpti-ta
FUTURE	nulúkessúpni-ta	nulúkessúpti-ta
PAST FUTURE	nulúlósskessúpni-ta	nulúlósskessúpti-ta

PROPOSITIVE
IMPERATIVE

INFORMAL *Familiar*

	INDICATIVE	RETROSPECTIVE
DECLARATIVE/		
INTERROGATIVE		
PRESENT	nulù-ne/-nka	nulù-te/-tónka
PAST	nulúlóss-ne/-núnka	nulúlóss-te
REMOTE PAST	nulúlóssóss-ne	nulúlóssóss-te
FUTURE	nulúkess-ne	nulúkess-te
PAST FUTURE	nulúlósskess-ne	nulúlósskess-te

PROPOSITIVE
IMPERATIVE

	INFORMAL *Intimate* INDICATIVE	INFORMAL *Casual* INDICATIVE
DECLARATIVE/		
INTERROGATIVE		
PRESENT	nulúl-ó	nulù-ci
PAST	nulúlóss-ó	nulúlóss-ci
REMOTE PAST	nulúlóssóss-ó	nulúlóssóss-ci
FUTURE	nulúkess-ó	nulúkess-ci
PAST FUTURE	nulúlósskess-ó	nulúlósskess-ci

PROPOSITIVE
IMPERATIVE

CAUSATIVE: *PASSIVE:*

FORMAL *Plain*

DECLARATIVE/ INTERROGATIVE	INDICATIVE	RETROSPECTIVE
PRESENT	nulù-n.ta	nulù-tóla/-tónya
PAST	nullóss-ta	nullóss-tóla
REMOTE PAST	nullóssóss-ta	nullóssóss-tóla
FUTURE	nulùkess-ta	nulùkess-tóla
PAST FUTURE	nullósskess-ta	nullósskess-tóla
PROPOSITIVE	nulù-ca	
IMPERATIVE	null-óla	

FORMAL *Polite*

DECLARATIVE/ INTERROGATIVE	INDICATIVE	RETROSPECTIVE
PRESENT	nulùpni-ta/-kka	nulùpti-ta/-kka
PAST	nullóssùpni-ta	nullóssùpti-ta
REMOTE PAST	nullóssóssùpni-ta	nullóssóssùpti-ta
FUTURE	nulùkessùpni-ta	nulùkessùpti-ta
PAST FUTURE	nullósskessùpni-ta	nullósskessùpti-ta
PROPOSITIVE		
IMPERATIVE		

INFORMAL *Familiar*

DECLARATIVE/ INTERROGATIVE	INDICATIVE	RETROSPECTIVE
PRESENT	nulù-ne/-nùnka	nulù-te/-tónka
PAST	nullóss-ne	nullóss-te
REMOTE PAST	nullóssóss-ne	nullóssóss-te
FUTURE	nulùkess-ne	nulùkess-te
PAST FUTURE	nullósskess-ne	nullósskess-te
PROPOSITIVE	nulù-se	
IMPERATIVE	nulù-ke	

DECLARATIVE/ INTERROGATIVE	INFORMAL *Intimate* INDICATIVE	INFORMAL *Casual* INDICATIVE
PRESENT	null-ó	nulù-ci
PAST	nullóss-ó	nullóss-ci
REMOTE PAST	nullóssóss-ó	nullóssóss-ci
FUTURE	nulùkess-ó	nulùkess-ci
PAST FUTURE	nullósskess-ó	nullósskess-ci
PROPOSITIVE *IMPERATIVE*	null-ó	nulù-ci

CAUSATIVE:

PASSIVE: NULLI.TA
to be pressed,
to be oppressed

FORMAL *Plain*

	INDICATIVE	RETROSPECTIVE
DECLARATIVE/ *INTERROGATIVE*		
PRESENT	nup-nún.ta/-núnya	nup-tóla/-tónya
PAST	nuwóss-ta	nuwóss-tóla
REMOTE PAST	nuwóssóss-ta	nuwóssóss-tóla
FUTURE	nupkess-ta	nupkess-tóla
PAST FUTURE	nuwósskess-ta	nuwósskess-tóla
PROPOSITIVE	nup-ca	
IMPERATIVE	nuw-ó.la	

FORMAL *Polite*

	INDICATIVE	RETROSPECTIVE
DECLARATIVE/ *INTERROGATIVE*		
PRESENT	nupsúpni-ta/-kka	nupsúpti-ta/-kka
PAST	nuwóssúpni-ta	nuwóssúpti-ta
REMOTE PAST	nuwóssóssúpni-ta	nuwóssóssúpti-ta
FUTURE	nupkessúpni-ta	nupkessúpti-ta
PAST FUTURE	nuwósskessúpni-ta	nuwósskessúpti-ta
PROPOSITIVE	nuúpsi-ta	
IMPERATIVE	nuú(si)psi-o	

INFORMAL *Familiar*

	INDICATIVE	RETROSPECTIVE
DECLARATIVE/ *INTERROGATIVE*		
PRESENT	nup-ne/-núnka	nup-te/-tónya
PAST	nuwóss-ne	nuwóss-te
REMOTE PAST	nuwóssóss-ne	nuwóssóss-te
FUTURE	nupkess-ne	nupkess-te
PAST FUTURE	nuwósskess-ne	nuwósskess-te
PROPOSITIVE	nuú-se	
IMPERATIVE	nup-ke	

	INFORMAL *Intimate* INDICATIVE	INFORMAL *Casual* INDICATIVE
DECLARATIVE/ *INTERROGATIVE*		
PRESENT	nu.w-ó	nup-ci
PAST	nuwóss-ó	nuwóss-ci
REMOTE PAST	nuwóssóss-ó	nuwóssóss-ci
FUTURE	nupkess-ó	nupkess-ci
PAST FUTURE	nuwósskess-ó	nuwósskess-ci
PROPOSITIVE		
IMPERATIVE		

CAUSATIVE: *PASSIVE:*

NUT.TA
to get scorched, to burn   INTRANSITIVE   눋다

FORMAL *Plain*

	INDICATIVE	RETROSPECTIVE
DECLARATIVE/ *INTERROGATIVE*		
PRESENT	nut-nún.ta/-núnya	nut-tóla/-tónya
PAST	nulóss-ta	nulóss-tóla
REMOTE PAST	nulóssóss-ta	nulóssóss-tóla
FUTURE	nutkess-ta	nutkess-tóla
PAST FUTURE	nulósskess-ta	nulósskess-tóla

PROPOSITIVE
IMPERATIVE

FORMAL *Polite*

	INDICATIVE	RETROSPECTIVE
DECLARATIVE/ *INTERROGATIVE*		
PRESENT	nutsúpni-ta/-kka	nutsúpti-ta/-kka
PAST	nulóssúpni-ta	nulóssúpti-ta
REMOTE PAST	nulóssóssúpni-ta	nulóssóssúpti-ta
FUTURE	nutkessúpni-ta	nutkessúpti-ta
PAST FUTURE	nulósskessúpni-ta	nulósskessúpti-ta

PROPOSITIVE
IMPERATIVE

INFORMAL *Familiar*

	INDICATIVE	RETROSPECTIVE
DECLARATIVE/ *INTERROGATIVE*		
PRESENT	nut-ne/-núnka	nut-te/-tónka
PAST	nulóss-ne	nulóss-te
REMOTE PAST	nulóssóss-ne	nulóssóss-te
FUTURE	nutkess-ne	nutkess-te
PAST FUTURE	nulósskess-ne	nulósskess-te

PROPOSITIVE
IMPERATIVE

	INFORMAL *Intimate* INDICATIVE	INFORMAL *Casual* INDICATIVE
DECLARATIVE/ *INTERROGATIVE*		
PRESENT	nul-ó	nut-ci
PAST	nulóss-ó	nulóss-ci
REMOTE PAST	nulóssóss-ó	nulóssóss-ci
FUTURE	nutkess-ó	nutkess-ci
PAST FUTURE	nulósskess-ó	nulósskess-ci

PROPOSITIVE
IMPERATIVE

CAUSATIVE: *PASSIVE:*

NÚC.TA   늦다
1) to be late   2) to be loose   DESCRIPTIVE
_____
                              FORMAL *Plain*

                   INDICATIVE   RETROSPECTIVE

DECLARATIVE/
INTERROGATIVE

      PRESENT   nùc-ta/-ùnya   nùc-tóla/-tónya
      PAST   nùcóss-ta/-nùnya   nùcóss-tóla
      REMOTE PAST nùcóssóss-ta   nucóssóss-tóla
      FUTURE   nùckess-ta   nùckess-tóla
      PAST FUTURE nùcósskess-ta   nùcósskess-tóla

PROPOSITIVE
IMPERATIVE

                              FORMAL *Polite*

                   INDICATIVE   RETROSPECTIVE

DECLARATIVE/
INTERROGATIVE

      PRESENT   nùcsùpni-ta/-kka   nùcsùpti-ta/-kka
      PAST   nùcóssùpni-ta   nùcóssùpti-ta
      REMOTE PAST nùcóssóssùpni-ta   nùcóssóssùpti-ta
      FUTURE   nùckessùpni-ta   nùckessùpti-ta
      PAST FUTURE nùcósskessùpni-ta   nùcósskessùpti-ta

PROPOSITIVE
IMPERATIVE

                             INFORMAL *Familiar*

                   INDICATIVE   RETROSPECTIVE

DECLARATIVE/
INTERROGATIVE

      PRESENT   nùc-ne/-ùnka   nùc-te/-tónka
      PAST   nùcóss-ne/-nùnka   nùcóss-te
      REMOTE PAST nùcóssóss-ne   nùcóssóss-te
      FUTURE   nùckess-ne   nùckess-te
      PAST FUTURE nùcósskess-ne   nùcósskess-te

PROPOSITIVE
IMPERATIVE

                   INFORMAL *Intimate*   INFORMAL *Casual*
                   INDICATIVE   INDICATIVE

DECLARATIVE/
INTERROGATIVE

      PRESENT   nùc-ó   nùc-ci
      PAST   nùcóss-ó   nùcóss-ci
      REMOTE PAST nùcóssóss-ó   nùcóssóss-ci
      FUTURE   nùckess-ó   nùckess-ci
      PAST FUTURE nùcósskess-ó   nùcósskess-ci

PROPOSITIVE
IMPERATIVE
_____
          CAUSATIVE: NÚC.CHU.TA   *PASSIVE:*
                        to loosen, to slacken,
                        to extend

                                                                      121

FORMAL *Plain*

	INDICATIVE	RETROSPECTIVE
DECLARATIVE/ INTERROGATIVE		
PRESENT	núc-núnta/-núnya	núc-tóla/-tónya
PAST	núcóss-ta	núcóss-tóla
REMOTE PAST	núcóssóss-ta	núcóssóss-tóla
FUTURE	núckess-ta	núckess-tóla
PAST FUTURE	núcósskess-ta	núcósskess-tóla

PROPOSITIVE
IMPERATIVE

FORMAL *Polite*

	INDICATIVE	RETROSPECTIVE
DECLARATIVE/ INTERROGATIVE		
PRESENT	núcsúpni-ta/-kka	núcsúpti-ta/-kka
PAST	núcóssúpni-ta	núcóssúpti-ta
REMOTE PAST	núcóssóssúpni-ta	núcóssóssúpti-ta
FUTURE	núckessúpni-ta	núckessúpti-ta
PAST FUTURE	núcósskessúpni-ta	núcósskessúpti-ta

PROPOSITIVE
IMPERATIVE

INFORMAL *Familiar*

	INDICATIVE	RETROSPECTIVE
DECLARATIVE/ INTERROGATIVE		
PRESENT	núc-ne/-núnka	núc-te/-tónka
PAST	núcóss-ne	núcóss-te
REMOTE PAST	núcóssóss-ne	núcóssóss-te
FUTURE	núckess-ne	núckess-te
PAST FUTURE	núcósskess-ne	núcósskess-te

PROPOSITIVE
IMPERATIVE

	INFORMAL *Intimate* INDICATIVE	INFORMAL *Casual* INDICATIVE
DECLARATIVE/ INTERROGATIVE		
PRESENT	núc-ó	núc-ci
PAST	núcóss-ó	núcóss-ci
REMOTE PAST	núcóssóss-ó	núcóssóss-ci
FUTURE	núckess-ó	núckess-ci
PAST FUTURE	núcósskess-ó	núcósskess-ci

PROPOSITIVE
IMPERATIVE

CAUSATIVE: *PASSIVE:*

NÙLK.TA
to become (grow) old   INTRANSITIVE   늙다

FORMAL *Plain*

	INDICATIVE	RETROSPECTIVE
DECLARATIVE/ *INTERROGATIVE*		
PRESENT	nùlk-nùnta/-nùnya	nùlk-tòla/-tònya
PAST	nùlkòss-ta	nùlkòss-tòla
REMOTE PAST	nùlkòssòss-ta	nùlkòssòss-tòla
FUTURE	nùlkkess-ta	nùlkkess-tòla
PAST FUTURE	nùlkòsskess-ta	nùlkòsskess-tòla
PROPOSITIVE	nùlk-ca	
IMPERATIVE	nùlk-òla	

FORMAL *Polite*

	INDICATIVE	RETROSPECTIVE
DECLARATIVE/ *INTERROGATIVE*		
PRESENT	nùlksùpni-ta/-kka	nùlksùpti-ta/-kka
PAST	nùlkòssùpni-ta	nùlkòssùpti-ta
REMOTE PAST	nùlkòssòssùpni-ta	nùlkòssòssùpti-ta
FUTURE	nùlkkessùpni-ta	nùlkkessùpti-ta
PAST FUTURE	nùlkòsskessùpni-ta	nùlkòsskessùpti-ta
PROPOSITIVE	nùlkùpsi-ta	
IMPERATIVE	nùlkù(si)psi-o	

INFORMAL *Familiar*

	INDICATIVE	RETROSPECTIVE
DECLARATIVE/ *INTERROGATIVE*		
PRESENT	nùlk-ne/-nùnka	nùlk-te/-tònka
PAST	nùlkòss-ne	nùlkòss-te
REMOTE PAST	nùlkòssòss-ne	nùlkòssòss-te
FUTURE	nùlkkess-ne	nùlkkess-te
PAST FUTURE	nùlkòsskess-ne	nùlkòsskess-te
PROPOSITIVE	nùlk-se	
IMPERATIVE	nùlk-ke	

	INFORMAL *Intimate* INDICATIVE	INFORMAL *Casual* INDICATIVE
DECLARATIVE/ *INTERROGATIVE*		
PRESENT	nùlk-ò	nùlk-ci
PAST	nùlkòss-ò	nùlkòss-ci
REMOTE PAST	nùlkòssòss-ò	nùlkòssòss-ci
FUTURE	nùlkkess-ò	nùlkkess-ci
PAST FUTURE	nùlkòsskess-ò	nùlkòsskess-ci
PROPOSITIVE	nùlk-ò	nùlk-ci
IMPERATIVE		

CAUSATIVE: *PASSIVE:*

123

FORMAL *Plain*

	INDICATIVE	RETROSPECTIVE
DECLARATIVE/		
INTERROGATIVE		
PRESENT	o-n.ta/-nùnya	o-tóla/-tónya
PAST	wass-ta	wass-tóla
REMOTE PAST	wassóss-ta	wassóss-tóla
FUTURE	okess-ta	okess-tóla
PAST FUTURE	wasskess-ta	wasskess-tóla
PROPOSITIVE	o-ca	
IMPERATIVE	wa-la~ o-nóla	

FORMAL *Polite*

	INDICATIVE	RETROSPECTIVE
DECLARATIVE/		
INTERROGATIVE		
PRESENT	opni-ta/-kka	opti-ta/-kka
PAST	wassùpni-ta	wassùpti-ta
REMOTE PAST	wassóssùpni-ta	wassóssùpti-ta
FUTURE	okessùpni-ta	okessùpti-ta
PAST FUTURE	wasskessùpni-ta	wasskessùpti-ta
PROPOSITIVE	opsi-ta	
IMPERATIVE	o(si)psi-o	

INFORMAL *Familiar*

	INDICATIVE	RETROSPECTIVE
DECLARATIVE/		
INTERROGATIVE		
PRESENT	o-ne/-nùnka	o-te/-tónka
PAST	wass-ne	wass-te
REMOTE PAST	wassóss-ne	wassóss-te
FUTURE	okess-ne	okess-te
PAST FUTURE	wasskess-ne	wasskess-te
PROPOSITIVE	o-se	
IMPERATIVE	o-ke	

	INFORMAL *Intimate* INDICATIVE	INFORMAL *Casual* INDICATIVE
DECLARATIVE/		
INTERROGATIVE		
PRESENT	wa	o-ci
PAST	wass-ó	wass-ci
REMOTE PAST	wassóss-ó	wassóss-ci
FUTURE	okess-ó	okess-ci
PAST FUTURE	wasskess-ó	wasskess-ci
PROPOSITIVE	wa	o-ci
IMPERATIVE		

CAUSATIVE: *PASSIVE:*

OLH.TA   옳다
to be right, to be just   DESCRIPTIVE

FORMAL *Plain*

	INDICATIVE	RETROSPECTIVE
DECLARATIVE/ *INTERROGATIVE*		
PRESENT	olh-ta/-únya	olh-tóla/-tónya
PAST	olhass-ta/-núnya	olhass-tóla
REMOTE PAST	olhassóss-ta	olhassóss-tóla
FUTURE	olhkess-ta	olhkess-tóla
PAST FUTURE	olhasskess-ta	olhasskess-tóla

PROPOSITIVE
IMPERATIVE

FORMAL *Polite*

	INDICATIVE	RETROSPECTIVE
DECLARATIVE/ *INTERROGATIVE*		
PRESENT	olhsúpni-ta/-kka	olhsúpti-ta/-kka
PAST	olhassúpni-ta	olhassúpti-ta
REMOTE PAST	olhassóssúpni-ta	olhassóssúpti-ta
FUTURE	olhkessúpni-ta	olhkessúpti-ta
PAST FUTURE	olhasskessúpni-ta	olhasskessúpti-ta

PROPOSITIVE
IMPERATIVE

INFORMAL *Familiar*

	INDICATIVE	RETROSPECTIVE
DECLARATIVE/ *INTERROGATIVE*		
PRESENT	olh-ne/-únka	olh-te/-tónka
PAST	olhass-ne/-núnka	olhass-te
REMOTE PAST	olhassóss-ne	olhassóss-te
FUTURE	olhkess-ne	olhkess-te
PAST FUTURE	olhasskess-ne	olhasskess-te

PROPOSITIVE
IMPERATIVE

	INFORMAL *Intimate* INDICATIVE	INFORMAL *Casual* INDICATIVE
DECLARATIVE/ *INTERROGATIVE*		
PRESENT	olh-a	olh-ci
PAST	olhass-ó	olhass-ci
REMOTE PAST	olhassóss-ó	olhassóss-ci
FUTURE	olhkess-ó	olhkess-ci
PAST FUTURE	ólhasskess-ó	olhasskess-ci

PROPOSITIVE
IMPERATIVE

CAUSATIVE: *PASSIVE:*

```
OLM.TA                                                               읊다
to be infected    INTRANSITIVE
```

FORMAL *Plain*

	INDICATIVE	RETROSPECTIVE
DECLARATIVE/ *INTERROGATIVE*		
PRESENT	olm-núnta/-núnya	olm-tóla/-tónya
PAST	olmass-ta	olmass-tóla
REMOTE PAST	olmassóss-ta	olmassóss-tóla
FUTURE	olmkess-ta	olmkess-tóla
PAST FUTURE	olmasskess-ta	olmasskess-tóla

PROPOSITIVE
IMPERATIVE

FORMAL *Polite*

	INDICATIVE	RETROSPECTIVE
DECLARATIVE/ *INTERROGATIVE*		
PRESENT	olmsúpni-ta/-kka	olmsúpti-ta/-kka
PAST	olmassúpni-ta	olmassúpti-ta
REMOTE PAST	olmassóssúpni-ta	olmassóssúpti-ta
FUTURE	olmkessúpni-ta	olmkessúpti-ta
PAST FUTURE	olmasskessúpni-ta	olmasskessúpti-ta

PROPOSITIVE
IMPERATIVE

INFORMAL *Familiar*

	INDICATIVE	RETROSPECTIVE
DECLARATIVE/ *INTERROGATIVE*		
PRESENT	olm-ne/-núnka	olm-te/-tónka
PAST	olmass-ne	olmass-te
REMOTE PAST	olmassóss-ne	olmassóss-te
FUTURE	olmkess-ne	olmkess-te
PAST FUTURE	olmasskess-ne	olmasskess-te

PROPOSITIVE
IMPERATIVE

	INFORMAL *Intimate* INDICATIVE	INFORMAL *Casual* INDICATIVE
DECLARATIVE/ *INTERROGATIVE*		
PRESENT	olm-a	olm-ci
PAST	olmass-ó	olmass-ci
REMOTE PAST	olmassóss-ó	olmassóss-ci
FUTURE	olmkess-ó	olmkess-ci
PAST FUTURE	olmasskess-ó	olmasskess-ci

PROPOSITIVE
IMPERATIVE

CAUSATIVE: OLMKI.TA   *PASSIVE:*
              to move it, to transfer

ÔPS.TA
to not exist, to not have   EXISTENTIAL (NEG)   없다

FORMAL *Plain*

	INDICATIVE	RETROSPECTIVE
DECLARATIVE/		
INTERROGATIVE		
PRESENT	óps-ta/-núnya	óps-tóla/-tónya
PAST	ópsóss-ta	ópsóss-tóla
REMOTE PAST	ópsóssóss-ta	ópsóssóss-tóla
FUTURE	ópskess-ta	ópskess-tóla
PAST FUTURE	ópsósskess-ta	ópsósskess-tóla

PROPOSITIVE
IMPERATIVE

FORMAL *Polite*

	INDICATIVE	RETROSPECTIVE
DECLARATIVE/		
INTERROGATIVE		
PRESENT	ópssúpni-ta/-kka	ópssúpti-ta/-kka
PAST	ópsóssúpni-ta	ópsóssúpti-ta
REMOTE PAST	ópsóssóssúpni-ta	ópsóssóssúpti-ta
FUTURE	ópskessúpni-ta	ópskessúpti-ta
PAST FUTURE	ópsósskessúpni-ta	ópsósskessúpti-ta

PROPOSITIVE
IMPERATIVE

INFORMAL *Familiar*

	INDICATIVE	RETROSPECTIVE
DECLARATIVE/		
INTERROGATIVE		
PRESENT	óps-ne/-núnka	óps-te/-tónka
PAST	ópsóss-ne	ópsóss-te
REMOTE PAST	ópsóssóss-ne	ópsóssóss-te
FUTURE	ópskess-ne	ópskess-te
PAST FUTURE	ópsósskess-ne	ópsósskess-te

PROPOSITIVE
IMPERATIVE

	INFORMAL *Intimate*	INFORMAL *Casual*
	INDICATIVE	INDICATIVE
DECLARATIVE/		
INTERROGATIVE		
PRESENT	óps-ó	óps-ci
PAST	ópsóss-ó	ópsóss-ci
REMOTE PAST	ópsóssóss-ó	ópsóssóss-ci
FUTURE	ópskess-ó	ópskess-ci
PAST FUTURE	ópsósskess-ó	ópsósskess-ci

PROPOSITIVE
IMPERATIVE

CAUSATIVE: ÔPSAE.TA   *PASSIVE:*
              to make nonexistent,
              to do away with

to be a certain way, to be how (in interrogative)

FORMAL *Plain*

DECLARATIVE/ INTERROGATIVE	INDICATIVE	RETROSPECTIVE
PRESENT	ŏttŏ-h.ta/-nya	ŏttŏh-tŏla/-tŏnya
PAST	ŏttaess-ta/-nŭnya	ŏttaess-tŏla
REMOTE PAST	ŏttaessŏss-ta	ŏttaessŏss-tŏla
FUTURE	ŏttŏhkess-ta	ŏttŏhkess-tŏla
PAST FUTURE	ŏttaesskess-ta	ŏttaesskess-tŏla

PROPOSITIVE
IMPERATIVE

FORMAL *Polite*

DECLARATIVE/ INTERROGATIVE	INDICATIVE	RETROSPECTIVE
PRESENT	ŏttŏhsŭpni-ta/-kka	ŏttŏhsŭpti-ta/-kka
PAST	ŏttaessŭpni-ta	ŏttaessŭpti-ta
REMOTE PAST	ŏttaessŏssŭpni-ta	ŏttaessŏssŭpti-ta
FUTURE	ŏttŏhkessŭpni-ta	ŏttŏhkessŭpti-ta
PAST FUTURE	ŏttaesskessŭpni-ta	ŏttaesskessŭpti-ta

PROPOSITIVE
IMPERATIVE

INFORMAL *Familiar*

DECLARATIVE/ INTERROGATIVE	INDICATIVE	RETROSPECTIVE
PRESENT	ŏttŏ-h.ne/-nka	ŏttŏh-te/-tŏnka
PAST	ŏttaess-ne/-nŭnka	ŏttaess-te
REMOTE PAST	ŏttaessŏss-ne	ŏttaessŏss-te
FUTURE	ŏttŏhkess-ne	ŏttŏhkess-te
PAST FUTURE	ŏttaesskess-ne	ŏttaesskess-te

PROPOSITIVE
IMPERATIVE

DECLARATIVE/ INTERROGATIVE	INFORMAL *Intimate* INDICATIVE	INFORMAL *Casual* INDICATIVE
PRESENT	ŏttae	ŏttŏh-ci
PAST	ŏttaess-ŏ	ŏttaess-ci
REMOTE PAST	ŏttaessŏss-ŏ	ŏttaessŏss-ci
FUTURE	ŏttŏhkess-ŏ	ŏttŏhkess-ci
PAST FUTURE	ŏttaesskess-ŏ	

PROPOSITIVE
IMPERATIVE

CAUSATIVE: *PASSIVE:*

ÔTUP.TA
to be dark, to be dim, to be gloomy   DESCRIPTIVE

FORMAL *Plain*

	INDICATIVE	RETROSPECTIVE
DECLARATIVE/ *INTERROGATIVE*		
PRESENT	ótu-p.ta/-unya	ótup-tóla/-tónya
PAST	ótuwòss-ta/-nùnya	ótuwòss-tóla
REMOTE PAST	ótuwòssòss-ta	ótuwòssòss-tóla
FUTURE	ótupkess-ta	ótupkess-tóla
PAST FUTURE	ótuwòsskess-ta	ótuwòsskess-tóla

PROPOSITIVE
IMPERATIVE

FORMAL *Polite*

	INDICATIVE	RETROSPECTIVE
DECLARATIVE/ *INTERROGATIVE*		
PRESENT	ótupsùpni-ta/-kka	ótupsùpti-ta/-kka
PAST	ótuwòssùpni-ta	ótuwòssùpti-ta
REMOTE PAST	ótuwòssòssùpni-ta	ótuwòssòssùpti-ta
FUTURE	ótupkessùpni-ta	ótupkessùpti-ta
PAST FUTURE	ótuwòsskessùpni-ta	ótuwòsskessùpti-ta

PROPOSITIVE
IMPERATIVE

INFORMAL *Familiar*

	INDICATIVE	RETROSPECTIVE
DECLARATIVE/ *INTERROGATIVE*		
PRESENT	ótu-p.ne/-unka	ótup-te/-tónka
PAST	ótuwòss-ne/-nùnka	ótuwòss-te
REMOTE PAST	ótuwòssòss-ne	ótuwòssòss-te
FUTURE	ótupkess-ne	ótupkess-te
PAST FUTURE	ótuwòsskess-ne	ótuwòsskess-te

PROPOSITIVE
IMPERATIVE

	INFORMAL *Intimate* INDICATIVE	INFORMAL *Casual* INDICATIVE
DECLARATIVE/ *INTERROGATIVE*		
PRESENT	ótu.w-ò	ótup-ci
PAST	ótuwòss-ò	ótuwòss-ci
REMOTE PAST	ótuwòssòss-ò	ótuwòssòss-ci
FUTURE	ótupkess-ò	ótupkess-ci
PAST FUTURE	ótuwòsskess-ò	ótuwòsskess-ci

PROPOSITIVE
IMPERATIVE

CAUSATIVE: *PASSIVE:*

PALK.TA   밝다
1) to be light, to be bright   DESCRIPTIVE
_____
                                  FORMAL *Plain*
                    INDICATIVE   RETROSPECTIVE
DECLARATIVE/
INTERROGATIVE

     PRESENT   palk-ta/-únya   palk-tóla/-tónya
     PAST   palkass-ta/-núnya   palkass-tóla
     REMOTE PAST palkassóss-ta   palkassóss-tóla
     FUTURE   palkkess-ta   palkess-tóla
     PAST FUTURE palkasskess-ta   palkasskess-tóla

PROPOSITIVE
IMPERATIVE

                                  FORMAL *Polite*
                    INDICATIVE   RETROSPECTIVE
DECLARATIVE/
INTERROGATIVE

     PRESENT   palksúpni-ta/-kka   palksúpti-ta/-kka
     PAST   palkassúpni-ta   palkassúpti-ta
     REMOTE PAST palkassóssúpni-ta   palkassóssúpti-ta
     FUTURE   palkkessúpni-ta   palkkessúpti-ta
     PAST FUTURE palkasskessúpni-ta   palkasskessúpti-ta

PROPOSITIVE
IMPERATIVE

                                 INFORMAL *Familiar*
                    INDICATIVE   RETROSPECTIVE
DECLARATIVE/
INTERROGATIVE

     PRESENT   palk-ne/-únka   palk-te/-tónka
     PAST   palkass-ne/-núnka   palkass-te
     REMOTE PAST palkassóss-ne   palkassóss-te
     FUTURE   palkkess-ne   palkkess-te
     PAST FUTURE palkasskess-ne   palkasskess-te

PROPOSITIVE
IMPERATIVE

                    INFORMAL *Intimate*   INFORMAL *Casual*
                    INDICATIVE   INDICATIVE
DECLARATIVE/
INTERROGATIVE

     PRESENT   palk-a   palk-ci
     PAST   palkass-ó   palkass-ci
     REMOTE PAST palkassóss-ó   palkassóss-ci
     FUTURE   palkkess-ó   palkkess-ci
     PAST FUTURE palkasskess-ó   palkasskess-ci

PROPOSITIVE
IMPERATIVE
_____
     CAUSATIVE: PALKHI.TA   *PASSIVE:*
                   1) to make it clear

130

FORMAL *Plain*

	INDICATIVE	RETROSPECTIVE
DECLARATIVE/ *INTERROGATIVE*		
PRESENT	palp-nún.ta/-núnya	palp-tóla/-tónya
PAST	palpass-ta	palpass-tóla
REMOTE PAST	palpassóss-ta	palpassóss-tóla
FUTURE	palpkess-ta	palpkess-tóla
PAST FUTURE	palpasskess-ta	palpasskess-tóla
PROPOSITIVE	palp-ca	
IMPERATIVE	palp-ala	

FORMAL *Polite*

	INDICATIVE	RETROSPECTIVE
DECLARATIVE/ *INTERROGATIVE*		
PRESENT	palpsúpni-ta/-kka	palpsúpti-ta/-kka
PAST	palpassúpni-ta	palpassúpti-ta
REMOTE PAST	palpassóssúpni-ta	palpassóssúpti-ta
FUTURE	palpkessúpni-ta	palpkessúpti-ta
PAST FUTURE	palpasskessúpni-ta	palpasskessúpti-ta
PROPOSITIVE		
IMPERATIVE		

INFORMAL *Familiar*

	INDICATIVE	RETROSPECTIVE
DECLARATIVE/ *INTERROGATIVE*		
PRESENT	palp-ne/-núnka	palp-te/-tónka
PAST	palpass-ne	palpass-te
REMOTE PAST	palpassóss-ne	palpassóss-te
FUTURE	palpkess-ne	palpkess-te
PAST FUTURE	palpasskess-ne	palpasskess-te
PROPOSITIVE		
IMPERATIVE		

	INFORMAL *Intimate* INDICATIVE	INFORMAL *Casual* INDICATIVE
DECLARATIVE/ *INTERROGATIVE*		
PRESENT	palp-a	palp-ci
PAST	palpass-ó	palpass-ci
REMOTE PAST	palpassóss-ó	palpassóss-ci
FUTURE	palpkess-ó	palpkess-ci
PAST FUTURE	palpasskess-ó	palpasskess-ci
PROPOSITIVE	palp-a	
IMPERATIVE		

CAUSATIVE: *PASSIVE:* PALPHI.TA
                              to be stepped on

PALÙ.TA
to apply (an ointment/oil) to, to stick, to paint

FORMAL *Plain*

	INDICATIVE	RETROSPECTIVE
DECLARATIVE/ *INTERROGATIVE*		
PRESENT	palù-n.ta/-nùnya	palù-tóla/-tónya
PAST	pallass-ta	pallass-tóla
REMOTE PAST	pallassóss-ta	pallassóss-tóla
FUTURE	palùkess-ta	palùkess-tóla
PAST FUTURE	pallasskess-ta	pallasskess-tóla
PROPOSITIVE	palù-ca	
IMPERATIVE	pall-ala	

FORMAL *Polite*

	INDICATIVE	RETROSPECTIVE
DECLARATIVE/ *INTERROGATIVE*		
PRESENT	palùpni-ta/-kka	palùpti-ta/-kka
PAST	pallassùpni-ta	pallassùpti-ta
REMOTE PAST	pallassóssùpni-ta	pallassóssùpti-ta
FUTURE	palùkessùpni-ta	palùkessùpti-ta
PAST FUTURE	pallasskessùpni-ta	pallasskessùpti-ta
PROPOSITIVE	palùpsi-ta	
IMPERATIVE	palù(si)psi-o	

INFORMAL *Familiar*

	INDICATIVE	RETROSPECTIVE
DECLARATIVE/ *INTERROGATIVE*		
PRESENT	palù-ne/-nùnka	palù-te/-tónka
PAST	pallass-ne	pallass-te
REMOTE PAST	pallassóss-ne	pallassóss-te
FUTURE	palùkess-ne	palùkess-te
PAST FUTURE	pallasskess-ne	pallasskess-te
PROPOSITIVE	palù-se	
IMPERATIVE	palù-ke	

	INFORMAL *Intimate* INDICATIVE	INFORMAL *Casual* INDICATIVE
DECLARATIVE/ *INTERROGATIVE*		
PRESENT	pall-a	palù-ci
PAST	pallass-ò	pallass-ci
REMOTE PAST	pallassóss-ò	pallassóss-ci
FUTURE	palùkess-ò	palùkess-ci
PAST FUTURE	pallasskess-ò	pallasskess-ci
PROPOSITIVE *IMPERATIVE*	pall-a	palù-ci

CAUSATIVE:

PASSIVE: PALLI.TA
to be applied (to)
(paste, oil, etc.)

FORMAL *Plain*

	INDICATIVE	RETROSPECTIVE
DECLARATIVE/ *INTERROGATIVE*		
PRESENT	panka-p.ta/-unya	pankap-tóla/-tónya
PAST	pankawass-ta/-núnya	pankawass-tóla
REMOTE PAST	pankawassóss-ta	pankawassóss-tóla
FUTURE	pankapkess-ta	pankapkess-tóla
PAST FUTURE	pankawasskess-ta	pankawasskess-tóla
PROPOSITIVE		
IMPERATIVE		

FORMAL *Polite*

	INDICATIVE	RETROSPECTIVE
DECLARATIVE/ *INTERROGATIVE*		
PRESENT	pankapsúpni-ta/-kka	pankapsúpti-ta/-kka
PAST	pankawassúpni-ta	pankawassúpti-ta
REMOTE PAST	pankawassóssúpni-ta	pankawassóssúpti-ta
FUTURE	pankapkessúpni-ta	pankapkessúpti-ta
PAST FUTURE	pankawasskessúpni-ta	pankawasskessúpti-ta
PROPOSITIVE		
IMPERATIVE		

INFORMAL *Familiar*

	INDICATIVE	RETROSPECTIVE
DECLARATIVE/ *INTERROGATIVE*		
PRESENT	panka-p.ne/-unka	pankap-te/-tónka
PAST	pankawass-ne/-núnka	pankawass-te
REMOTE PAST	pankawassóss-ne	pankawassóss-te
FUTURE	pankapkess-ne	pankapkess-te
PAST FUTURE	pankawasskess-ne	pankawasskess-te
PROPOSITIVE		
IMPERATIVE		

	INFORMAL *Intimate* INDICATIVE	INFORMAL *Casual* INDICATIVE
DECLARATIVE/ *INTERROGATIVE*		
PRESENT	panka.w-a	pankap-ci
PAST	pankawass-ó	pankawass-ci
REMOTE PAST	pankawassóss-ó	pankawassóss-ci
FUTURE	pankapkess-ó	pankapkess-ci
PAST FUTURE	pankawasskess-ó	pankawasskess-ci
PROPOSITIVE		
IMPERATIVE		

CAUSATIVE: *PASSIVE:*

PO.TA
to see, to look at
보다

FORMAL *Plain*

	INDICATIVE	RETROSPECTIVE
DECLARATIVE/ *INTERROGATIVE*		
PRESENT	po-n.ta/-núnya	po-tóla/-tónya
PAST	poass-ta	poass-tóla
REMOTE PAST	poassóss-ta	poassóss-tóla
FUTURE	pokess-ta	pokess-tóla
PAST FUTURE	poasskess-ta	poasskess-tóla
PROPOSITIVE	po-ca	
IMPERATIVE	po-ala	

FORMAL *Polite*

	INDICATIVE	RETROSPECTIVE
DECLARATIVE/ *INTERROGATIVE*		
PRESENT	popni-ta/-kka	popti-ta/-kka
PAST	poassúpni-ta	poassúpti-ta
REMOTE PAST	poassóssúpni-ta	poassóssúpti-ta
FUTURE	pokessúpni-ta	pokessúpti-ta
PAST FUTURE	poasskessúpni-ta	poasskessúpti-ta
PROPOSITIVE	popsi-ta	
IMPERATIVE	po(si)psi-o	

INFORMAL *Familiar*

	INDICATIVE	RETROSPECTIVE
DECLARATIVE/ *INTERROGATIVE*		
PRESENT	po-ne/-núnka	po-te/-tónka
PAST	poass-ne	poass-te
REMOTE PAST	poassóss-ne	poassóss-te
FUTURE	pokess-ne	pokess-te
PAST FUTURE	poasskess-ne	poasskess-te
PROPOSITIVE	po-se	
IMPERATIVE	po-ke	

	INFORMAL *Intimate* INDICATIVE	INFORMAL *Casual* INDICATIVE
DECLARATIVE/ *INTERROGATIVE*		
PRESENT	po-a	po-ci
PAST	poass-ó	poass-ci
REMOTE PAST	poassóss-ó	poassóss-ci
FUTURE	pokess-ó	pokess-ci
PAST FUTURE	poasskess-ó	poasskess-ci
PROPOSITIVE *IMPERATIVE*	po-a	po-ci

CAUSATIVE: POI.TA
to let (a person) see,
to show

PASSIVE: POI.TA
to be seen,
to be visible

	FORMAL *Plain*	
	INDICATIVE	RETROSPECTIVE
DECLARATIVE/ *INTERROGATIVE*		
PRESENT	pu-n.ta/-núnya	pul-tóla/-tónya
PAST	pulóss-ta	pulóss-tóla
REMOTE PAST	pulóssóss-ta	pulóssóss-tóla
FUTURE	pulkess-ta	pulkess-tóla
PAST FUTURE	pulósskess-ta	pulósskess-tóla
PROPOSITIVE	pul-ca	
IMPERATIVE	pul-óla	

	FORMAL *Polite*	
	INDICATIVE	RETROSPECTIVE
DECLARATIVE/ *INTERROGATIVE*		
PRESENT	pupni-ta/-kka	pupti-ta/-kka
PAST	pulóssúpni-ta	pulóssúpti-ta
REMOTE PAST	pulóssóssúpni-ta	pulóssóssúpti-ta
FUTURE	pulkessúpni-ta	pulkessúpti-ta
PAST FUTURE	pulósskessúpni-ta	pulósskessúpti-ta
PROPOSITIVE	pupsi-ta	
IMPERATIVE	pu(si)psi-o	

	INFORMAL *Familiar*	
	INDICATIVE	RETROSPECTIVE
DECLARATIVE/ *INTERROGATIVE*		
PRESENT	pu-ne/-núnka	pul-te/-tónka
PAST	pulóss-ne	pulóss-te
REMOTE PAST	pulóssóss-ne	pulóssóss-te
FUTURE	pulkess-ne	pulkess-te
PAST FUTURE	pulósskess-ne	pulósskess-te
PROPOSITIVE	pu-se	
IMPERATIVE	pul-ke	

	INFORMAL *Intimate* INDICATIVE	INFORMAL *Casual* INDICATIVE
DECLARATIVE/ *INTERROGATIVE*		
PRESENT	pul-ó	pul-ci
PAST	pulóss-ó	pulóss-ci
REMOTE PAST	pulóssóss-ó	pulóssóss-ci
FUTURE	pulkess-ó	pulkess-ci
PAST FUTURE	pulósskess-ó	pulósskess-ci
PROPOSITIVE *IMPERATIVE*	pul-ó	pul-ci

CAUSATIVE: PULLI.TA
to make (a person) blow

PASSIVE: PULLI.TA
to be blown
(by the wind)

FORMAL *Plain*

	INDICATIVE	RETROSPECTIVE
DECLARATIVE/ *INTERROGATIVE*		
PRESENT	pulù-n.ta/-nùnya	pulù-tóla/-tónya
PAST	pullóss-ta	pullóss-tóla
REMOTE PAST	pullóssóss-ta	pullóssóss-tóla
FUTURE	pulùkess-ta	pulùkess-tóla
PAST FUTURE	pullósskess-ta	pullósskess-tóla
PROPOSITIVE	pulù-ca	
IMPERATIVE	pull-óla	

FORMAL *Polite*

	INDICATIVE	RETROSPECTIVE
DECLARATIVE/ *INTERROGATIVE*		
PRESENT	pulùpni-ta/-kka	pulùpti-ta/-kka
PAST	pullóssùpni-ta	pullóssùptí-ta
REMOTE PAST	pullóssóssùpni-ta	pullóssóssùpti-ta
FUTURE	pulùkessùpni-ta	pulùkessùpti-ta
PAST FUTURE	pullósskessùpni-ta	pullósskessùpti-ta
PROPOSITIVE	pulùpsi-ta	
IMPERATIVE	pulù(si)psi-o	

INFORMAL *Familiar*

	INDICATIVE	RETROSPECTIVE
DECLARATIVE/ *INTERROGATIVE*		
PRESENT	pulù-ne/-nùnka	pulù-te/-tónka
PAST	pullóss-ne	pullóss-te
REMOTE PAST	pullóssóss-ne	pullóssóss-te
FUTURE	pulùkess-ne	pulùkess-te
PAST FUTURE	pullósskess-ne	pullósskess-te
PROPOSITIVE	pulù-se	
IMPERATIVE	pulù-ke	

	INFORMAL *Intimate* INDICATIVE	INFORMAL *Casual* INDICATIVE
DECLARATIVE/ *INTERROGATIVE*		
PRESENT	pull-ó	pulù-ci
PAST	pullóss-ó	pullóss-ci
REMOTE PAST	pullóssóss-ó	pullóssóss-ci
FUTURE	pulùkess-ó	pulùkess-ci
PAST FUTURE	pullósskess-ó	pullósskess-ci
PROPOSITIVE *IMPERATIVE*	pull-ó	

CAUSATIVE:

PASSIVE: PULLI.TA
to be called

to be shameful, to be shy   DESCRIPTIVE

FORMAL *Plain*

	INDICATIVE	RETROSPECTIVE
DECLARATIVE/ *INTERROGATIVE*		
PRESENT	pukkùlò-p.ta/-unya	pukkùlòp-tòla/-tònya
PAST	pukkùlòwòss-ta/-nùnya	pukkùlòwòss-tòla
REMOTE PAST	pukkùlòwòssòss-ta	pukkùlòwòssòss-tòla
FUTURE	pukkùlòpkess-ta	pukkùlòpkess-tòla
PAST FUTURE	pukkùlòwòsskess-ta	pukkùlòwòsskess-tòla

PROPOSITIVE
IMPERATIVE

FORMAL *Polite*

	INDICATIVE	RETROSPECTIVE
DECLARATIVE/ *INTERROGATIVE*		
PRESENT	pukkùlòpsùpni-ta/-kka	pukkùlòpsùpti-ta/-kka
PAST	pukkùlòwòssùpni-ta	pukkùlòwòssùpti-ta
REMOTE PAST	pukkùlòwòssòssùpni-ta	pukkùlòwòssòssùpti-ta
FUTURE	pukkùlòpkessùpni-ta	pukkùlòpkessùpti-ta
PAST FUTURE	pukkùlòwòsskessùpni-ta	pukkùlòwòsskessùpti-ta

PROPOSITIVE
IMPERATIVE

INFORMAL *Familiar*

	INDICATIVE	RETROSPECTIVE
DECLARATIVE/ *INTERROGATIVE*		
PRESENT	pukkùlò-p.ne/-unka	pukkùlòp-te/-tònka
PAST	pukkùlòwòss-ne/-nùnka	pukkùlòwòss-te
REMOTE PAST	pukkùlòwòssòss-ne	pukkùlòwòssòss-te
FUTURE	pukkùlòpkess-ne	pukkùlòpkess-te
PAST FUTURE	pukkùlòwòsskess-ne	pukkùlòwòsskess-te

PROPOSITIVE
IMPERATIVE

	INFORMAL *Intimate* INDICATIVE	INFORMAL *Casual* INDICATIVE
DECLARATIVE/ *INTERROGATIVE*		
PRESENT	pukkùlò.w-ò	pukkùlòp-ci
PAST	pukkùlòwòss-ò	pukkùlòwòss-ci
REMOTE PAST	pukkùlòwòssòss-ò	pukkùlòwòssòss-ci
FUTURE	pukkùlòpkess-ò	pukkùlòpkess-ci
PAST FUTURE	pukkùlòwòsskess-ò	pukkùlòwòsskess-ci

PROPOSITIVE
IMPERATIVE

CAUSATIVE: *PASSIVE:*

1) to swell up (a part of the body) INTRANSITIVE   2) to pour   붓다

FORMAL *Plain*

	INDICATIVE	RETROSPECTIVE
DECLARATIVE/ *INTERROGATIVE*		
PRESENT	pus-nŭn.ta/-nŭnya	pus-tóla/-tónya
PAST	puóss-ta	puóss-tóla
REMOTE PAST	puóssóss-ta	puóssóss-tóla
FUTURE	puskess-ta	puskess-tóla
PAST FUTURE	puósskess-ta	puósskess-tóla
PROPOSITIVE	pus-ca (2)	
IMPERATIVE	pu-óla (2)	

FORMAL *Polite*

	INDICATIVE	RETROSPECTIVE
DECLARATIVE/ *INTERROGATIVE*		
PRESENT	pussŭpni-ta/-kka	pussŭpti-ta/-kka
PAST	puóssŭpni-ta	puóssŭpti-ta
REMOTE PAST	puóssóssŭpni-ta	puóssóssŭpti-ta
FUTURE	puskessŭpni-ta	puskessŭpti-ta
PAST FUTURE	puósskessŭpni-ta	puósskessŭpti-ta
PROPOSITIVE	puŭpsi-ta (2)	
IMPERATIVE	puŭ(si)psi-o (2)	

INFORMAL *Familiar*

	INDICATIVE	RETROSPECTIVE
DECLARATIVE/ *INTERROGATIVE*		
PRESENT	pus-ne/-nŭnka	pus-te/-tónka
PAST	puóss-ne	puóss-te
REMOTE PAST	puóssóss-ne	puóssóss-te
FUTURE	puskess-ne	puskess-te
PAST FUTURE	puósskess-ne	puósskess-te
PROPOSITIVE	pus-se (2)	
IMPERATIVE	pus-ke (2)	

	INFORMAL *Intimate* INDICATIVE	INFORMAL *Casual* INDICATIVE
DECLARATIVE/ *INTERROGATIVE*		
PRESENT	pu-ó	pus-ci
PAST	puóss-ó	puóss-ci
REMOTE PAST	puóssóss-ó	puóssóss-ci
FUTURE	puskess-ó	puskess-ci
PAST FUTURE	puósskess-ó	puósskess-ci
PROPOSITIVE *IMPERATIVE*	pu-ó	pus-ci

CAUSATIVE: *PASSIVE:*

PUT.TA
to swell, to increase INTRANSITIVE

붇다

FORMAL Plain

	INDICATIVE	RETROSPECTIVE
DECLARATIVE/ *INTERROGATIVE*		
PRESENT	put-nún.ta/-núnya	put-tóla/-tónya
PAST	pulóss-ta	pulóss-tóla
REMOTE PAST	pulóssóss-ta	pulóssóss-tóla
FUTURE	putkess-ta	putkess-tóla
PAST FUTURE	pulósskess-ta	pulósskess-tóla

PROPOSITIVE
IMPERATIVE

FORMAL Polite

	INDICATIVE	RETROSPECTIVE
DECLARATIVE/ *INTERROGATIVE*		
PRESENT	putsúpni-ta/-kka	putsúpti-ta/-kka
PAST	pulóssúpni-ta	pulóssúpti-ta
REMOTE PAST	pulóssóssúpni-ta	pulóssóssúpti-ta
FUTURE	putkessúpni-ta	putkessúpti-ta
PAST FUTURE	pulósskessúpni-ta	pulósskessúpti-ta

PROPOSITIVE
IMPERATIVE

INFORMAL Familiar

	INDICATIVE	RETROSPECTIVE
DECLARATIVE/ *INTERROGATIVE*		
PRESENT	put-ne/-núnka	put-te/-tónka
PAST	pulóss-ne	pulóss-te
REMOTE PAST	pulóssóss-ne	pulóssóss-te
FUTURE	putkess-ne	putkess-te
PAST FUTURE	pulósskess-ne	pulósskess-te

PROPOSITIVE
IMPERATIVE

	INFORMAL *Intimate* INDICATIVE	INFORMAL *Casual* INDICATIVE
DECLARATIVE/ *INTERROGATIVE*		
PRESENT	pul-ó	put-ci
PAST	pulóss-ó	pulóss-ci
REMOTE PAST	pulóssóss-ó	pulóssóss-ci
FUTURE	putkess-ó	putkess-ci
PAST FUTURE	pulósskess-ó	pulósskess-ci

PROPOSITIVE
IMPERATIVE

CAUSATIVE: PULLI.TA   *PASSIVE:*
to increase it

FORMAL *Plain*

DECLARATIVE/ INTERROGATIVE	INDICATIVE	RETROSPECTIVE
PRESENT	pha-n.ta/-nùnya	pha-tóla/-tónya
PAST	phass-ta	phass-tóla
REMOTE PAST	phassóss-ta	phassóss-tóla
FUTURE	phakess-ta	phakess-tóla
PAST FUTURE	phasskess-ta	phasskess-tóla
PROPOSITIVE	pha-ca	
IMPERATIVE	pha-la	

FORMAL *Polite*

DECLARATIVE/ INTERROGATIVE	INDICATIVE	RETROSPECTIVE
PRESENT	phapni-ta/-kka	phapti-ta/-kka
PAST	phassùpni-ta	phassùpti-ta
REMOTE PAST	phassóssùpni-ta	phassóssùpti-ta
FUTURE	phakessùpni-ta	phakessùpti-ta
PAST FUTURE	phasskessùpni-ta	phasskessùpti-ta
PROPOSITIVE	phapsi-ta	
IMPERATIVE	pha(si)psi-o	

INFORMAL *Familiar*

DECLARATIVE/ INTERROGATIVE	INDICATIVE	RETROSPECTIVE
PRESENT	pha-ne/-nùnka	pha-te/-tónka
PAST	phass-ne	phass-te
REMOTE PAST	phassóss-ne	phassóss-te
FUTURE	phakess-ne	phakess-te
PAST FUTURE	phasskess-ne	phasskess-te
PROPOSITIVE	pha-se	
IMPERATIVE	pha-ke	

DECLARATIVE/ INTERROGATIVE	INFORMAL *Intimate* INDICATIVE	INFORMAL *Casual* INDICATIVE
PRESENT	pha	pha-ci
PAST	phass-ó	phass-ci
REMOTE PAST	phassóss-ó	phassóss-ci
FUTURE	phakess-ó	phakess-ci
PAST FUTURE	phasskess-ó	phasskess-ci
PROPOSITIVE IMPERATIVE	pha	pha-ci

CAUSATIVE: PHAE.TA
to have a person dig

PASSIVE: PHAE.TA
to be hollowed out

PHAE.TA   패다
1) to split, to chop up (with an axe)   2) to beat, to assault

FORMAL *Plain*

	INDICATIVE	RETROSPECTIVE
DECLARATIVE/ *INTERROGATIVE*		
PRESENT	phae-n.ta/-núnya	phae-tóla/-tónya
PAST	phaess-ta	phaess-tóla
REMOTE PAST	phaessóss-ta	phaessóss-tóla
FUTURE	phaekess-ta	phaekess-tóla
PAST FUTURE	phaesskess-ta	phaesskess-tóla
PROPOSITIVE	phae-ca	
IMPERATIVE	phae-la	

FORMAL *Polite*

	INDICATIVE	RETROSPECTIVE
DECLARATIVE/ *INTERROGATIVE*		
PRESENT	phaepni-ta/-kka	phaepti-ta/-kka
PAST	phaessúpni-ta	phaessúpti-ta
REMOTE PAST	phaessóssúpni-ta	phaessóssúpti-ta
FUTURE	phaekessúpni-ta	phaekessúpti-ta
PAST FUTURE	phaesskessúpni-ta	phaesskessúpti-ta
PROPOSITIVE	phaepsi-ta	
IMPERATIVE	phae(si)psi-o	

INFORMAL *Familiar*

	INDICATIVE	RETROSPECTIVE
DECLARATIVE/ *INTERROGATIVE*		
PRESENT	phae-ne/-núnka	phae-te/-tónka
PAST	phaess-ne	phaess-te
REMOTE PAST	phaessóss-ne	phaessóss-te
FUTURE	phaekess-ne	phaekess-te
PAST FUTURE	phaesskess-ne	phaesskess-te
PROPOSITIVE	phae-se	
IMPERATIVE	phae-ke	

	INFORMAL *Intimate* INDICATIVE	INFORMAL *Casual* INDICATIVE
DECLARATIVE/ *INTERROGATIVE*		
PRESENT	phae	phae-ci
PAST	phaess-ó	phaess-ci
REMOTE PAST	phaessóss-ó	phaessóss-ci
FUTURE	phaekess-ó	phaekess-ci
PAST FUTURE	phaesskess-ó	phaesskess-ci
PROPOSITIVE *IMPERATIVE*	phae	phae-ci

CAUSATIVE: *PASSIVE:*

141

FORMAL *Plain*

	INDICATIVE	RETROSPECTIVE
DECLARATIVE/ INTERROGATIVE		
PRESENT	pha-n.ta/-núnya	phal-tóla/-tónya
PAST	phalass-ta	phalass-tóla
REMOTE PAST	phalassóss-ta	phalassóss-tóla
FUTURE	phalkess-ta	phalkess-tóla
PAST FUTURE	phalasskess-ta	phalasskess-tóla
PROPOSITIVE	phal-ca	
IMPERATIVE	phal-ala	

FORMAL *Polite*

	INDICATIVE	RETROSPECTIVE
DECLARATIVE/ INTERROGATIVE		
PRESENT	phapni-ta/-kka	phapti-ta/-kka
PAST	phalassúpni-ta	phalassúpti-ta
REMOTE PAST	phalassóssúpni-ta	phalassóssúpti-ta
FUTURE	phalkessúpni-ta	phalkessúpti-ta
PAST FUTURE	phalasskessúpni-ta	phalasskessúpti-ta
PROPOSITIVE	phapsi-ta	
IMPERATIVE	pha(si)psi-o	

INFORMAL *Familiar*

	INDICATIVE	RETROSPECTIVE
DECLARATIVE/ INTERROGATIVE		
PRESENT	pha-ne/-núnka	phal-te/-tónka
PAST	phalass-ne	phalass-te
REMOTE PAST	phalassóss-ne	phalassóss-te
FUTURE	phalkess-ne	phalkess-te
PAST FUTURE	phalasskess-ne	phalasskess-te
PROPOSITIVE	pha-se	
IMPERATIVE	phal-ke	

	INFORMAL *Intimate* INDICATIVE	INFORMAL *Casual* INDICATIVE
DECLARATIVE/ INTERROGATIVE		
PRESENT	phal-a	phal-ci
PAST	phalass-ó	phalass-ci
REMOTE PAST	phalassóss-ó	phalassóss-ci
FUTURE	phalkess-ó	phalkess-ci
PAST FUTURE	phalasskess-ó	phalasskess-ci
PROPOSITIVE *IMPERATIVE*	phal-a	phal-ci

CAUSATIVE: *PASSIVE:* PHALLI.TA
                                          to be sold

to be green, to be deep blue   DESCRIPTIVE

FORMAL *Plain*

	INDICATIVE	RETROSPECTIVE
DECLARATIVE/ *INTERROGATIVE*		
PRESENT	phala-h.ta/-nya	phalah-tóla/-tónya
PAST	phalaess-ta/-núnya	phalaess-tóla
REMOTE PAST	phalaessóss-ta	phalaessóss-tóla
FUTURE	phalahkess-ta	phalahkess-tóla
PAST FUTURE	phalaesskess-ta	phalaesskess-tóla

PROPOSITIVE
IMPERATIVE

FORMAL *Polite*

	INDICATIVE	RETROSPECTIVE
DECLARATIVE/ *INTERROGATIVE*		
PRESENT	phalahsúpni-ta/-kka	phalahsúpti-ta/-kka
PAST	phalaessúpni-ta	phalaessúpti-ta
REMOTE PAST	phalaessóssúpni-ta	phalaessóssúpti-ta
FUTURE	phalahkessúpni-ta	phalahkessúpti-ta
PAST FUTURE	phalaesskessúpni-ta	phalaesskessúpti-ta

PROPOSITIVE
IMPERATIVE

INFORMAL *Familiar*

	INDICATIVE	RETROSPECTIVE
DECLARATIVE/ *INTERROGATIVE*		
PRESENT	phala-h.ne/-nka	phalah-te/-tónka
PAST	phalaess-ne/-núnka	phalaess-te
REMOTE PAST	phalaessóss-ne	phalaessóss-te
FUTURE	phalahkess-ne	phalahkess-te
PAST FUTURE	phalaesskess-ne	phalaesskess-te

PROPOSITIVE
IMPERATIVE

	INFORMAL *Intimate* INDICATIVE	INFORMAL *Casual* INDICATIVE
DECLARATIVE/ *INTERROGATIVE*		
PRESENT	phalae	phalah-ci
PAST	phalaess-ó	phalaess-ci
REMOTE PAST	phalaessóss-ó	phalaessóss-ci
FUTURE	phalahkess-ó	phalahkess-ci
PAST FUTURE	phalaesskess-ó	phalaesskess-ci

PROPOSITIVE
IMPERATIVE

CAUSATIVE: *PASSIVE:*

1) to spread it out, to unfold   2) to bloom   INTRANSITIVE

FORMAL *Plain*

	INDICATIVE	RETROSPECTIVE
DECLARATIVE/ *INTERROGATIVE*		
PRESENT	phi-n.ta/-núnya	phi-tóla/-tónya
PAST	phyóss-ta	phyóss-tóla
REMOTE PAST	phyóssóss-ta	phyóssóss-tóla
FUTURE	phikess-ta	phikess-tóla
PAST FUTURE	phyósskess-ta	phyósskess-tóla
PROPOSITIVE	phi-ca (1)	
IMPERATIVE	phy-ó.la (1)	

FORMAL *Polite*

	INDICATIVE	RETROSPECTIVE
DECLARATIVE/ *INTERROGATIVE*		
PRESENT	phipni-ta/-kka	phipti-ta/-kka
PAST	phyóssúpni-ta	phyóssúpti-ta
REMOTE PAST	phyóssóssúpni-ta	phyóssóssúpti-ta
FUTURE	phikessúpni-ta	phikessúpti-ta
PAST FUTURE	phyósskessúpni-ta	phyósskessúpti-ta
PROPOSITIVE	phipsi-ta (1)	
IMPERATIVE	phi(si)psi-o (1)	

INFORMAL *Familiar*

	INDICATIVE	RETROSPECTIVE
DECLARATIVE/ *INTERROGATIVE*		
PRESENT	phi-ne/-núnka	phi-te/-tónka
PAST	phyóss-ne	phyóss-te
REMOTE PAST	phyóssóss-ne	phyóssóss-te
FUTURE	phikess-ne	phikess-te
PAST FUTURE	phyósskess-ne	phyósskess-te
PROPOSITIVE	phi-se (1)	
IMPERATIVE	phi-ke (1)	

	INFORMAL *Intimate* INDICATIVE	INFORMAL *Casual* INDICATIVE
DECLARATIVE/ *INTERROGATIVE*		
PRESENT	phy-ó	phi-ci
PAST	phyóss-ó	phyóss-ci
REMOTE PAST	phyóssóss-ó	phyóssóss-ci
FUTURE	phikess-ó	phikess-ci
PAST FUTURE	phyósskess-ó	phyósskess-ci
PROPOSITIVE *IMPERATIVE*	phy-ó (1)	phi-ci (1)

CAUSATIVE: *PASSIVE:*

1) to smoke, to burn   2) to play (tricks)

FORMAL *Plain*

	INDICATIVE	RETROSPECTIVE
DECLARATIVE/ *INTERROGATIVE*		
PRESENT	phiu-n.ta/-nunya	phiu-tola/-tonya
PAST	phiwoss-ta	phiwoss-tola
REMOTE PAST	phiwossoss-ta	phiwossoss-tola
FUTURE	phiukess-ta	phiukess-tola
PAST FUTURE	phiwosskess-ta	phiwosskess-tola
PROPOSITIVE	phiu-ca	
IMPERATIVE	phiw-ola	

FORMAL *Polite*

	INDICATIVE	RETROSPECTIVE
DECLARATIVE/ *INTERROGATIVE*		
PRESENT	phiupni-ta/-kka	phiupti-ta/-kka
PAST	phiwossupni-ta	phiwossupti-ta
REMOTE PAST	phiwossossupni-ta	phiwossossupti-ta
FUTURE	phiukessupni-ta	phiukessuti-ta
PAST FUTURE	phiwosskessupni-ta	phiwosskessupti-ta
PROPOSITIVE	phiupsi-ta	
IMPERATIVE	phiu(si)psi-o	

INFORMAL *Familiar*

	INDICATIVE	RETROSPECTIVE
DECLARATIVE/ *INTERROGATIVE*		
PRESENT	phiu-ne/-nunka	phiu-te/-tonka
PAST	phiwoss-ne	phiwoss-te
REMOTE PAST	phiwossoss-ne	phiwossoss-te
FUTURE	phiukess-ne	phiukess-te
PAST FUTURE	phiwosskess-ne	phiwosskess-te
PROPOSITIVE	phiu-se	
IMPERATIVE	phiu-ke	

	INFORMAL *Intimate* INDICATIVE	INFORMAL *Casual* INDICATIVE
DECLARATIVE/ *INTERROGATIVE*		
PRESENT	phi.w-o	phiu-ci
PAST	phiwoss-o	phiwoss-ci
REMOTE PAST	phiwossoss-o	phiwossoss-ci
FUTURE	phiukess-o	phiukess-ci
PAST FUTURE	phiwosskess-o	phiwosskess-ci
PROPOSITIVE *IMPERATIVE*	phi.w-o	phiu-ci

CAUSATIVE: *PASSIVE:*

FORMAL *Plain*

	INDICATIVE	RETROSPECTIVE
DECLARATIVE/ INTERROGATIVE		
PRESENT	phu-n.ta/-nûnya	phu-tóla/-tónya
PAST	phóss-ta	phóss-tóla
REMOTE PAST	phóssóss-ta	phóssóss-tóla
FUTURE	phukess-ta	phukess-tóla
PAST FUTURE	phósskess-ta	phósskess-tóla
PROPOSITIVE	phu-ca	
IMPERATIVE	phó-la	

FORMAL *Polite*

	INDICATIVE	RETROSPECTIVE
DECLARATIVE/ INTERROGATIVE		
PRESENT	phupni-ta/-kka	phupti-ta/-kka
PAST	phóssúpni-ta	phóssúpti-ta
REMOTE PAST	phóssóssúpni-ta	phóssóssúpti-ta
FUTURE	phukessúpni-ta	phukessúpti-ta
PAST FUTURE	phósskessúpni-ta	phósskessúpti-ta
PROPOSITIVE	phupsi-ta	
IMPERATIVE	phu(si)psi-o	

INFORMAL *Familiar*

	INDICATIVE	RETROSPECTIVE
DECLARATIVE/ INTERROGATIVE		
PRESENT	phu-ne/-nûnka	phu-te/-tónka
PAST	phóss-ne	phóss-te
REMOTE PAST	phóssóss-ne	phóssóss-te
FUTURE	phukess-ne	phukess-te
PAST FUTURE	phósskess-ne	phósskess-te
PROPOSITIVE	phu-se	
IMPERATIVE	phu-ke	

	INFORMAL *Intimate* INDICATIVE	INFORMAL *Casual* INDICATIVE
DECLARATIVE/ INTERROGATIVE		
PRESENT	phó	phu-ci
PAST	phóss-ó	phóss-ci
REMOTE PAST	phóssóss-ó	phóssóss-ci
FUTURE	phukess-ó	phukess-ci
PAST FUTURE	phósskess-ó	phósskess-ci
PROPOSITIVE IMPERATIVE	phó	phu-ci

CAUSATIVE: *PASSIVE:*

	FORMAL *Plain*	
	INDICATIVE	RETROSPECTIVE
DECLARATIVE/ *INTERROGATIVE*		
PRESENT	phu-n.ta/-núnya	phul-tóla/-tónya
PAST	phulóss-ta	phulóss-tóla
REMOTE PAST	phulóssóss-ta	phulóssóss-tóla
FUTURE	phulkess-ta	phulkess-tóla
PAST FUTURE	phulósskess-ta	phulósskess-tóla
PROPOSITIVE	phul-ca	
IMPERATIVE	phul-óla	

	FORMAL *Polite*	
	INDICATIVE	RETROSPECTIVE
DECLARATIVE/ *INTERROGATIVE*		
PRESENT	phupni-ta/-kka	phupti-ta/-kka
PAST	phulóssúpni-ta	phulóssúpti-ta
REMOTE PAST	phulóssóssúpni-ta	phulóssóssúpti-ta
FUTURE	phulkessúpni-ta	phulkessúpti-ta
PAST FUTURE	phulósskessúpni-ta	phulósskessúpti-ta
PROPOSITIVE	phupsi-ta	
IMPERATIVE	phu(si)psi-o	

	INFORMAL *Familiar*	
	INDICATIVE	RETROSPECTIVE
DECLARATIVE/ *INTERROGATIVE*		
PRESENT	phu-ne/-núnka	phul-te/-tónka
PAST	phulóss-ne	phulóss-te
REMOTE PAST	phulóssóss-ne	phulóssóss-te
FUTURE	phulkess-ne	phulkess-te
PAST FUTURE	phulósskess-ne	phulósskess-te
PROPOSITIVE	phu-se	
IMPERATIVE	phul-ke	

	INFORMAL *Intimate* INDICATIVE	INFORMAL *Casual* INDICATIVE
DECLARATIVE/ *INTERROGATIVE*		
PRESENT	phul-ó	phul-ci
PAST	phulóss-ó	phulóss-ci
REMOTE PAST	phulóssóss-ó	phulóssóss-ci
FUTURE	phulkess-ó	phulkess-ci
PAST FUTURE	phulósskess-ó	phulósskess-ci
PROPOSITIVE *IMPERATIVE*	phul-ó	phul-ci

CAUSATIVE:

PASSIVE: PHULLI.TA
to get untied,
to be disentangled

PHULÙ.TA
to be blue, to be green   DESCRIPTIVE   푸르다

FORMAL *Plain*

	INDICATIVE	RETROSPECTIVE
DECLARATIVE/ *INTERROGATIVE*		
PRESENT	phulù-ta/-nya	phulù-tóla/-tónya
PAST	phulùlóss-ta/-nùnya	phulùlóss-tóla
REMOTE PAST	phulùlóssòss-ta	phulùlóssòss-tóla
FUTURE	phulùkess-ta	phulùkess-tóla
PAST FUTURE	phulùlósskess-ta	phulùlósskess-tóla

PROPOSITIVE
IMPERATIVE

FORMAL *Polite*

	INDICATIVE	RETROSPECTIVE
DECLARATIVE/ *INTERROGATIVE*		
PRESENT	phulùpni-ta/-kka	phulùpti-ta/-kka
PAST	phulùlóssùpni-ta	phulùlóssùpti-ta
REMOTE PAST	phulùlóssòssùpni-ta	phulùlóssòssùpti-ta
FUTURE	phulùkessùpni-ta	phulùkessùpti-ta
PAST FUTURE	phulùlósskessùpni-ta	phulùlósskessùpti-ta

PROPOSITIVE
IMPERATIVE

INFORMAL *Familiar*

	INDICATIVE	RETROSPECTIVE
DECLARATIVE/ *INTERROGATIVE*		
PRESENT	phulù-ne/-nka	phulù-te/-tónka
PAST	phulùlóss-ne/-nùnka	phulùlóss-te
REMOTE PAST	phulùlóssòss-ne	phulùlóssòss-te
FUTURE	phulùkess-ne	phulùkess-te
PAST FUTURE	phulùlósskess-ne	phulùlósskess-te

PROPOSITIVE
IMPERATIVE

	INFORMAL *Intimate* INDICATIVE	INFORMAL *Casual* INDICATIVE
DECLARATIVE/ *INTERROGATIVE*		
PRESENT	phulùl-ó	phulù-ci
PAST	phulùlóss-ó	phulùlóss-ci
REMOTE PAST	phulùlóssòss-ó	phulùlóssòss-ci
FUTURE	phulùkess-ó	phulùkess-ci
PAST FUTURE	phulùlósskess-ó	phulùlósskess-ci

PROPOSITIVE
IMPERATIVE

CAUSATIVE: *PASSIVE:*

FORMAL *Plain*

	INDICATIVE	RETROSPECTIVE
DECLARATIVE/ *INTERROGATIVE*		
PRESENT	phum-núnta/-núnya	phum-tóla/-tónya
PAST	phumóss-ta	phumóss-tóla
REMOTE PAST	phumóssóss-ta	phumóssóss-tóla
FUTURE	phumkess-ta	phumkess-tóla
PAST FUTURE	phumósskess-ta	phumósskess-tóla
PROPOSITIVE	phum-ca	
IMPERATIVE	phum-óla	

FORMAL *Polite*

	INDICATIVE	RETROSPECTIVE
DECLARATIVE/ *INTERROGATIVE*		
PRESENT	phumsúpni-ta/-kka	phumsúpti-ta/-kka
PAST	phumóssúpni-ta	phumóssúpti-ta
REMOTE PAST	phumóssóssúpni-ta	phumóssóssúpti-ta
FUTURE	phumkessúpni-ta	phumkessúpti-ta
PAST FUTURE	phumósskessúpni-ta	phumósskessúpti-ta
PROPOSITIVE	phumúpsi-ta	
IMPERATIVE	phumú(si)psi-o	

INFORMAL *Familiar*

	INDICATIVE	RETROSPECTIVE
DECLARATIVE/ *INTERROGATIVE*		
PRESENT	phum-ne/-núnka	phum-te/-tónka
PAST	phumóss-ne	phumóss-te
REMOTE PAST	phumóssóss-ne	phumóssóss-te
FUTURE	phumkess-ne	phumkess-te
PAST FUTURE	phumósskess-ne	phumósskess-te
PROPOSITIVE	phum-se	
IMPERATIVE	phum-ke	

	INFORMAL *Intimate* INDICATIVE	INFORMAL *Casual* INDICATIVE
DECLARATIVE/ *INTERROGATIVE*		
PRESENT	phum-ó	phum-ci
PAST	phumóss-ó	phumóss-ci
REMOTE PAST	phumóssóss-ó	phumóssóss-ci
FUTURE	phumkess-ó	phumkess-ci
PAST FUTURE	phumósskess-ó	phumósskess-ci
PROPOSITIVE *IMPERATIVE*	phum-ó	phum-ci

CAUSATIVE: *PASSIVE:*

FORMAL *Plain*

	INDICATIVE	RETROSPECTIVE
DECLARATIVE/ *INTERROGATIVE*		
PRESENT	phungki-n.ta/-nŭnya	phungki-tŏla/-tŏnya
PAST	phungkyŏss-ta	phungkyŏss-tŏla
REMOTE PAST	phungkyŏssŏss-ta	phungkyŏssŏss-tŏla
FUTURE	phungkikess-ta	phungkikess-tŏla
PAST FUTURE	phungkyŏsskess-ta	phungkyŏsskess-tŏla
PROPOSITIVE	phungki-ca	
IMPERATIVE	phungky-ŏ.la	

FORMAL *Polite*

	INDICATIVE	RETROSPECTIVE
DECLARATIVE/ *INTERROGATIVE*		
PRESENT	phungkipni-ta/-kka	phungkipti-ta/-kka
PAST	phungkyŏssŭpni-ta	phungkyŏssŭpti-ta
REMOTE PAST	phungkyŏssŏssŭpni-ta	phungkyŏssŏssŭpti-ta
FUTURE	phungkikessŭpni-ta	phungkikessŭpti-ta
PAST FUTURE	phungkyŏsskessŭpni-ta	phungkyŏsskessŭpti-ta
PROPOSITIVE	phungkipsi-ta	
IMPERATIVE	phungki(si)psi-o	

INFORMAL *Familiar*

	INDICATIVE	RETROSPECTIVE
DECLARATIVE/ *INTERROGATIVE*		
PRESENT	phungki-ne/-nŭnka	phungki-te/-tŏnka
PAST	phungkyŏss-ne	phungkyŏss-te
REMOTE PAST	phungkyŏssŏss-ne	phungkyŏssŏss-te
FUTURE	phungkikess-ne	phungkikess-te
PAST FUTURE	phungkyŏsskess-ne	phungkyŏsskess-te
PROPOSITIVE	phungki-se	
IMPERATIVE	phungki-ke	

	INFORMAL *Intimate* INDICATIVE	INFORMAL *Casual* INDICATIVE
DECLARATIVE/ *INTERROGATIVE*		
PRESENT	phungk.y-ŏ	phungki-ci
PAST	phungkyŏss-ŏ	phungkyŏss-ci
REMOTE PAST	phungkyŏssŏss-ŏ	phungkyŏssŏss-ci
FUTURE	phungkikess-ŏ	phungkikess-ci
PAST FUTURE	phungkyŏsskess-ŏ	phungkyŏsskess-ci
PROPOSITIVE *IMPERATIVE*	phungk.y-ŏ	phungki-ci

CAUSATIVE: *PASSIVE:*

FORMAL *Plain*

	INDICATIVE	RETROSPECTIVE
DECLARATIVE/		
INTERROGATIVE		
PRESENT	ppah-nún.ta/-núnya	ppah-tóla/-tónya
PAST	ppahass-ta	ppahass-tóla
REMOTE PAST	ppahassóss-ta	ppahassóss-tóla
FUTURE	ppahkess-ta	ppahkess-tóla
PAST FUTURE	ppahasskess-ta	ppahasskess-tóla
PROPOSITIVE	ppah-ca	
IMPERATIVE	ppah-ala	

FORMAL *Polite*

	INDICATIVE	RETROSPECTIVE
DECLARATIVE/		
INTERROGATIVE		
PRESENT	ppahsúpni-ta/-kka	ppahsúpti-ta/-kka
PAST	ppahassúpni-ta	ppahassúpti-ta
REMOTE PAST	ppahassóssúpni-ta	ppahassóssúpti-ta
FUTURE	ppahkessúpni-ta	ppahkessúpti-ta
PAST FUTURE	ppahasskessúpni-ta	ppahasskessúpti-ta
PROPOSITIVE	ppahúpsi-ta	
IMPERATIVE	ppahú(si)psi-o	

INFÓRMAL *Familiar*

	INDICATIVE	RETROSPECTIVE
DECLARATIVE/		
INTERROGATIVE		
PRESENT	ppah-ne/-núnka	ppah-te/-tónya
PAST	ppahass-ne	ppahass-te
REMOTE PAST	ppahassóss-ne	ppahassóss-te
FUTURE	ppahkess-ne	ppahkess-te
PAST FUTURE	ppahasskess-ne	ppahasskess-te
PROPOSITIVE	ppah-se	
IMPERATIVE	ppah-ke	

	INFORMAL *Intimate*	INFORMAL *Casual*
	INDICATIVE	INDICATIVE
DECLARATIVE/		
INTERROGATIVE		
PRESENT	ppah-a	ppah-ci
PAST	ppahass-ó	ppahass-ci
REMOTE PAST	ppahassóss-ó	ppahassóss-ci
FUTURE	ppahkess-ó	ppahkess-ci
PAST FUTURE	ppahasskess-ó	ppahasskess-ci
PROPOSITIVE	ppah-a	ppah-ci
IMPERATIVE		

CAUSATIVE: *PASSIVE:*

FORMAL *Plain*

	INDICATIVE	RETROSPECTIVE
DECLARATIVE/ *INTERROGATIVE*		
PRESENT	ppalú-ta/-nya	ppalú-tóla/-tónya
PAST	ppallass-ta/-núnya	ppallass-tóla
REMOTE PAST	ppallassóss-ta	ppallassóss-tóla
FUTURE	ppalúkess-ta	ppalúkess-tóla
PAST FUTURE	ppallasskess-ta	ppallasskess-tóla

PROPOSITIVE
IMPERATIVE

FORMAL *Polite*

	INDICATIVE	RETROSPECTIVE
DECLARATIVE/ *INTERROGATIVE*		
PRESENT	ppalúpni-ta/-kka	ppalúpti-ta/-kka
PAST	ppallassúpni-ta	ppallassúpti-ta
REMOTE PAST	ppallassóssúpni-ta	ppallassóssúpti-ta
FUTURE	ppalúkessúpni-ta	ppalúkessúpti-ta
PAST FUTURE	ppallasskessúpni-ta	ppallasskessúpti-ta

PROPOSITIVE
IMPERATIVE

INFORMAL *Familiar*

	INDICATIVE	RETROSPECTIVE
DECLARATIVE/ *INTERROGATIVE*		
PRESENT	ppalú-ne/-nka	ppalú-te/-tónka
PAST	ppallass-ne/-núnka	ppallass-te
REMOTE PAST	ppallassóss-ne	ppallassóss-te
FUTURE	ppalúkess-ne	ppalúkess-te
PAST FUTURE	ppallasskess-ne	ppallasskess-te

PROPOSITIVE
IMPERATIVE

	INFORMAL *Intimate* INDICATIVE	INFORMAL *Casual* INDICATIVE
DECLARATIVE/ *INTERROGATIVE*		
PRESENT	ppall-a	ppalú-ci
PAST	ppallass-ó	ppallass-ci
REMOTE PAST	ppallassóss-ó	ppallassóss-ci
FUTURE	ppalúkess-ó	ppalúkess-ci
PAST FUTURE	ppallasskess-ó	ppallasskess-ci

PROPOSITIVE
IMPERATIVE

CAUSATIVE: *PASSIVE:*

SA.TA
to buy

FORMAL *Plain*

	INDICATIVE	RETROSPECTIVE
DECLARATIVE/		
INTERROGATIVE		
PRESENT	sa-n.ta/-núnya	sa-tóla/-tónya
PAST	sass-ta	sass-tóla
REMOTE PAST	sassóss-ta	sassóss-tóla
FUTURE	sakess-ta	sakess-tóla
PAST FUTURE	sasskess-ta	sasskess-tóla
PROPOSITIVE	sa-ca	
IMPERATIVE	sa-la	

FORMAL *Polite*

	INDICATIVE	RETROSPECTIVE
DECLARATIVE/		
INTERROGATIVE		
PRESENT	sapni-ta/-kka	sapti-ta/-kka
PAST	sassúpni-ta	sassúpti-ta
REMOTE PAST	sassóssúpni-ta	sassóssúpti-ta
FUTURE	sakessúpni-ta	sakessúpti-ta
PAST FUTURE	sasskessúpni-ta	sasskessúpti-ta
PROPOSITIVE	sapsi-ta	
IMPERATIVE	sa(si)psi-o	

INFORMAL *Familiar*

	INDICATIVE	RETROSPECTIVE
DECLARATIVE/		
INTERROGATIVE		
PRESENT	sa-ne/-núnka	sa-te/-tónka
PAST	sass-ne	sass-te
REMOTE PAST	sassóss-ne	sassóss-te
FUTURE	sakess-ne	sakess-te
PAST FUTURE	sasskess-ne	sasskess-te
PROPOSITIVE		
IMPERATIVE		

	INFORMAL *Intimate* INDICATIVE	INFORMAL *Casual* INDICATIVE
DECLARATIVE/		
INTERROGATIVE		
PRESENT	sa	sa-ci
PAST	sass-ó	sass-ci
REMOTE PAST	sassóss-ó	sassóss-ci
FUTURE	sakess-ó	sakess-ci
PAST FUTURE	sasskess-ó	sasskess-ci
PROPOSITIVE	sa	sa-ci
IMPERATIVE		

CAUSATIVE: *PASSIVE:*

153

FORMAL *Plain*

	INDICATIVE	RETROSPECTIVE
DECLARATIVE/ *INTERROGATIVE*		
PRESENT	saelo-p.ta/-unya	saelop-tóla/-tónya
PAST	saelowass-ta/-núnya	saelowass-tóla
REMOTE PAST	saelowassóss-ta	saelowasskess-tóla
FUTURE	saelopkess-ta	saelopkess-tóla
PAST FUTURE	saelowasskess-ta	saelowasskess-tóla
PROPOSITIVE		
IMPERATIVE		

FORMAL *Polite*

	INDICATIVE	RETROSPECTIVE
DECLARATIVE/ *INTERROGATIVE*		
PRESENT	saelopsúpni-ta/-kka	saelopsúpti-ta/-kka
PAST	saelowassúpni-ta	saelowassúpti-ta
REMOTE PAST	saelowassóssúpni-ta	saelowassóssúpti-ta
FUTURE	saelopkessúpni-ta	saelopkessúpti-ta
PAST FUTURE	saelowasskessúpni-ta	saelowasskessúpti-ta
PROPOSITIVE		
IMPERATIVE		

INFORMAL *Familiar*

	INDICATIVE	RETROSPECTIVE
DECLARATIVE/ *INTERROGATIVE*		
PRESENT	saelo-p.ne/-unka	saelop-te/-tónka
PAST	saelowass-ne/-núnka	saelowass-te
REMOTE PAST	salowassóss-ne	saelowassóss-te
FUTURE	saelopkess-ne	saelopkess-te
PAST FUTURE	saelowasskess-ne	saelowasskess-te
PROPOSITIVE		
IMPERATIVE		

	INFORMAL *Intimate* INDICATIVE	INFORMAL *Casual* INDICATIVE
DECLARATIVE/ *INTERROGATIVE*		
PRESENT	saelo.w-a	saelop-ci
PAST	saelowass-ó	saelowass-ci
REMOTE PAST	saelwassóss-ó	saelowassóss-ci
FUTURE	saelopkess-ó	saelopkess-ci
PAST FUTURE	saelowasskess-ó	saelowasskess-ci
PROPOSITIVE		
IMPERATIVE		

CAUSATIVE: *PASSIVE:*

SAL.TA   살다
to live, to be alive, to dwell

FORMAL Plain

	INDICATIVE	RETROSPECTIVE
DECLARATIVE/ INTERROGATIVE		
PRESENT	sa-n.ta/-nʉnya	sal-tóla/-tònya
PAST	salass-ta	salass-tóla
REMOTE PAST	salassóss-ta	salassóss-tóla
FUTURE	salkess-ta	salkess-tóla
PAST FUTURE	salassóss-ta	salasskess-tóla
PROPOSITIVE	sal-ca	
IMPERATIVE	sal-ala	

FORMAL Polite

	INDICATIVE	RETROSPECTIVE
DECLARATIVE/ INTERROGATIVE		
PRESENT	sapni-ta/-kka	sapti-ta/-kka
PAST	salassʉpni-ta	salassʉpti-ta
REMOTE PAST	salassóssʉpni-ta	salassóssʉpti-ta
FUTURE	salkessʉpni-ta	salkessʉpti-ta
PAST FUTURE	salasskessʉpni-ta	salasskessʉpti-ta
PROPOSITIVE	sapsi-ta	
IMPERATIVE	sa(si)psi-o	

INFORMAL Familiar

	INDICATIVE	RETROSPECTIVE
DECLARATIVE/ INTERROGATIVE		
PRESENT	sa-ne/-nʉnka	sal-te/-tònka
PAST	salass-ne	salass-te
REMOTE PAST	salassóss-ne	salassóss-te
FUTURE	salkess-ne	salkess-te
PAST FUTURE	salasskess-ne	salasskess-te
PROPOSITIVE	sa-se	
IMPERATIVE	sal-ke	

	INFORMAL <i>Intimate</i> INDICATIVE	INFORMAL <i>Casual</i> INDICATIVE
DECLARATIVE/ INTERROGATIVE		
PRESENT	sal-a	sal-ci
PAST	salass-ó	salass-ci
REMOTE PAST	salassóss-ó	salassóss-ci
FUTURE	salkess-ó	salkess-ci
PAST FUTURE	salasskess-ó	salasskess-ci
PROPOSITIVE *IMPERATIVE*	sal-a	sal-ci

CAUSATIVE: SALLI.TA   *PASSIVE:*
          to save. to rescue

FORMAL *Plain*

	INDICATIVE	RETROSPECTIVE
DECLARATIVE/ *INTERROGATIVE*		
PRESENT	salm-núnta/-núnya	salm-tóla/-tónya
PAST	salmass-ta	salmass-tóla
REMOTE PAST	salmassóss-ta	salmassóss-tóla
FUTURE	salmkess-ta	salmkess-tóla
PAST FUTURE	salmasskess-ta	salmasskess-tóla
PROPOSITIVE	salm-ca	
IMPERATIVE	salm-ala	

FORMAL *Polite*

	INDICATIVE	RETROSPECTIVE
DECLARATIVE/ *INTERROGATIVE*		
PRESENT	salmsúpni-ta/-kka	salmsúpti-ta/-kka
PAST	salmassúpni-ta	salmassúpti-ta
REMOTE PAST	salmassóssúpni-ta	salmassóssúpti-ta
FUTURE	salmkessúpni-ta	salmkessúpti-ta
PAST FUTURE	salmasskessúpni-ta	salmasskessúpti-ta
PROPOSITIVE	salmúpsi-ta	
IMPERATIVE	salmú(si)psi-ó	

INFORMAL *Familiar*

	INDICATIVE	RETROSPECTIVE
DECLARATIVE/ *INTERROGATIVE*		
PRESENT	salm-ne/-núnka	salm-te/-tónka
PAST	salmass-ne	salmass-te
REMOTE PAST	salmassóss-ne	salmassóss-te
FUTURE	salmkess-ne	salmkess-te
PAST FUTURE	salmasskess-ne	salmasskess-te
PROPOSITIVE	salm-se	
IMPERATIVE	salm-ke	

	INFORMAL *Intimate* INDICATIVE	INFORMAL *Casual* INDICATIVE
DECLARATIVE/ *INTERROGATIVE*		
PRESENT	salm-a	salm-ci
PAST	salmass-ó	salmass-ci
REMOTE PAST	salmassóss-ó	salmassóss-ci
FUTURE	salmkess-ó	salmkess-ci
PAST FUTURE	salmasskess-ó	salmasskess-ci
PROPOSITIVE *IMPERATIVE*	salm-a	salm-ci

CAUSATIVE: *PASSIVE:*

FORMAL *Plain*

	INDICATIVE	RETROSPECTIVE
DECLARATIVE/ *INTERROGATIVE*		
PRESENT	silh-ta/-únya	silh-tóla/-tònya
PAST	silhóss-ta/-núnya	silhóss-tóla
REMOTE PAST	silhóssóss-ta	silhóssóss-tóla
FUTURE	silhkess-ta	silhkess-tóla
PAST FUTURE	silhósskess-ta	silhósskess-tóla
PROPOSITIVE		
IMPERATIVE		

FORMAL *Polite*

	INDICATIVE	RETROSPECTIVE
DECLARATIVE/ *INTERROGATIVE*		
PRESENT	silhsúpni-ta/-kka	silhsúpti-ta/-kka
PAST	silhóssúpni-ta	silhóssúpti-ta
REMOTE PAST	silhóssóssúpni-ta	silkóssóssúpti-ta
FUTURE	silhkessúpni-ta	silhkessúpti-ta
PAST FUTURE	silhósskessúpni-ta	silhósskessúpti-ta
PROPOSITIVE		
IMPERATIVE		

INFORMAL *Familiar*

	INDICATIVE	RETROSPECTIVE
DECLARATIVE/ *INTERROGATIVE*		
PRESENT	silh-ne/-únka	silh-te/-tònka
PAST	silhóss-ne/-núnka	silhóss-te
REMOTE PAST	silhóssóss-ne	silhóssóss-te
FUTURE	silhkess-ne	silhkess-te
PAST FUTURE	silhósskess-ne	silhósskess-te
PROPOSITIVE		
IMPERATIVE		

	INFORMAL *Intimate* INDICATIVE	INFORMAL *Casual* INDICATIVE
DECLARATIVE/ *INTERROGATIVE*		
PRESENT	silh-ó	silh-ci
PAST	silhóss-ó	silhóss-ci
REMOTE PAST	silhóssóss-ó	silhóssóss-ci
FUTURE	silhkess-ó	silhkess-ci
PAST FUTURE	silhósskess-ó	silhósskess-ci
PROPOSITIVE		
IMPERATIVE		

CAUSATIVE: *PASSIVE:*

FORMAL *Plain*

	INDICATIVE	RETROSPECTIVE
DECLARATIVE/ *INTERROGATIVE*		
PRESENT	sin-nŭnta/-nŭnya	sin-tóla/-tónya
PAST	sinóss-ta	sinóss-tóla
REMOTE PAST	sinóssóss-ta	sinóssóss-tóla
FUTURE	sinkess-ta	sinkess-tóla
PAST FUTURE	sinósskess-ta	sinósskess-tóla
PROPOSITIVE	sin-ca	
IMPERATIVE	sin-óla	

FORMAL *Polite*

	INDICATIVE	RETROSPECTIVE
DECLARATIVE/ *INTERROGATIVE*		
PRESENT	sinsŭpni-ta/-kka	sinsŭpti-ta/-kka
PAST	sinóssŭpni-ta	sinóssŭpti-ta
REMOTE PAST	sinóssóssŭpni-ta	sinóssóssŭpti-ta
FUTURE	sinkessŭpni-ta	sinkessŭpti-ta
PAST FUTURE	sinósskessŭpni-ta	sinósskessŭpti-ta
PROPOSITIVE	sinŭpsi-ta	
IMPERATIVE	sinŭ(si)psi-o	

INFORMAL *Familiar*

	INDICATIVE	RETROSPECTIVE
DECLARATIVE/ *INTERROGATIVE*		
PRESENT	sin-ne/-nŭnka	sin-te/-tónka
PAST	sinóss-ne	sinóss-te
REMOTE PAST	sinóssóss-ne	sinóssóss-te
FUTURE	sinkess-ne	sinkess-te
PAST FUTURE	sinósskess-ne	sinósskess-te
PROPOSITIVE	sin-se	
IMPERATIVE	sin-ke	

	INFORMAL *Intimate* INDICATIVE	INFORMAL *Casual* INDICATIVE
DECLARATIVE/ *INTERROGATIVE*		
PRESENT	sin-ó	sin-ci
PAST	sinóss-ó	sinóss-ci
REMOTE PAST	sinóssóss-ó	sinóssóss-ci
FUTURE	sinkess-ó	sinkess-ci
PAST FUTURE	sinósskess-ó	sinósskess-ci
PROPOSITIVE *IMPERATIVE*	sin-ó	sin-ci

CAUSATIVE: SINKI.TA *PASSIVE:*
to put (footwear) on (a person)

SIT.TA   실다
1) to load, to carry   2) to record, to carry (something written)

	FORMAL *Plain*	
	INDICATIVE	RETROSPECTIVE
DECLARATIVE/ *INTERROGATIVE*		
PRESENT	sit-nún.ta/-núnya	sit-tóla/-tónya
PAST	silóss-ta	silóss-tóla
REMOTE PAST	silóssóss-ta	silóssóss-tóla
FUTURE	sitkess-ta	sitkess-tóla
PAST FUTURE	silósskess-ta	silósskess-tóla
PROPOSITIVE	sit-ca	
IMPERATIVE	sil-óla	

	FORMAL *Polite*	
	INDICATIVE	RETROSPECTIVE
DECLARATIVE/ *INTERROGATIVE*		
PRESENT	sitsúpni-ta/-kka	sitsúpti-ta/-kka
PAST	silóssúpni-ta	silóssúpti-ta
REMOTE PAST	silóssóssúpni-ta	silóssóssúpti-ta
FUTURE	sitkessúpni-ta	sitkessúpti-ta
PAST FUTURE	silósskessúpni-ta	silósskessúpti-ta
PROPOSITIVE	silúpsi-ta	
IMPERATIVE	silú(si)psi-o	

	INFORMAL *Familiar*	
	INDICATIVE	RETROSPECTIVE
DECLARATIVE/ *INTERROGATIVE*		
PRESENT	sit-ne/-núnka	sit-te/-tónka
PAST	silóss-ne	silóss-te
REMOTE PAST	silóssóss-ne	silóssóss-te
FUTURE	sitkess-ne	sitkess-te
PAST FUTURE	silósskess-ne	silósskess-te
PROPOSITIVE	sit-se	
IMPERATIVE	sit-ke	

	INFORMAL *Intimate* INDICATIVE	INFORMAL *Casual* INDICATIVE
DECLARATIVE/ *INTERROGATIVE*		
PRESENT	sil-ó	sit-ci
PAST	silóss-ó	silóss-ci
REMOTE PAST	silóssóss-ó	silóssóss-ci
FUTURE	sitkess-ó	sitkess-ci
PAST FUTURE	silósskess-ó	silósskess-ci
PROPOSITIVE *IMPERATIVE*	sil-ó	sit-ci

CAUSATIVE: *PASSIVE:*

159

to be refreshing, to be cool   DESCRIPTIVE   시원하다

FORMAL *Plain*

	INDICATIVE	RETROSPECTIVE
DECLARATIVE/ *INTERROGATIVE*		
PRESENT	siwònha-ta/-nya	siwònha-tòla/-tònya
PAST	siwònhaess-ta/-nùnya	siwònhaess-tòla
REMOTE PAST	siwònhaessòss-ta	siwònhaessòss-tòla
FUTURE	siwònhakess-ta	siwònhakess-tòla
PAST FUTURE	siwònhaesskess-ta	siwònhaesskess-tòla

PROPOSITIVE
IMPERATIVE

FORMAL *Polite*

	INDICATIVE	RETROSPECTIVE
DECLARATIVE/ *INTERROGATIVE*		
PRESENT	siwònhapni-ta/-kka	siwònhapti-ta/-kka
PAST	siwònhaessùpni-ta	siwònhaessùpti-ta
REMOTE PAST	siwònhaessòssùpni-ta	siwònhaessòssùpti-ta
FUTURE	siwònhakessùpni-ta	siwònhakessùpti-ta
PAST FUTURE	siwònhaesskessùpni-ta	siwònhaesskessùpti-ta

PROPOSITIVE
IMPERATIVE

INFORMAL *Familiar*

	INDICATIVE	RETROSPECTIVE
DECLARATIVE/ *INTERROGATIVE*		
PRESENT	siwònha-ne/-nka	siwònha-te/-tònka
PAST	siwònhaess-ne/-nùnka	siwònhaess-te
REMOTE PAST	siwònhaessòss-ne	siwònhaessòss-te
FUTURE	siwònhakess-ne	siwònhakess-te
PAST FUTURE	siwonhaesskess-ne	siwonhaesskess-te

PROPOSITIVE
IMPERATIVE

	INFORMAL *Intimate* INDICATIVE	INFORMAL *Casual* INDICATIVE
DECLARATIVE/ *INTERROGATIVE*		
PRESENT	siwònhae	siwònha-ci
PAST	siwònhaess-ò	siwònhaess-ci
REMOTE PAST	siwònhaessòss-ò	siwònhaessòss-ci
FUTURE	siwònhakess-ò	siwònhakess-ci
PAST FUTURE	siwònhaesskess-ò	siwònhaesskess-ci

PROPOSITIVE
IMPERATIVE

CAUSATIVE: *PASSIVE:*

FORMAL *Plain*

	INDICATIVE	RETROSPECTIVE
DECLARATIVE/ INTERROGATIVE		
PRESENT	sok-nûn.ta/-nûnya	sok-tóla/-tónya
PAST	sokass-ta	sokass-tóla
REMOTE PAST	sokassóss-ta	sokassóss-tóla
FUTURE	sokkess-ta	sokkess-tóla
PAST FUTURE	sokasskess-ta	sokasskess-tóla
PROPOSITIVE	sok-ca	
IMPERATIVE	sok-ala	

FORMAL *Polite*

	INDICATIVE	RETROSPECTIVE
DECLARATIVE/ INTERROGATIVE		
PRESENT	soksûpni-ta/-kka	soksûpti-ta/-kka
PAST	sokassûpni-ta	sokassûpti-ta
REMOTE PAST	sokassóssûpni-ta	sokassóssûpti-ta
FUTURE	sokkessûpni-ta	sokkessûpti-ta
PAST FUTURE	sokasskessûpni-ta	sokasskessûpti-ta
PROPOSITIVE	sokûpsi-ta	
IMPERATIVE	sokû(si)psi-o	

INFORMAL *Familiar*

	INDICATIVE	RETROSPECTIVE
DECLARATIVE/ INTERROGATIVE		
PRESENT	sok-ne/-nûnka	sok-te/-tónka
PAST	sokass-ne	sokass-te
REMOTE PAST	sokassóss-ne	sokassóss-te
FUTURE	sokkess-ne	sokkess-te
PAST FUTURE	sokasskess-ne	sokasskess-te
PROPOSITIVE	sok-se	
IMPERATIVE	sok-ke	

	INFORMAL *Intimate* INDICATIVE	INFORMAL *Casual* INDICATIVE
DECLARATIVE/ INTERROGATIVE		
PRESENT	sok-a	sok-ci
PAST	sokass-ó	sokass-ci
REMOTE PAST	sokassóss-ó	sokassóss-ci
FUTURE	sokkess-ó	sokkess-ci
PAST FUTURE	sokasskess-ó	sokasskess-ci
PROPOSITIVE *IMPERATIVE*	sok-a	sok-ci

CAUSATIVE: SOKI.TA
to falsify, to lie about

PASSIVE:

FORMAL *Plain*

	INDICATIVE	RETROSPECTIVE
DECLARATIVE/		
INTERROGATIVE		
PRESENT	só-n.ta/-núnya	só-tóla/-tónya
PAST	sóss-ta	sóss-tóla
REMOTE PAST	sóssóss-ta	sóssóss-tóla
FUTURE	sókess-ta	sókess-tóla
PAST FUTURE	sósskess-ta	sósskess-tóla
PROPOSITIVE	só-ca	
IMPERATIVE	só-la	

FORMAL *Polite*

	INDICATIVE	RETROSPECTIVE
DECLARATIVE/		
INTERROGATIVE		
PRESENT	sópni-ta/-kka	sópti-ta/-kka
PAST	sóssúpni-ta	sóssúpti-ta
REMOTE PAST	sóssóssúpni-ta	sóssóssúpti-ta
FUTURE	sókessúpni-ta	sókessúpti-ta
PAST FUTURE	sósskessúpni-ta	sósskessúpti-ta
PROPOSITIVE	sópsi-ta	
IMPERATIVE	só(si)psi-o	

INFORMAL *Familiar*

	INDICATIVE	RETROSPECTIVE
DECLARATIVE/		
INTERROGATIVE		
PRESENT	só-ne/-núnka	só-te/-tónka
PAST	sóss-ne	sóss-te
REMOTE PAST	sóssóss-ne	sóssóss-te
FUTURE	sókess-ne	sókess-te
PAST FUTURE	sósskess-ne	sósskess-te
PROPOSITIVE	só-se	
IMPERATIVE	só-ke	

	INFORMAL *Intimate*	INFORMAL *Casual*
	INDICATIVE	INDICATIVE
DECLARATIVE/		
INTERROGATIVE		
PRESENT	só	só-ci
PAST	sóss-ó	sóss-ci
REMOTE PAST	sóssóss-ó	sóssóss-ci
FUTURE	sókess-ó	sókess-ci
PAST FUTURE	sósskess-ó	sósskess-ci
PROPOSITIVE	só	só-ci
IMPERATIVE		

CAUSATIVE: SEU.TA   *PASSIVE:*
            to make stand, to erect

FORMAL *Plain*

	INDICATIVE	RETROSPECTIVE
DECLARATIVE/ *INTERROGATIVE*		
PRESENT	swi-p.tá/-unya	swip-tóla/-tónya
PAST	swiwóss-ta/-núnya	swiwóss-tóla
REMOTE PAST	swiwóssóss-ta	swiwóssóss-tóla
FUTURE	swipkess-ta	swipkess-tóla
PAST FUTURE	swiwósskess-ta	swiwósskess-tóla

PROPOSITIVE
IMPERATIVE

FORMAL *Polite*

	INDICATIVE	RETROSPECTIVE
DECLARATIVE/ *INTERROGATIVE*		
PRESENT	swipsúpni-ta/-kka	swipsúpti-ta/-kka
PAST	swiwóssúpni-ta	swiwóssúpti-ta
REMOTE PAST	swiwóssóssúpni-ta	swisóssóssúpti-ta
FUTURE	swipkessúpni-ta	swipkessúpti-ta
PAST FUTURE	swiwósskessúpni-ta	swiwósskessúpti-ta

PROPOSITIVE
IMPERATIVE

INFORMAL *Familiar*

	INDICATIVE	RETROSPECTIVE
DECLARATIVE/ *INTERROGATIVE*		
PRESENT	swi-p.ne/-unka	swip-te/-tónka
PAST	swiwóss-ne/-núnka	swiwóss-te
REMOTE PAST	swiwóssóss-ne	swiwóssóss-te
FUTURE	swipkess-ne	swipkess-te
PAST FUTURE	swiwósskess-ne	swiwósskess-te

PROPOSITIVE
IMPERATIVE

	INFORMAL *Intimate* INDICATIVE	INFORMAL *Casual* INDICATIVE
DECLARATIVE/ *INTERROGATIVE*		
PRESENT	swi.w-ó	swip-ci
PAST	swiwóss-ó	swiwóss-ci
REMOTE PAST	swiwóssóss-ó	swiwóssóss-ci
FUTURE	swipkess-ó	swipkess-ci
PAST FUTURE	swiwósskess-ó	swiwósskess-ci

PROPOSITIVE
IMPERATIVE

CAUSATIVE: *PASSIVE:*

to be cheap, to be inexpensive   DESCRIPTIVE

FORMAL *Plain*

	INDICATIVE	RETROSPECTIVE
DECLARATIVE/ *INTERROGATIVE*		
PRESENT	ssa.ta/-nya	ssa-tóla/-tónya
PAST	ssass-ta/-núnya	ssass-tóla
REMOTE PAST	ssassóss-ta	ssassóss-tóla
FUTURE	ssakess-ta	ssakess-tóla
PAST FUTURE	ssasskess-ta	ssasskess-tóla

PROPOSITIVE
IMPERATIVE

FORMAL *Polite*

	INDICATIVE	RETROSPECTIVE
DECLARATIVE/ *INTERROGATIVE*		
PRESENT	ssapni-ta/-kka	ssapti-ta/-kka
PAST	ssassúpni-ta	ssassúpti-ta
REMOTE PAST	ssassóssúpni-ta	ssassóssúpti-ta
FUTURE	ssakessúpni-ta	ssakessúpti-ta
PAST FUTURE	ssasskessúpni-ta	ssasskessúpti-ta

PROPOSITIVE
IMPERATIVE

INFORMAL *Familiar*

	INDICATIVE	RETROSPECTIVE
DECLARATIVE/ *INTERROGATIVE*		
PRESENT	ssa-ne/-nka	ssa-te/-tónka
PAST	ssass-ne/-núnka	ssass-te
REMOTE PAST	ssassóss-ne	ssassóss-te
FUTURE	ssakess-ne	ssakess-te
PAST FUTURE	ssasskess-ne	ssasskess-te

PROPOSITIVE
IMPERATIVE

	INFORMAL *Intimate* INDICATIVE	INFORMAL *Casual* INDICATIVE
DECLARATIVE/ *INTERROGATIVE*		
PRESENT	ssa	ssa-ci
PAST	ssass-ó	ssass-ci
REMOTE PAST	ssassóss-ó	ssassóss-ci
FUTURE	ssakess-ó	ssakess-ci
PAST FUTURE	ssasskess-ó	ssasskess-ci

PROPOSITIVE
IMPERATIVE

CAUSATIVE: *PASSIVE:*

SSA.TA   싸다
to wrap up, to pack

FORMAL Plain

	INDICATIVE	RETROSPECTIVE
DECLARATIVE/		
INTERROGATIVE		
PRESENT	ssa-n.ta/-núnya	ssa-tóla/-tónya
PAST	ssass-ta	ssass-tóla
REMOTE PAST	ssassóss-ta	ssassóss-tóla
FUTURE	ssakess-ta	ssakess-tóla
PAST FUTURE	ssasskess-ta	ssasskess-tóla
PROPOSITIVE	ssa-ca	
IMPERATIVE	ssa-la	

FORMAL Polite

	INDICATIVE	RETROSPECTIVE
DECLARATIVE/		
INTERROGATIVE		
PRESENT	ssapni-ta/-kka	ssapti-ta/kka
PAST	ssassúpni-ta	ssassúpti-ta
REMOTE PAST	ssassóssúpni-ta	ssassóssúpti-ta
FUTURE	ssakessúpni-ta	ssakessúpti-ta
PAST FUTURE	ssasskessúpni-ta	ssasskessúpti-ta
PROPOSITIVE	ssapsi-ta	
IMPERATIVE	ssa(si)psi-o	

INFORMAL Familiar

	INDICATIVE	RETROSPECTIVE
DECLARATIVE/		
INTERROGATIVE		
PRESENT	ssa-ne/-núnka	ssa-te/-tónka
PAST	ssass-ne	ssass-te
REMOTE PAST	ssassóss-ne	ssassóss-te
FUTURE	ssakess-ne	ssakess-te
PAST FUTURE	ssassókess-ne	ssasskess-te
PROPOSITIVE	ssa-se	
IMPERATIVE	ssa-ke	

	INFORMAL Intimate INDICATIVE	INFORMAL Casual INDICATIVE
DECLARATIVE/		
INTERROGATIVE		
PRESENT	ssa	ssa-ci
PAST	ssass-ó	ssass-ci
REMOTE PAST	ssassóss-ó	ssassóss-ci
FUTURE	ssakess-ó	ssakess-ci
PAST FUTURE	ssasskess-ó	ssasskess-ci
PROPOSITIVE	ssa	ssa-ci
IMPERATIVE		

CAUSATIVE: *PASSIVE:* SSAI.TA
                                                 to get wrapped up

SSAH.TA
to pile up, to build ‎쌓다

FORMAL *Plain*

	INDICATIVE	RETROSPECTIVE
DECLARATIVE/ *INTERROGATIVE*		
PRESENT	ssah-ta/-nùnya	ssah-tóla/-tónya
PAST	ssahass-ta	ssahass-tóla
REMOTE PAST	ssahassóss-ta	ssahassóss-tóla
FUTURE	ssahkess-ta	ssahkess-tóla
PAST FUTURE	ssahasskess-ta	ssahasskess-tóla
PROPOSITIVE	ssah-ca	
IMPERATIVE	ssah-ala	

FORMAL *Polite*

	INDICATIVE	RETROSPECTIVE
DECLARATIVE/ *INTERROGATIVE*		
PRESENT	ssahsùpni-ta/-kka	ssahsùpti-ta/-kka
PAST	ssahassùpni-ta	ssahassùpti-ta
REMOTE PAST	ssahassóssùpni-ta	ssahassóssùpti-ta
FUTURE	ssahkessùpni-ta	ssahkessùpti-ta
PAST FUTURE	ssahasskessùpni-ta	ssahasskessùpti-ta
PROPOSITIVE	ssahùpsi-ta	
IMPERATIVE	ssahù(si)psi-o	

INFORMAL *Familiar*

	INDICATIVE	RETROSPECTIVE
DECLARATIVE/ *INTERROGATIVE*		
PRESENT	ssah-ne/-nùnka	ssah-te/-tónka
PAST	ssahass-ne	ssahass-te
REMOTE PAST	ssahassóss-ne	ssahassóss-te
FUTURE	ssahkess-ne	ssahkess-te
PAST FUTURE	ssahasskess-ne	ssahasskess-te
PROPOSITIVE	ssah-se	
IMPERATIVE	ssah-ke	

	INFORMAL *Intimate* INDICATIVE	INFORMAL *Casual* INDICATIVE
DECLARATIVE/ *INTERROGATIVE*		
PRESENT	ssah-a	ssah-ci
PAST	ssahass-ó	ssahass-ci
REMOTE PAST	ssahassóss-ó	ssahassóss-ci
FUTURE	ssahkess-ó	ssahkess-ci
PAST FUTURE	ssahasskess-ó	ssahasskess-ci
PROPOSITIVE *IMPERATIVE*	ssah-a	ssah-ci

CAUSATIVE: *PASSIVE:* SSAHI.TA
to be piled up

FORMAL *Plain*

	INDICATIVE	RETROSPECTIVE
DECLARATIVE/ *INTERROGATIVE*		
PRESENT	tah-nún.ta/-núnya	tah-tóla/-tónya
PAST	tahass-ta	tahass-tóla
REMOTE PAST	tahassóss-ta	tahassóss-tóla
FUTURE	tahkess-ta	tahkess-tóla
PAST FUTURE	tahasskess-ta	tahasskess-tóla
PROPOSITIVE	tah-ca	
IMPERATIVE	tah-ala	

FORMAL *Polite*

	INDICATIVE	RETROSPECTIVE
DECLARATIVE/ *INTERROGATIVE*		
PRESENT	tahsúpni-ta/-kka	tahsúpti-ta/-kka
PAST	tahassúpni-ta	tahassúpti-ta
REMOTE PAST	tahassóssúpni-ta	tahassóssúpti-ta
FUTURE	tahkessúpni-ta	tahkessúpti-ta
PAST FUTURE	tahasskessúpni-ta	tahasskessúpti-ta
PROPOSITIVE	tahúpsi-ta	
IMPERATIVE	tahú(si)psi-o	

INFORMAL *Familiar*

	INDICATIVE	RETROSPECTIVE
DECLARATIVE/ *INTERROGATIVE*		
PRESENT	tah-ne/-núnka	tah-te/-tónka
PAST	tahass-ne	tahass-te
REMOTE PAST	tahassóss-ne	tahassóss-te
FUTURE	tahkess-ne	tahkess-te
PAST FUTURE	tahasskess-ne	tahasskess-te
PROPOSITIVE	tah-se	
IMPERATIVE	tah-ke	

	INFORMAL *Intimate* INDICATIVE	INFORMAL *Casual* INDICATIVE
DECLARATIVE/ *INTERROGATIVE*		
PRESENT	tah-a	tah-ci
PAST	tahass-ó	tahass-ci
REMOTE PAST	tahassóss-ó	tahassóss-ci
FUTURE	tahkess-ó	tahkess-ci
PAST FUTURE	tahasskess-ó	tahasskess-ci
PROPOSITIVE *IMPERATIVE*	tah-a	tah-ci

CAUSATIVE: *PASSIVE:*

FORMAL *Plain*

DECLARATIVE/ INTERROGATIVE	INDICATIVE	RETROSPECTIVE
PRESENT	takk-nûn.ta/-nûnya	takk-tóla/-tónya
PAST	takkass-ta	takkass-tóla
REMOTE PAST	takkassóss-ta	takkassóss-tóla
FUTURE	takkkess-ta	takkkess-tóla
PAST FUTURE	takkasskess-ta	takkasskess-tóla
PROPOSITIVE	takk-ca	
IMPERATIVE	takk-ala	

FORMAL *Polite*

DECLARATIVE/ INTERROGATIVE	INDICATIVE	RETROSPECTIVE
PRESENT	takksûpni-ta/-kka	takksûpti-ta/-kka
PAST	takkassûpni-ta	takkassûpti-ta
REMOTE PAST	takkassóssûpni-ta	takkassóssûpti-ta
FUTURE	takkkessûpni-ta	takkkessûpti-ta
PAST FUTURE	takkasskessûpni-ta	takkasskessûpti-ta
PROPOSITIVE	takkûpsi-ta	
IMPERATIVE	takkûp(si)psi-o	

INFORMAL *Familiar*

DECLARATIVE/ INTERROGATIVE	INDICATIVE	RETROSPECTIVE
PRESENT	takk-ne/-nûnka	takk-te/-tónka
PAST	takkass-ne	takkass-te
REMOTE PAST	takkassóss-ne	takkassóss-te
FUTURE	takkkess-ne	takkkess-te
PAST FUTURE	takkasskess-ne	takkasskess-te
PROPOSITIVE	takk-se	
IMPERATIVE	takk-ke	

DECLARATIVE/ INTERROGATIVE	INFORMAL *Intimate* INDICATIVE	INFORMAL *Casual* INDICATIVE
PRESENT	takk-a	takk-ci
PAST	takkass-ó	takkass-ci
REMOTE PAST	takkassóss-ó	takkassóss-ci
FUTURE	takkkess-ó	takkkess-ci
PAST FUTURE	takkasskess-ó	takkasskess-ci
PROPOSITIVE IMPERATIVE	takk-a	takk-ci

CAUSATIVE:

PASSIVE: TAKKI-TA
to be polished

TAL.TA
to be sweet   DESCRIPTIVE   달다

FORMAL *Plain*

	INDICATIVE	RETROSPECTIVE
DECLARATIVE/ INTERROGATIVE		
PRESENT	ta-l.ta/-nya	tal-tóla/-tónya
PAST	talass-ta/-núnya	talass-tóla
REMOTE PAST	talassóss-ta	talassóss-tóla
FUTURE	talkess-ta	talkess-tóla
PAST FUTURE	talasskess-ta	talasskess-tóla

PROPOSITIVE
IMPERATIVE

FORMAL *Polite*

	INDICATIVE	RETROSPECTIVE
DECLARATIVE/ INTERROGATIVE		
PRESENT	tapni-ta/-kka	tapti-ta/-kka
PAST	talassúpni-ta	talassúpti-ta
REMOTE PAST	talassóssúpni-ta	talassóssúpti-ta
FUTURE	talkessúpti-ta	talkessúpti-ta
PAST FUTURE	talasskessúpni-ta	talasskessúpti-ta

PROPOSITIVE
IMPERATIVE

INFORMAL *Familiar*

	INDICATIVE	RETROSPECTIVE
DECLARATIVE/ INTERROGATIVE		
PRESENT	ta-ne/-nka	tal-te/-tónka
PAST	talass-ne/-núnka	talass-te
REMOTE PAST	talassóss-ne	talassóss-te
FUTURE	talkess-ne	talkess-te
PAST FUTURE	talasskess-ne	talasskess-te

PROPOSITIVE
IMPERATIVE

	INFORMAL *Intimate* INDICATIVE	INFORMAL *Casual* INDICATIVE
DECLARATIVE/ INTERROGATIVE		
PRESENT	tal-a	tal-ci
PAST	talass-ó	talass-ci
REMOTE PAST	talassóss-ó	talassóss-ci
FUTURE	talkess-ó	talkess-ci
PAST FUTURE	talasskess-ó	talasskess-ci

PROPOSITIVE
IMPERATIVE

    CAUSATIVE: *PASSIVE:*

1) to hang, to attach 2) to weigh

FORMAL *Plain*

DECLARATIVE/ INTERROGATIVE	INDICATIVE	RETROSPECTIVE
PRESENT	ta-n.ta/-núnya	tal-tóla/-tónya
PAST	talass-ta	talass-tóla
REMOTE PAST	talassóss-ta	talassóss-tóla
FUTURE	talkess-ta	talkess-tóla
PAST FUTURE	talasskess-ta	talasskess-tóla
PROPOSITIVE	tal-ca	
IMPERATIVE	tal-ala	

FORMAL *Polite*

DECLARATIVE/ INTERROGATIVE	INDICATIVE	RETROSPECTIVE
PRESENT	tapni-ta/-kka	tapti-ta/-kka
PAST	talassúpni-ta	talassúpti-ta
REMOTE PAST	talassóssúpni-ta	talassóssúpti-ta
FUTURE	talkessúpni-ta	talkessúpti-ta
PAST FUTURE	talasskessúpni-ta	talasskessúpti-ta
PROPOSITIVE	tapsi-ta	
IMPERATIVE	ta(si)psi-o	

INFORMAL *Familiar*

DECLARATIVE/ INTERROGATIVE	INDICATIVE	RETROSPECTIVE
PRESENT	ta-ne/-núnka	tal-te/-tónka
PAST	talass-ne	talass-te
REMOTE PAST	talassóss-ne	talassóss-te
FUTURE	talkess-ne	talkess-te
PAST FUTURE	talasskess-ne	talasskess-te
PROPOSITIVE	ta-se	
IMPERATIVE	tal-ke	

DECLARATIVE/ INTERROGATIVE	INFORMAL *Intimate* INDICATIVE	INFORMAL *Casual* INDICATIVE
PRESENT	tal-a	tal-ci
PAST	talass-ó	talass-ci
REMOTE PAST	talassóss-ó	talassóss-ci
FUTURE	talkess-ó	talkess-ci
PAST FUTURE	talasskess-ó	talasskess-ci
PROPOSITIVE *IMPERATIVE*	tal-a	tal-ci

CAUSATIVE:	*PASSIVE:* TALLI.TA to hang, to weigh INTRANSITIVE

```
TALH.TA
to wear away (down)    INTRANSITIVE                                          닳다
```

FORMAL Plain

	INDICATIVE	RETROSPECTIVE
DECLARATIVE/ *INTERROGATIVE*		
PRESENT	talh-nún.ta/-núnya	talh-tóla/-tónya
PAST	talhass-ta	talhass-tóla
REMOTE PAST	talhassóss-ta	talhassóss-tóla
FUTURE	talhkess-ta	talhkess-tóla
PAST FUTURE	talhasskess-ta	talhasskess-tóla
PROPOSITIVE		
IMPERATIVE		

FORMAL Polite

	INDICATIVE	RETROSPECTIVE
DECLARATIVE/ *INTERROGATIVE*		
PRESENT	talhsúpni-ta/-kka	talhsúpti-ta/-kka
PAST	talhassúpni-ta	talhassúpti-ta
REMOTE PAST	talhassóssúpni-ta	talhassóssúpti-ta
FUTURE	talhkessúpni-ta	talhkessúpti-ta
PAST FUTURE	talhasskessúpni-ta	talhasskessúpti-ta
PROPOSITIVE		
IMPERATIVE		

INFORMAL Familiar

	INDICATIVE	RETROSPECTIVE
DECLARATIVE/ *INTERROGATIVE*		
PRESENT	talh-ne/-núnka	talh-te/-tónka
PAST	talhass-ne	talhass-te
REMOTE PAST	talhassóss-ne	talhassóss-te
FUTURE	talhkess-ne	talhkess-te
PAST FUTURE	talhasskess-ne	talhasskess-te
PROPOSITIVE		
IMPERATIVE		

	INFORMAL *Intimate* INDICATIVE	INFORMAL *Casual* INDICATIVE
DECLARATIVE/ *INTERROGATIVE*		
PRESENT	talh-a	talh-ci
PAST	talhass-ó	talhass-ci
REMOTE PAST	talhassóss-ó	talhassóss-ci
FUTURE	talhkess-ó	talhkess-ci
PAST FUTURE	talhasskess-ó	talhasskess-ci
PROPOSITIVE		
IMPERATIVE		

CAUSATIVE: TALHLI.TA   *PASSIVE:*
          to wear away

TALM-TA
to resemble, to be alike   닮다

	FORMAL *Plain*	
	INDICATIVE	RETROSPECTIVE
DECLARATIVE/ *INTERROGATIVE*		
PRESENT	talm-nún.ta/-núnya	talm-tóla/-tónya
PAST	talmass-ta	talmass-tóla
REMOTE PAST	talmassóss-ta	talmassóss-tóla
FUTURE	talmkess-ta	talmkess-tóla
PAST FUTURE	talmasskess-ta	talmasskess-tóla
PROPOSITIVE	talm-ca	
IMPERATIVE	talm-ala	

	FORMAL *Polite*	
	INDICATIVE	RETROSPECTIVE
DECLARATIVE/ *INTERROGATIVE*		
PRESENT	talmsúpni-ta/-kka	talmsúpti-ta/-kka
PAST	talmassúpni-ta	talmassúpti-ta
REMOTE PAST	talmassóssúpni-ta	talmassóssúpti-ta
FUTURE	talmkessúpni-ta	talmkessúpti-ta
PAST FUTURE	talmasskessúpni-ta	talmasskessúpti-ta
PROPOSITIVE	talmúpsi-ta	
IMPERATIVE	talmú(si)psi-o	

	INFORMAL *Familiar*	
	INDICATIVE	RETROSPECTIVE
DECLARATIVE/ *INTERROGATIVE*		
PRESENT	talm-ne/-núnka	talm-te/-tónka
PAST	talmass-ne	talmass-te
REMOTE PAST	talmassóss-ne	talmassóss-te
FUTURE	talmkess-ne	talmkess-te
PAST FUTURE	talmasskess-ne	talmasskess-te
PROPOSITIVE	talm-se	
IMPERATIVE	talm-ke	

	INFORMAL *Intimate* INDICATIVE	INFORMAL *Casual* INDICATIVE
DECLARATIVE/ *INTERROGATIVE*		
PRESENT	talm-a	talm-ci
PAST	talmass-ó	talmass-ci
REMOTE PAST	talmassóss-ó	talmassóss-ci
FUTURE	talmkess-ó	talmkess-ci
PAST FUTURE	talmasskess-ó	talmasskess-ci
PROPOSITIVE *IMPERATIVE*	talm-a	talm-ci

CAUSATIVE: *PASSIVE:*

FORMAL *Plain*

	INDICATIVE	RETROSPECTIVE
DECLARATIVE/ *INTERROGATIVE*		
PRESENT	talû-ta/-nya	talû-tóla/-tónya
PAST	tallass-ta/-nûnya	tallass-tóla
REMOTE PAST	tallassóss-ta	tallassóss-tóla
FUTURE	talûkess-ta	talûkess-tóla
PAST FUTURE	tallasskess-ta	tallasskess-tóla

PROPOSITIVE
IMPERATIVE

FORMAL *Polite*

	INDICATIVE	RETROSPECTIVE
DECLARATIVE/ *INTERROGATIVE*		
PRESENT	talûpni-ta/-kka	talûpti-ta/-kka
PAST	tallassûpni-ta	tallassûpti-ta
REMOTE PAST	tallassóssûpni-ta	tallassóssûpti-ta
FUTURE	talûkessûpni-ta	talûkessûpti-ta
PAST FUTURE	tallasskessûpni-ta	tallasskessûpti-ta

PROPOSITIVE
IMPERATIVE

INFORMAL *Familiar*

	INDICATIVE	RETROSPECTIVE
DECLARATIVE/ *INTERROGATIVE*		
PRESENT	talû-ne/-nka	talû-te/-tónka
PAST	tallass-ne/-nûnka	tallass-te
REMOTE PAST	tallassóss-ne	tallassóss-te
FUTURE	talûkess-ne	talûkess-te
PAST FUTURE	tallasskess-ne	tallasskess-te

PROPOSITIVE
IMPERATIVE

	INFORMAL *Intimate* INDICATIVE	INFORMAL *Casual* INDICATIVE
DECLARATIVE/ *INTERROGATIVE*		
PRESENT	tall-a	talû-ci
PAST	tallass-ó	tallass-ci
REMOTE PAST	tallassóss-ó	tallassóss-ci
FUTURE	talûkess-ó	talûkess-ci
PAST FUTURE	talasskess-ó	tallasskess-ci

PROPOSITIVE
IMPERATIVE

CAUSATIVE: *PASSIVE:*

to come and go, to commute   INTRANSITIVE

FORMAL *Plain*

	INDICATIVE	RETROSPECTIVE
DECLARATIVE/ *INTERROGATIVE*		
PRESENT	tani-n.ta/-nùnya	tani-tóla/-tónya
PAST	tanyóss-ta	tanyóss-tóla
REMOTE PAST	tanyóssóss-ta	tanyóssóss-tóla
FUTURE	tanikess-ta	tanykess-tóla
PAST FUTURE	tanyósskess-ta	tanyósskess-tóla
PROPOSITIVE	tani-ca	
IMPERATIVE	tany-ó.la	

FORMAL *Polite*

	INDICATIVE	RETROSPECTIVE
DECLARATIVE/ *INTERROGATIVE*		
PRESENT	tanipni-ta/-kka	tanipti-ta/-kka
PAST	tanyóssùpni-ta	tanyóssùpti-ta
REMOTE PAST	tanyóssóssùpni-ta	tanyóssóssùpti-ta
FUTURE	tanikessùpni-ta	tanikessùpti-ta
PAST FUTURE	tanyósskessùpni-ta	tanyósskessùpti-ta
PROPOSITIVE	tanipsi-ta	
IMPERATIVE	tani(si)psi-o	

INFORMAL *Familiar*

	INDICATIVE	RETROSPECTIVE
DECLARATIVE/ *INTERROGATIVE*		
PRESENT	tani-ne/-nùnka	tani-te/-tónka
PAST	tanyóss-ne	tanyóss-te
REMOTE PAST	tanyóssóss-ne	tanyóssóss-te
FUTURE	tanikess-ne	tanikess-te
PAST FUTURE	tanyósskess-ne	tanyósskess-te
PROPOSITIVE	tani-se	
IMPERATIVE	tani-ke	

	INFORMAL *Intimate* INDICATIVE	INFORMAL *Casual* INDICATIVE
DECLARATIVE/ *INTERROGATIVE*		
PRESENT	tan.y-ó	tani-ci
PAST	tanyóss-ó	tanyóss-ci
REMOTE PAST	tanyóssóss-ó	tanyóssóss-ci
FUTURE	tanikess-ó	tanikess-ci
PAST FUTURE	tanyósskess-ó	tanyósskess-ci
PROPOSITIVE *IMPERATIVE*	tan.y-ó	tani-ci

CAUSATIVE: *PASSIVE:*

FORMAL *Plain*

	INDICATIVE	RETROSPECTIVE
DECLARATIVE/ *INTERROGATIVE*		
PRESENT	tat-nún.ta/-núnya	tat-tóla/-tónya
PAST	tatass-ta	tatass-tóla
REMOTE PAST	tatassóss-ta	tatassóss-tóla
FUTURE	tatkess-ta	tatkess-tóla
PAST FUTURE	tatasskess-ta	tatasskess-tóla
PROPOSITIVE	tat-ca	
IMPERATIVE	tat-ala	

FORMAL *Polite*

	INDICATIVE	RETROSPECTIVE
DECLARATIVE/ *INTERROGATIVE*		
PRESENT	tatsúpni-ta/-kka	tatsúpti-ta/-kka
PAST	tatassúpni-ta	tatassúpti-ta
REMOTE PAST	tatassóssúpni-ta	tatassóssúpti-ta
FUTURE	tatkessúpni-ta	tatkessúpni-ta
PAST FUTURE	tatasskessúpni-ta	tatasskessúpti-ta
PROPOSITIVE	tatúpsi-ta	
IMPERATIVE	tatú(si)psi-o	

INFORMAL *Familiar*

	INDICATIVE	RETROSPECTIVE
DECLARATIVE/ *INTERROGATIVE*		
PRESENT	tat-ne/-núnka	tat-te/-tónka
PAST	tatass-ne	tatass-te
REMOTE PAST	tatassóss-ne	tatassóss-te
FUTURE	tatkess-ne	tatkess-te
PAST FUTURE	tatasskess-ne	tatasskess-te
PROPOSITIVE	tat-se	
IMPERATIVE	tat-ke	

	INFORMAL *Intimate* INDICATIVE	INFORMAL *Casual* INDICATIVE
DECLARATIVE/ *INTERROGATIVE*		
PRESENT	tat-a	tat-ci
PAST	tatass-ó	tatass-ci
REMOTE PAST	tatassóss-ó	tatassóss-ci
FUTURE	tatkess-ó	tatkess-ci
PAST FUTURE	tatasskess-ó	tatasskess-ci
PROPOSITIVE *IMPERATIVE*	tat-a	tat-ci

CAUSATIVE: *PASSIVE:*

FORMAL *Plain*

	INDICATIVE	RETROSPECTIVE
DECLARATIVE/ INTERROGATIVE		
PRESENT	toi-n.ta/-núnya	toi-tóla/-tónya
PAST	toioss-ta	toioss-tóla
REMOTE PAST	toiossóss-ta	toissóss-tóla
FUTURE	toikess-ta	toikess-tóla
PAST FUTURE	toiósskess-ta	toiósskess-tóla
PROPOSITIVE	toi-ca	
IMPERATIVE	toi-óla	

FORMAL *Polite*

	INDICATIVE	RETROSPECTIVE
DECLARATIVE/ INTERROGATIVE		
PRESENT	toipni-ta/-kka	toipti-ta/-kka
PAST	toióssúpni-ta	toióssúpti-ta
REMOTE PAST	toióssóssúpni-ta	toiósskessúpti-ta
FUTURE	toikessúpni-ta	toikessúpti-ta
PAST FUTURE	toiósskessúpni-ta	toiósskessúpti-ta
PROPOSITIVE	toipsi-ta	
IMPERATIVE	toi(si)psi-o	

INFORMAL *Familiar*

	INDICATIVE	RETROSPECTIVE
DECLARATIVE/ INTERROGATIVE		
PRESENT	toi-ne/-núnka	toi-te/-tónka
PAST	toióss-ne	toióss-te
REMOTE PAST	toióssóss-ne	toióssóss-te
FUTURE	toikess-ne	toikess-te ·
PAST FUTURE	toiósskess-ne	toiósskess-te
PROPOSITIVE	toi-se	
IMPERATIVE	toi-ke	

	INFORMAL *Intimate* INDICATIVE	INFORMAL *Casual* INDICATIVE
DECLARATIVE/ INTERROGATIVE		
PRESENT	toi-ó	toi-ci
PAST	toióss-ó	toióss-ci
REMOTE PAST	toióssóss-ó	toióssóss-ci
FUTURE	toikess-ó	toikess-ci
PAST FUTURE	toiósskess-ó	toiósskess-ci
PROPOSITIVE *IMPERATIVE*	toi-ó	toi-ci

CAUSATIVE: *PASSIVE:*

FORMAL *Plain*

	INDICATIVE	RETROSPECTIVE
DECLARATIVE/ *INTERROGATIVE*		
PRESENT	top-nùn.ta/-nùnya	top-tóla/-tónya
PAST	towass-ta	towass-tóla
REMOTE PAST	towassóss-ta	towassóss-tóla
FUTURE	topkess-ta	topkess-tóla
PAST FUTURE	towasskess-ta	towasskess-tóla
PROPOSITIVE	top-ca	
IMPERATIVE	tow-a.la	

FORMAL *Polite*

	INDICATIVE	RETROSPECTIVE
DECLARATIVE/ *INTERROGATIVE*		
PRESENT	topsùpni-ta/-kka	topsùpti-ta/-kka
PAST	towassùpni-ta	towassùpti-ta
REMOTE PAST	towassóssùpni-ta	towassóssùpti-ta
FUTURE	topkessùpni-ta	topkessùpti-ta
PAST FUTURE	towasskessùpni-ta	towasskessùpti-ta
PROPOSITIVE	toupsi-ta	
IMPERATIVE	tou(si)psi-o	

INFORMAL *Familiar*

	INDICATIVE	RETROSPECTIVE
DECLARATIVE/ *INTERROGATIVE*		
PRESENT	top-ne/-nùnka	top-te/-tónka
PAST	towass-ne	towass-te
REMOTE PAST	towassóss-ne	towassóss-te
FUTURE	topkess-ne	topkess-te
PAST FUTURE	towasskess-ne	towasskess-te
PROPOSITIVE	top-se	
IMPERATIVE	top-ke	

	INFORMAL *Intimate* INDICATIVE	INFORMAL *Casual* INDICATIVE
DECLARATIVE/ *INTERROGATIVE*		
PRESENT	to.w-a	top-ci
PAST	towass-ó	towass-ci
REMOTE PAST	towassóss-ó	towassóss-ci
FUTURE	topkess-ó	topkess-ci
PAST FUTURE	towasskess-ó	towasskess-ci
PROPOSITIVE *IMPERATIVE*	to.w-a	top-ci

CAUSATIVE: *PASSIVE:*

TÒL.TA   덜다
to subtract

FORMAL *Plain*

	INDICATIVE	RETROSPECTIVE
DECLARATIVE/ *INTERROGATIVE*		
PRESENT	tò-n.ta/-nùnya	tòl-tòla/-tònya
PAST	tòlòss-ta	tòlòss-tòla
REMOTE PAST	tòlòssòss-ta	tòlòssòss-tòla
FUTURE	tòlkess-ta	tòlkess-tòla
PAST FUTURE	tòlòsskess-ta	tòlòsskess-tòla
PROPOSITIVE	tòl-ca	
IMPERATIVE	tòl-òla	

FORMAL *Polite*

	INDICATIVE	RETROSPECTIVE
DECLARATIVE/ *INTERROGATIVE*		
PRESENT	tòpni-ta/-kka	tòpti-ta/-kka
PAST	tòlòssùpni-ta	tòlòssùpti-ta
REMOTE PAST	tòlòssòssùpni-ta	tòlòssòssùpti-ta
FUTURE	tòlkessùpni-ta	tòlkessùpti-ta
PAST FUTURE	tòlòsskessùpni-ta	tòlòsskessùpti-ta
PROPOSITIVE	tòpsi-ta	
IMPERATIVE	tò(si)psi-o	

INFORMAL *Familiar*

	INDICATIVE	RETROSPECTIVE
DECLARATIVE/ *INTERROGATIVE*		
PRESENT	tò-ne/-nùnka	tòl-te/-tònka
PAST	tòlòss-ne	tòlòss-te
REMOTE PAST	tòlòssòss-ne	tòlòssòss-te
FUTURE	tòlkess-ne	tòlkess-te
PAST FUTURE	tòlòsskess-ne	tòlòsskess-te
PROPOSITIVE	tò-se	
IMPERATIVE	tòl-ke	

	INFORMAL *Intimate* INDICATIVE	INFORMAL *Casual* INDICATIVE
DECLARATIVE/ *INTERROGATIVE*		
PRESENT	tòl-ò	tòl-ci
PAST	tòlòss-ò	tòlòss-ci
REMOTE PAST	tòlòssòss-ò	tòlòssòss-ci
FUTURE	tòlkess-ò	tòlkess-ci
PAST FUTURE	tòlòsskess-ò	tòlòsskess-ci
PROPOSITIVE *IMPERATIVE*	tòl-ò	tòl-ci

CAUSATIVE: *PASSIVE:* TOLLI.TA
                                                          to be subtracted

to be dirty, to be filthy   DESCRIPTIVE

FORMAL *Plain*

	INDICATIVE	RETROSPECTIVE
DECLARATIVE/ *INTERROGATIVE*		
PRESENT	tóló-p.ta/-unya	tólóp-tóla/-tónya
PAST	tólówòss-ta/-nùnya	tólówòss-tóla
REMOTE PAST	tólówòssòss-ta	tólówòssòss-tóla
FUTURE	tólópkess-ta	tólópkess-tóla
PAST FUTURE	tólówòsskess-ta	tólówòsskess-tóla

PROPOSITIVE
IMPERATIVE

FORMAL *Polite*

	INDICATIVE	RETROSPECTIVE
DECLARATIVE/ *INTERROGATIVE*		
PRESENT	tólópsùpni-ta/-kka	tólópsùpti-ta/-kka
PAST	tólówòssùpni-ta	tólówòssùpti-ta
REMOTE PAST	tólówòssòssùpni-ta	tólówòssòssùpti-ta
FUTURE	tólópkessùpni-ta	tólópkessùpti-ta
PAST FUTURE	tólówòsskessùpni-ta	tólówòsskessùpti-ta

PROPOSITIVE
IMPERATIVE

INFORMAL *Familiar*

	INDICATIVE	RETROSPECTIVE
DECLARATIVE/ *INTERROGATIVE*		
PRESENT	tóló-p.ne/-unka	tólóp-te/-tónka
PAST	tólówòss-ne/-nùnka	tólówòss-te
REMOTE PAST	tólówòssòss-ne	tólówòssòss-te
FUTURE	tólópkess-ne	tólópkess-te
PAST FUTURE	tólówòsskess-ne	tólówòsskess-te

PROPOSITIVE
IMPERATIVE

	INFORMAL *Intimate* INDICATIVE	INFORMAL *Casual* INDICATIVE
DECLARATIVE/ *INTERROGATIVE*		
PRESENT	tóló.w-ò	tólóp-ci
PAST	tólówòss-ò	tólówòss-ci
REMOTE PAST	tólówòssòss-ò	tólówòssòss-ci
FUTURE	tólópkess-ò	tólópkess-ci
PAST FUTURE	tólówòsskess-ò	tólówòsskess-ci

PROPOSITIVE
IMPERATIVE

CAUSATIVE: *PASSIVE:*

to be hot, to be warm   DESCRIPTIVE

FORMAL *Plain*

	INDICATIVE	RETROSPECTIVE
DECLARATIVE/ *INTERROGATIVE*		
PRESENT	tó-p.ta/-unya	tòp-tóla/-tónya
PAST	tówóss-ta/-núnya	tòwóss-tóla
REMOTE PAST	tówóssóss-ta	tòwóssóss-tóla
FUTURE	tópkess-ta	tópkess-tóla
PAST FUTURE	tówósskess-ta	tòwósskess-tóla

PROPOSITIVE
IMPERATIVE

FORMAL *Polite*

	INDICATIVE	RETROSPECTIVE
DECLARATIVE/ *INTERROGATIVE*		
PRESENT	tópsúpni-ta/-kka	tópsúpti-ta/-kka
PAST	tówssúpni-ta	tòwóssúpti-ta
REMOTE PAST	tówóssóssúpni-ta	tòwóssóssúpnti-ta
FUTURE	tópkessúpni-ta	tópkessúpti-ta
PAST FUTURE	tówósskessúpni-ta	tòwósskessúpti-ta

PROPOSITIVE
IMPERATIVE

INFORMAL *Familiar*

	INDICATIVE	RETROSPECTIVE
DECLARATIVE/ *INTERROGATIVE*		
PRESENT	tó-p.ne/-unka	tòp-te/-tónka
PAST	tówóss-ne/-núnka	tòwóss-te
REMOTE PAST	tówóssóss-ne	tòwóssóss-te
FUTURE	tópkess-ne	tópkess-te
PAST FUTURE	tówósskess-ne	tòwósskess-te

PROPOSITIVE
IMPERATIVE

	INFORMAL *Intimate* INDICATIVE	INFORMAL *Casual* INDICATIVE
DECLARATIVE/ *INTERROGATIVE*		
PRESENT	tó.w-ó	tòp-ci
PAST	tówóss-ó	tòwóss-ci
REMOTE PAST	tówóssóss-ó	tòwóssóss-ci
FUTURE	tópkesss-ó	tópkess-ci
PAST FUTURE	tówósskess-ó	tòwósskess-ci

PROPOSITIVE
IMPERATIVE

     CAUSATIVE: *PASSIVE:*

to surround, to wear (wrap) about one

FORMAL *Plain*

	INDICATIVE	RETROSPECTIVE
DECLARATIVE/ *INTERROGATIVE*		
PRESENT	tulú-n.ta/-núnya	tulú-tóla/-tónya
PAST	tullóss-ta	tullóss-tóla
REMOTE PAST	tullóssóss-ta	tullóssóss-tóla
FUTURE	tulúkess-ta	tulúkess-tóla
PAST FUTURE	tullósskess-ta	tullósskess-tóla
PROPOSITIVE	tulú-ca	
IMPERATIVE	tulló-la	

FORMAL *Polite*

	INDICATIVE	RETROSPECTIVE
DECLARATIVE/ *INTERROGATIVE*		
PRESENT	tulúpni-ta/-kka	tulúpti-ta/-kka
PAST	tullóssúpni-ta	tullóssúpti-ta
REMOTE PAST	tullóssóssúpni-ta	tullóssóssúpti-ta
FUTURE	tulúkessúpni-ta	tulúkessúpti-ta
PAST FUTURE	tullósskessúpni-ta	tullósskessúpti-ta
PROPOSITIVE	tulúpsi-ta	
IMPERATIVE	tulú(si)psi-o	

INFORMAL *Familiar*

	INDICATIVE	RETROSPECTIVE
DECLARATIVE/ *INTERROGATIVE*		
PRESENT	tulú-ne/-núnka	tulú-te/-tónka
PAST	tullóss-ne	tullóss-te
REMOTE PAST	tullóssóss-ne	tullóssóss-te
FUTURE	tulúkess-ne	tulúkess-te
PAST FUTURE	tullósskess-ne	tullósskess-te
PROPOSITIVE	tulú-se	
IMPERATIVE	tulú-ke	

	INFORMAL *Intimate* INDICATIVE	INFORMAL *Casual* INDICATIVE
DECLARATIVE/ *INTERROGATIVE*		
PRESENT	tull-ó	tulú-ci
PAST	tullóss-ó	tullóss-ci
REMOTE PAST	tullóssóss-ó	tullóssóss-ci
FUTURE	tulúkess-ó	tulúkess-ci
PAST FUTURE	tullósskess-ó	tullósskess-ci
PROPOSITIVE *IMPERATIVE*	tull-ó	tulú-ci

CAUSATIVE: *PASSIVE:*

FORMAL *Plain*

	INDICATIVE	RETROSPECTIVE
DECLARATIVE/ *INTERROGATIVE*		
PRESENT	tù-n.ta/-nùnya	tùl-tóla/-tònya
PAST	tùlòss-ta	tùlòss-tóla
REMOTE PAST	tùlòssòss-ta	tùlòssòss-tóla
FUTURE	tùlkess-ta	tùlkess-tóla
PAST FUTURE	tùlòsskess-ta	tùlòsskess-tóla
PROPOSITIVE	tùl-ca (1)	
IMPERATIVE	tùl-óla (1)	

FORMAL *Polite*

	INDICATIVE	RETROSPECTIVE
DECLARATIVE/ *INTERROGATIVE*		
PRESENT	tùpni-ta/-kka	tùpti-ta/-kka
PAST	tùlòssùpni-ta	tùlòssùpti-ta
REMOTE PAST	tùlòssòssùpni-ta	tùlòssòssùpti-ta
FUTURE	tùlkessùpni-ta	tùlkessùpti-ta
PAST FUTURE	tùlòsskessùpni-ta	tùlòsskessùpti-ta
PROPOSITIVE	tùpsi-ta (1)	
IMPERATIVE	tù(si)psi-o (1)	

INFORMAL *Familiar*

	INDICATIVE	RETROSPECTIVE
DECLARATIVE/ *INTERROGATIVE*		
PRESENT	tù-ne/-nùnka	tùl-te/-tònka
PAST	tùlòss-ne	tùlòss-te
REMOTE PAST	tùlòssòss-ne	tùlòssòss-te
FUTURE	tùlkess-ne	tùlkess-te
PAST FUTURE	tùlòsskess-ne	tùlòsskess-te
PROPOSITIVE	tù-se (1)	
IMPERATIVE	tùl-ke (1)	

	INFORMAL *Intimate* INDICATIVE	INFORMAL *Casual* INDICATIVE
DECLARATIVE/ *INTERROGATIVE*		
PRESENT	tùl-o	tùl-ci
PAST	tùlòss-ò	tùlòss-ci
REMOTE PAST	tùlòssòss-ò	tùlòssòss-ci
FUTURE	tùlkess-ò	tùlkess-ci
PAST FUTURE	tùlòsskess-ò	tùlòsskess-ci
PROPOSITIVE *IMPERATIVE*	tùl-ò (1)	tùl-ci (1)

CAUSATIVE: *PASSIVE:*

TUT.TA
to hear, to listen to   듣다

FORMAL *Plain*

	INDICATIVE	RETROSPECTIVE
DECLARATIVE/ *INTERROGATIVE*		
PRESENT	tút-nún.ta/-núnya	tút-tóla/-tónya
PAST	túlóss-ta	túlóss-tóla
REMOTE PAST	túlóssóss-ta	túlóssóss-tóla
FUTURE	tútkess-ta	tútkess-tóla
PAST FUTURE	túlósskess-ta	túlósskess-tóla
PROPOSITIVE	tút-ca	
IMPERATIVE	túl-óla	

FORMAL *Polite*

	INDICATIVE	RETROSPECTIVE
DECLARATIVE/ *INTERROGATIVE*		
PRESENT	tútsúpni-ta/-kka	tútsúpti-ta/-kka
PAST	túlóssúpni-ta	túlóssúpti-ta
REMOTE PAST	túlóssóssúpni-ta	túlóssóssúpti-ta
FUTURE	tútkessúpni-ta	tútkessúpti-ta
PAST FUTURE	túlósskessúpni-ta	tólósskessúpti-ta
PROPOSITIVE	túlúpsi-ta	
IMPERATIVE	túlú(si)psi-o	

INFORMAL *Familiar*

	INDICATIVE	RETROSPECTIVE
DECLARATIVE/ *INTERROGATIVE*		
PRESENT	tút-ne/-núnka	tút-te/-tónka
PAST	túlóss-ne	túlóss-te
REMOTE PAST	túlóssóss-ne	túlóssóss-te
FUTURE	tútkess-ne	tútkess-te
PAST FUTURE	túlósskess-ne	túlósskess-te
PROPOSITIVE	tút-se	
IMPERATIVE	tút-ke	

	INFORMAL *Intimate* INDICATIVE	INFORMAL *Casual* INDICATIVE
DECLARATIVE/ *INTERROGATIVE*		
PRESENT	túl-ó	tút-ci
PAST	túlóss-ó	túlóss-ci
REMOTE PAST	túlóssóss-ó	túlóssóss-ci
FUTURE	tútkess-ó	tútkess-ci
PAST FUTURE	túlósskess-ó	túlósskess-ci
PROPOSITIVE *IMPERATIVE*	túl-ó	tút-ci

CAUSATIVE: *PASSIVE:*

1) to burn, to blaze 2) to ride (in or on) 3) to add, to mix

FORMAL *Plain*

	INDICATIVE	RETROSPECTIVE
DECLARATIVE/ *INTERROGATIVE*		
PRESENT	tha-n.ta/-nûnya	tha-tóla/-tónya
PAST	thass-ta	thass-tóla
REMOTE PAST	thassóss-ta	thassóss-tóla
FUTURE	thakess-ta	thakess-tóla
PAST FUTURE	thasskess-ta	thasskess-tóla
PROPOSITIVE	tha-ca (2,3)	
IMPERATIVE	tha-la (2,3)	

FORMAL *Polite*

	INDICATIVE	RETROSPECTIVE
DECLARATIVE/ *INTERROGATIVE*		
PRESENT	thapni-ta/-kka	thapti-ta/-kka
PAST	thassúpni-ta	thassúpti-ta
REMOTE PAST	thassóssúpni-ta	thassóssúpti-ta
FUTURE	thakessúpni-ta	thakessúpti-ta
PAST FUTURE	thasskessúpni-ta	thasskessúpti-ta
PROPOSITIVE	thapsi-ta (2,3)	
IMPERATIVE	tha(si)psi-o (2,3)	

INFORMAL *Familiar*

	INDICATIVE	RETROSPECTIVE
DECLARATIVE/ *INTERROGATIVE*		
PRESENT	tha-ne/-nûnka	tha-te/-tónke
PAST	thass-ne	thass-te
REMOTE PAST	thassóss-ne	thassóss-te
FUTURE	thakess-ne	thakess-te
PAST FUTURE	thasskess-ne	thasskess-te
PROPOSITIVE	tha-se (2,3)	
IMPERATIVE	tha-ke (2,3)	

	INFORMAL *Intimate* INDICATIVE	INFORMAL *Casual* INDICATIVE
DECLARATIVE/ *INTERROGATIVE*		
PRESENT	tha	tha-ci
PAST	thass-ó	thass-ci
REMOTE PAST	thassóss-ó	thassóss-ci
FUTURE	thakess-ó	thakess-ci
PAST FUTURE	thasskess-ó	thasskess-ci
PROPOSITIVE *IMPERATIVE*	tha (2,3)	tha-ci (2,3)

CAUSATIVE: THAEU.TA   *PASSIVE:*
1) to burn it
2) to give a ride

FORMAL *Plain*

	INDICATIVE	RETROSPECTIVE
DECLARATIVE/ *INTERROGATIVE*		
PRESENT	thóci-n.ta/-núnya	thóci-tóla/-tónya
PAST	thócyóss-ta	thócyóss-tóla
REMOTE PAST	thócyóssóss-ta	thócyóssóss-tóla
FUTURE	thócikess-ta	thócikess-tóla
PAST FUTURE	thócyósskess-ta	thócyósskess-tóla

PROPOSITIVE
IMPERATIVE

FORMAL *Polite*

	INDICATIVE	RETROSPECTIVE
DECLARATIVE/ *INTERROGATIVE*		
PRESENT	thócipni-ta/-kka	thócipti-ta/-kka
PAST	thócyóssúpni-ta	thócyóssúpti-ta
REMOTE PAST	thócyóssóssúpni-ta	thócyóssóssúpti-ta
FUTURE	thócikessúpni-ta	thócikessúpti-ta
PAST FUTURE	thócyósskessúpni-ta	thócyósskessúpti-ta

PROPOSITIVE
IMPERATIVE

INFORMAL *Familiar*

	INDICATIVE	RETROSPECTIVE
DECLARATIVE/ *INTERROGATIVE*		
PRESENT	thóci-ne/-núnka	thóci-te/-tónka
PAST	thócyóss-ne	thócyóss-te
REMOTE PAST	thócyóssóss-ne	thócyóssóss-te
FUTURE	thócikess-ne	thócikess-te
PAST FUTURE	thócyósskess-ne	thócyósskess-te

PROPOSITIVE
IMPERATIVE

	INFORMAL *Intimate* INDICATIVE	INFORMAL *Casual* INDICATIVE
DECLARATIVE/ *INTERROGATIVE*		
PRESENT	thóc.y-ó	thóci-ci
PAST	thócyóss-ó	thócyóss-ci
REMOTE PAST	thócyóssóss-ó	thócyóssóss-ci
FUTURE	thócikess-ó	thócikess-ci
PAST FUTURE	thócyósskess-ó	thócyósskess-ci

PROPOSITIVE
IMPERATIVE

CAUSATIVE: *PASSIVE:*

	FORMAL *Plain*	
	INDICATIVE	RETROSPECTIVE

DECLARATIVE/
INTERROGATIVE

	INDICATIVE	RETROSPECTIVE
PRESENT	thò-n.ta/-nùnya	thòl-tóla/-tónya
PAST	thòloss-ta	thòloss-tóla
REMOTE PAST	thòlóssóss-ta	thòlóssóss-tóla
FUTURE	thòlkess-ta	thòlkess-tóla
PAST FUTURE	thòlósskess-ta	thòlósskess-tóla

PROPOSITIVE	thòl-ca
IMPERATIVE	thòl-óla

FORMAL *Polite*

	INDICATIVE	RETROSPECTIVE

DECLARATIVE/
INTERROGATIVE

	INDICATIVE	RETROSPECTIVE
PRESENT	thòpni-ta/-kka	thòpti-ta/-kka
PAST	thòlóssùpni-ta	thòlóssùpti-ta
REMOTE PAST	thòlóssóssùpni-ta	thòlóssóssùpti-ta
FUTURE	thòlkessùpni-ta	thòlkessùpti-ta
PAST FUTURE	thòlósskessùpni-ta	thòlósskessùpti-ta

PROPOSITIVE	thòpsi-ta
IMPERATIVE	thò(si)psi-o

INFORMAL *Familiar*

	INDICATIVE	RETROSPECTIVE

DECLARATIVE/
INTERROGATIVE

	INDICATIVE	RETROSPECTIVE
PRESENT	thò-ne/-nùnka	thòl-te/-tónka
PAST	thòlóss-ne	thòlóss-te
REMOTE PAST	thòlóssóss-ne	thòlóssóss-te
FUTURE	thòlkess-ne	thòlkess-te
PAST FUTURE	thòlósskess-ne	thòlósskess-te

PROPOSITIVE	thò-se
IMPERATIVE	thòl-ke

	INFORMAL *Intimate* INDICATIVE	INFORMAL *Casual* INDICATIVE

DECLARATIVE/
INTERROGATIVE

	INFORMAL *Intimate* INDICATIVE	INFORMAL *Casual* INDICATIVE
PRESENT	thòl-ó	thòl-ci
PAST	thòlóss-ó	thòlóss-ci
REMOTE PAST	thòlóssóss-ó	thòlóssóss-ci
FUTURE	thòlkess-ó	thòlkess-ci
PAST FUTURE	thòlósskess-ó	thòlósskess-ci

PROPOSITIVE *IMPERATIVE*	thòl-ó	thòl-ci

CAUSATIVE:	*PASSIVE:* THOLLI.TA
	to get shaken off

	FORMAL *Plain*	
	INDICATIVE	RETROSPECTIVE

DECLARATIVE/
INTERROGATIVE

	INDICATIVE	RETROSPECTIVE
PRESENT	thòttúli-n.ta/-núnya	thòttúli-tóla/-tónya
PAST	thòttúlyóss-ta	thòttúlyóss-tóla
REMOTE PAST	thòttúlyóssóss-ta	thòttúlyóssóss-tóla
FUTURE	thòttúlikess-ta	thòttúlikess-tóla
PAST FUTURE	thòttúlyósskess-ta	thòttúlyósskess-tóla

PROPOSITIVE   thòttúli-ca
IMPERATIVE   thòttúly-ò.la

	FORMAL *Polite*	
	INDICATIVE	RETROSPECTIVE

DECLARATIVE/
INTERROGATIVE

	INDICATIVE	RETROSPECTIVE
PRESENT	thòttúlipni-ta/-kka	thòttúlipti-ta/-kka
PAST	thòttúlyóssúpni-ta	thòttúlyóssúpti-ta
REMOTE PAST	thòttúlyóssóssúpni-ta	thòttúlyóssóssúpti-ta
FUTURE	thòttúlikessúpni-ta	thòttúlikessúpti-ta
PAST FUTURE	thòttúlyósskessúpni-ta	thòttúlyósskessúpti-ta

PROPOSITIVE   thòttúlipsi-ta
IMPERATIVE   thòttúli(si)psi-o

	INFORMAL *Familiar*	
	INDICATIVE	RETROSPECTIVE

DECLARATIVE/
INTERROGATIVE

	INDICATIVE	RETROSPECTIVE
PRESENT	thòttúli-ne/-núnka	thòttúli-te/-tónka
PAST	thòttúlyóss-ne	thòttúlyóss-te
REMOTE PAST	thòttúlyóssóss-ne	thòttúlyóssóss-te
FUTURE	thòttúlikess-ne	thòttúlikess-te
PAST FUTURE	thòttúlyósskess-ne	thòttúlyósskess-te

PROPOSITIVE   thòttúli-se
IMPERATIVE   thòttúli-ke

	INFORMAL *Intimate*	INFORMAL *Casual*
	INDICATIVE	INDICATIVE

DECLARATIVE/
INTERROGATIVE

	INDICATIVE	INDICATIVE
PRESENT	thòttúl.y-ò	thòttúli-ci
PAST	thòttúlyóss-ò	thòttúlyóss-ci
REMOTE PAST	thòttúlyóssóss-ò	thòttúlyóssóss-ci
FUTURE	thòttúlikess-ò	thòttúlikess-ci
PAST FUTURE	thòttúlyósskess-ò	thòtúlyósskess-ci

PROPOSITIVE   thòttúl.y-ò   thòttúli-ci
IMPERATIVE

CAUSATIVE: *PASSIVE:*

1) to sprout, to bud out 2) to break it open

FORMAL *Plain*

	INDICATIVE	RETROSPECTIVE
DECLARATIVE/ *INTERROGATIVE*		
PRESENT	thú-n.ta/-núnya	thú-tóla/-tónya
PAST	thóss-ta	thóss-tóla
REMOTE PAST	thóssóss-ta	thóssóss-tóla
FUTURE	thúkess-ta	thúkess-tóla
PAST FUTURE	thósskess-ta	thósskess-tóla
PROPOSITIVE	thú-ca (2)	
IMPERATIVE	thó-la (2)	

FORMAL *Polite*

	INDICATIVE	RETROSPECTIVE
DECLARATIVE/ *INTERROGATIVE*		
PRESENT	thúpni-ta/-kka	thúpti-ta/-kka
PAST	thóssúpni-ta	thóssúpti-ta
REMOTE PAST	thóssóssúpni-ta	thóssóssúpti-ta
FUTURE	thúkessúpni-ta	thúkessúpti-ta
PAST FUTURE	thósskessúpni-ta	thósskessúpti-ta
PROPOSITIVE	thúpsi-ta (2)	
IMPERATIVE	thú(si)psi-o (2)	

INFORMAL *Familiar*

	INDICATIVE	RETROSPECTIVE
DECLARATIVE/ *INTERROGATIVE*		
PRESENT	thú-ne/-núnka	thú-te/-tónka
PAST	thóss-ne	thóss-te
REMOTE PAST	thóssóss-ne	thóssóss-te
FUTURE	thúkess-ne	thúkess-te
PAST FUTURE	thósskess-ne	thósskess-te
PROPOSITIVE		
IMPERATIVE		

	INFORMAL *Intimate* INDICATIVE	INFORMAL *Casual* INDICATIVE
DECLARATIVE/ *INTERROGATIVE*		
PRESENT	thó	thú-ci
PAST	thóss-ó	thóss-ci
REMOTE PAST	thóssóss-ó	thóssóss-ci
FUTURE	thúkess-ó	thúkess-ci
PAST FUTURE	thósskess-ó	thósskess-ci
PROPOSITIVE *IMPERATIVE*	thó (2)	thú-ci (2)

CAUSATIVE: *PASSIVE:* THÙI.TA
                                     to be opened, to get
                                     cleared

	FORMAL *Plain*	
	INDICATIVE	RETROSPECTIVE
DECLARATIVE/ *INTERROGATIVE*		
PRESENT	thú-n.ta/-núnya	thúl-tóla/-tónya
PAST	thúlóss-ta	thúlóss-tóla
REMOTE PAST	thúlóssóss-ta	thúlóssóss-tóla
FUTURE	thúlkess-ta	thúlkess-tóla
PAST FUTURE	thúlósskess-ta	thúlósskess-tóla
PROPOSITIVE	thúl-ca	
IMPERATIVE	thúl-óla	

	FORMAL *Polite*	
	INDICATIVE	RETROSPECTIVE
DECLARATIVE/ *INTERROGATIVE*		
PRESENT	thúpni-ta/-kka	thúpti-ta/-kka
PAST	thúlóssúpni-ta	thúlóssúpti-ta
REMOTE PAST	thúlóssóssúpni-ta	thúlóssóssúpti-ta
FUTURE	thúlkessúpni-ta	thúkessúpti-ta
PAST FUTURE	thúlósskessúpni-ta	thúlósskessúpti-ta
PROPOSITIVE	thúpsi-ta	
IMPERATIVE	thú(si)psi-o	

	INFORMAL *Familiar*	
	INDICATIVE	RETROSPECTIVE
DECLARATIVE/ *INTERROGATIVE*		
PRESENT	thú-ne/-núnka	thúl-te/-tónka
PAST	thúlóss-ne	thúlóss-te
REMOTE PAST	thúlóssóss-ne	thúlóssóss-te
FUTURE	thúlkess-ne	thúlkess-te
PAST FUTURE	thúlósskess-ne	thúlósskess-te
PROPOSITIVE	thú-se	
IMPERATIVE	thúl-ke	

	INFORMAL *Intimate* INDICATIVE	INFORMAL *Casual* INDICATIVE
DECLARATIVE/ *INTERROGATIVE*		
PRESENT	thúl-ó	thúl-ci
PAST	thúlóss-ó	thúlóss-ci
REMOTE PAST	thúlóssóss-ó	thúlóssoss-ci
FUTURE	thúlkess-ó	thúlkess-ci
PAST FUTURE	thúlósskess-ó	thúlósskess-ci
PROPOSITIVE *IMPERATIVE*	thúl-ó	thúl-ci

CAUSATIVE: THULLI.TA
  to get it wound,
  to have it turned

PASSIVE: THÚLLI.TA
  to get turned,
  to get wound

THULLI.TA
to go wrong, to fall out (with), to be mistaken

FORMAL *Plain*

	INDICATIVE	RETROSPECTIVE
DECLARATIVE/ INTERROGATIVE		
PRESENT	thúlli-n.ta/-núnya	thúlli-tóla/-tónka
PAST	thúllyóss-ta	thúllyóss-tóla
REMOTE PAST	thúllyóssóss-ta	thúllyóssóss-tóla
FUTURE	thúllikess-ta	thúllikess-tóla
PAST FUTURE	thúllyósskess-ta	thúllyósskess-tóla
PROPOSITIVE	thúlli-ca	
IMPERATIVE	thúlly-ó.la	

FORMAL *Polite*

	INDICATIVE	RETROSPECTIVE
DECLARATIVE/ INTERROGATIVE		
PRESENT	thúllipni-ta/-kka	thúllipti-ta/-kka
PAST	thúllyóssúpni-ta	thúllyóssúpti-ta
REMOTE PAST	thúllyóssóssúpni-ta	thúllyóssóssúpti-ta
FUTURE	thúllikessúpni-ta	thúllikessúpti-ta
PAST FUTURE	thúllyósskessúpni-ta	thúllyósskessúpti-ta
PROPOSITIVE	thúllipsi-ta	
IMPERATIVE	thúlli(si)psi-o	

INFORMAL *Familiar*

	INDICATIVE	RETROSPECTIVE
DECLARATIVE/ INTERROGATIVE		
PRESENT	thúlli-ne/-núnka	thúlli-te/-tónka
PAST	thúllyóss-ne	thúllyóss-te
REMOTE PAST	thúllyóssóss-ne	thúllyóssóss-te
FUTURE	thúllikess-ne	thúllikess-te
PAST FUTURE	thúllyósskess-ne	thúllyósskess-te
PROPOSITIVE	thúlli-se	
IMPERATIVE	thúlli-ke	

	INFORMAL *Intimate* INDICATIVE	INFORMAL *Casual* INDICATIVE
DECLARATIVE/ INTERROGATIVE		
PRESENT	thúll.y-ó	thúlli-ci
PAST	thúllyóss-ó	thúllyóss-ci
REMOTE PAST	thúllyóssóss-ó	thúllyóssóss-ci
FUTURE	thúllikess-ó	thúllikess-ci
PAST FUTURE	thúllyósskess-ó	thúllyósskess-ci
PROPOSITIVE	thúll.y-ó	thúlli-ci
IMPERATIVE		

CAUSATIVE:

PASSIVE:

THWI.TA   튀다
1) to spring, to bounce 2) to run away

FORMAL *Plain*

	INDICATIVE	RETROSPECTIVE
DECLARATIVE/ *INTERROGATIVE*		
PRESENT	thwi-n.ta/-núnya	thwi-tóla/-tónya
PAST	thwióss-ta	thwióss-tóla
REMOTE PAST	thwióssóss-ta	thwióssóss-tóla
FUTURE	thwikess-ta	thwikess-tóla
PAST FUTURE	thwiósskess-ta	thwiósskess-tóla
PROPOSITIVE	thwi-ca (2)	
IMPERATIVE	thwi-óla (2)	

FORMAL *Polite*

	INDICATIVE	RETROSPECTIVE
DECLARATIVE/ *INTERROGATIVE*		
PRESENT	thwipni-ta/-kka	thwipti-ta/-kka
PAST	thwióssúpni-ta	thwióssúpti-ta
REMOTE PAST	thwióssóssúpni-ta	thwióssóssúpti-ta
FUTURE	thwikessúpni-ta	thwikessúpti-ta
PAST FUTURE	thwiósskessúpni-ta	thwiósskessúpti-ta
PROPOSITIVE	thwipsi-ta (2)	
IMPERATIVE	thwi(si)psi-o (2)	

INFORMAL *Familiar*

	INDICATIVE	RETROSPECTIVE
DECLARATIVE/ *INTERROGATIVE*		
PRESENT	thwi-ne/-núnka	thwi-te/-tónka
PAST	thwióss-ne	thwióss-te
REMOTE PAST	thwióssóss-ne	thwióssóss-te
FUTURE	thwikess-ne	thwikess-te
PAST FUTURE	thwiósskess-ne	thwiósskess-te
PROPOSITIVE	thwi-se (2)	
IMPERATIVE	thwi-ke (2)	

	INFORMAL *Intimate* INDICATIVE	INFORMAL *Casual* INDICATIVE
DECLARATIVE/ *INTERROGATIVE*		
PRESENT	thwi-ó	thwi-ci
PAST	thwióss-ó	thwióss-ci
REMOTE PAST	thwióssóss-ó	thwióssóss-ci
FUTURE	thwikess-ó	thwikess-ci
PAST FUTURE	thwiósskess-ó	thwiósskess-ci
PROPOSITIVE *IMPERATIVE*	thwi-ó (2)	thwi-ci (2)

CAUSATIVE: THWIKI.TA   *PASSIVE:*
                    to scare away.
                    to splash (water)

TTALÚ.TA   따르다
1) to follow, to go after   2) to pour (out, into)

FORMAL *Plain*

	INDICATIVE	RETROSPECTIVE
DECLARATIVE/ *INTERROGATIVE*		
PRESENT	ttalú-n.ta/-núnya	ttalú-tóla/-tònya
PAST	ttalass-ta	ttalass-tóla
REMOTE PAST	ttalassóss-ta	ttalassóss-tóla
FUTURE	ttalúkess-ta	ttalúkess-tóla
PAST FUTURE	ttalasskess-ta	ttalasskess-tóla
PROPOSITIVE	ttalú-ca	
IMPERATIVE	ttal-ala	

FORMAL *Polite*

	INDICATIVE	RETROSPECTIVE
DECLARATIVE/ *INTERROGATIVE*		
PRESENT	ttalúpni-ta/-kka	ttalúpti-ta/-kka
PAST	ttalassúpni-ta	ttalassúpti-ta
REMOTE PAST	ttalassóssúpni-ta	ttalassóssúpti-ta
FUTURE	ttalúkessúpni-ta	ttalúkessúpti-ta
PAST FUTURE	ttalasskessúpni-ta	ttalasskessúpti-ta
PROPOSITIVE	ttalúpsi-ta	
IMPERATIVE	ttalú(si)psi-o	

INFORMAL *Familiar*

	INDICATIVE	RETROSPECTIVE
DECLARATIVE/ *INTERROGATIVE*		
PRESENT	ttalú-ne/-núnka	ttalú-te/-tónka
PAST	ttalass-ne	ttalass-te
REMOTE PAST	ttalassóss-ne	ttalassóss-te
FUTURE	ttalúkess-ne	ttalúkess-te
PAST FUTURE	ttalasskess-ne	ttalasskess-te
PROPOSITIVE	ttalú-se	
IMPERATIVE	ttalú-ke	

	INFORMAL *Intimate* INDICATIVE	INFORMAL *Casual* INDICATIVE
DECLARATIVE/ *INTERROGATIVE*		
PRESENT	ttal-a	ttalú-ci
PAST	ttalass-ó	ttalass-ci
REMOTE PAST	ttalassóss-ó	ttalassóss-ci
FUTURE	ttalúkess-ó	ttalúkess-ci
PAST FUTURE	ttalasskess-ó	ttalasskess-ci
PROPOSITIVE *IMPERATIVE*	ttal-a	ttalú-ci

CAUSATIVE: *PASSIVE:*

FORMAL *Plain*

	INDICATIVE	RETROSPECTIVE
DECLARATIVE/ *INTERROGATIVE*		
PRESENT	ttólp-ta/-únya	ttólp-tóla/-tónya
PAST	ttólpóss-ta/-núnya	ttólpóss-tóla
REMOTE PAST	ttólpóssóss-ta	ttólpóssóss-tóla
FUTURE	ttólpkess-ta	ttólpkess-tóla
PAST FUTURE	ttólpósskess-ta	ttólpósskess-tóla

PROPOSITIVE
IMPERATIVE

FORMAL *Polite*

	INDICATIVE	RETROSPECTIVE
DECLARATIVE/ *INTERROGATIVE*		
PRESENT	ttólpsúpni-ta/-kka	ttólpsúpti-ta/-kka
PAST	ttólpóssúpni-ta	ttólpóssúpti-ta
REMOTE PAST	ttólpóssóssúpni-ta	ttólpóssóssúpti-ta
FUTURE	ttólpkessúpni-ta	ttólpkessúpti-ta
PAST FUTURE	ttólpósskessúpni-ta	ttólpósskessúpti-ta

PROPOSITIVE
IMPERATIVE

INFORMAL *Familiar*

	INDICATIVE	RETROSPECTIVE
DECLARATIVE/ *INTERROGATIVE*		
PRESENT	ttólp-ne/-unka	ttólp-te/-tónka
PAST	ttólpóss-ne/-núnka	ttólpóss-te
REMOTE PAST	ttólpóssóss-ne	ttólpóssóss-te
FUTURE	ttólpkess-ne	ttólpkess-te
PAST FUTURE	ttólpósskess-ne	ttólpósskess-te

PROPOSITIVE
IMPERATIVE

	INFORMAL *Intimate* INDICATIVE	INFORMAL *Casual* INDICATIVE
DECLARATIVE/ *INTERROGATIVE*		
PRESENT	ttólp-ó	ttólp-ci
PAST	ttólpóss-ó	ttólpóss-ci
REMOTE PAST	ttólpóssóss-ó	ttólpóssóss-ci
FUTURE	ttólpkess-ó	ttólpkess-ci
PAST FUTURE	ttólpósskess-ó	ttólpósskess-ci

PROPOSITIVE
IMPERATIVE

CAUSATIVE: *PASSIVE:*

FORMAL *Plain*

	INDICATIVE	RETROSPECTIVE
DECLARATIVE/ *INTERROGATIVE*		
PRESENT	ttulh-nún.ta/-núnya	ttulh-tóla/-tónya
PAST	ttulhóss-ta	ttulhóss-tóla
REMOTE PAST	ttulhóssóss-ta	ttulhóssóss-tóla
FUTURE	ttulhkess-ta	ttulhkess-tóla
PAST FUTURE	ttulhósskess-ta	ttulhósskess-tóla
PROPOSITIVE	ttulh-ca	
IMPERATIVE	ttulh-óla	

FORMAL *Polite*

	INDICATIVE	RETROSPECTIVE
DECLARATIVE/ *INTERROGATIVE*		
PRESENT	ttulhsúpni-ta/-kka	ttulhsúpti-ta/-kka
PAST	ttulhóssúpni-ta	ttulhóssúpti-ta
REMOTE PAST	ttulhóssóssúpni-ta	ttulhóssóssúpti-ta
FUTURE	ttulhkessúpni-ta	ttulhkessúpti-ta
PAST FUTURE	ttulhósskessúpni-ta	ttulhósskessúpti-ta
PROPOSITIVE	ttulhúpsi-ta	
IMPERATIVE	ttulhú(si)psi-o	

INFORMAL *Familiar*

	INDICATIVE	RETROSPECTIVE
DECLARATIVE/ *INTERROGATIVE*		
PRESENT	ttulh-ne/-núnka	ttulh-te/-tónka
PAST	ttulhóss-ne	ttulhóss-te
REMOTE PAST	ttulhóssóss-ne	ttulhóssóss-te
FUTURE	ttulhkess-ne	ttulhkess-te
PAST FUTURE	ttulhósskess-ne	ttulhósskess-te
PROPOSITIVE	ttulh-se	
IMPERATIVE	ttulh-ke	

	INFORMAL *Intimate* INDICATIVE	INFORMAL *Casual* INDICATIVE
DECLARATIVE/ *INTERROGATIVE*		
PRESENT	ttulh-ó	ttulh-ci
PAST	ttulhóss-ó	ttulhóss-ci
REMOTE PAST	ttulhóssóss-ó	ttulhóssóss-ci
FUTURE	ttulhkess-ó	ttulhkess-ci
PAST FUTURE	ttulhósskess-ó	ttulhósskess-ci
PROPOSITIVE *IMPERATIVE*	ttulh-ó	ttulh-ci

CAUSATIVE:

PASSIVE: TTULHLI.TA
to be pierced,
to get opened up

FORMAL *Plain*

	INDICATIVE	RETROSPECTIVE
DECLARATIVE/ *INTERROGATIVE*		
PRESENT	u-n.ta/-núnya	ul-tóla/-tónya
PAST	ulóss-ta	ulóss-tóla
REMOTE PAST	ulóssóss-ta	ulóssóss-tóla
FUTURE	ulkess-ta	ulkess-tóla
PAST FUTURE	ulósskess-ta	ulósskess-tóla
PROPOSITIVE	ul-ca	
IMPERATIVE	ul-óla	

FORMAL *Polite*

	INDICATIVE	RETROSPECTIVE
DECLARATIVE/ *INTERROGATIVE*		
PRESENT	upni-ta/-kka	upti-ta/-kka
PAST	ulóssúpni-ta	ulóssúpti-ta
REMOTE PAST	ulóssóssúpni-ta	ulóssóssúpti-ta
FUTURE	ulkessúpni-ta	ulkessúpti-ta
PAST FUTURE	ulósskessúpni-ta	ulósskessúpti-ta
PROPOSITIVE	upsi-ta	
IMPERATIVE	u(si)psi-o	

INFORMAL *Familiar*

	INDICATIVE	RETROSPECTIVE
DECLARATIVE/ *INTERROGATIVE*		
PRESENT	u-ne/-núnka	ul-te/-tónka
PAST	ulóss-ne	ulóss-te
REMOTE PAST	ulóssóss-ne	ulóssóss-te
FUTURE	ulkess-ne	ulkess-te
PAST FUTURE	ulósskess-ne	ulósskess-te
PROPOSITIVE	u-se	
IMPERATIVE	ul-ke	

	INFORMAL *Intimate* INDICATIVE	INFORMAL *Casual* INDICATIVE
DECLARATIVE/ *INTERROGATIVE*		
PRESENT	ul-ó	ul-ci
PAST	ulóss-ó	ulóss-ci
REMOTE PAST	ulóssóss-ó	ulóssóss-ci
FUTURE	ulkess-ó	ulkess-ci
PAST FUTURE	ulósskess-ó	ulósskess-ci
PROPOSITIVE *IMPERATIVE*	ul-ó	ul-ci

CAUSATIVE: ULLI.TA
    to make (a person) cry

PASSIVE:

FORMAL *Plain*

	INDICATIVE	RETROSPECTIVE
DECLARATIVE/ *INTERROGATIVE*		
PRESENT	us-nún.ta/-núnya	us-tóla/-tònya
PAST	usóss-ta	usóss-tóla
REMOTE PAST	usóssóss-ta	usóssóss-tóla
FUTURE	uskess-ta	uskess-tóla
PAST FUTURE	usósskess-ta	usósskess-tóla
PROPOSITIVE	us-ca	
IMPERATIVE	us-óla	

FORMAL *Polite*

	INDICATIVE	RETROSPECTIVE
DECLARATIVE/ *INTERROGATIVE*		
PRESENT	ussúpni-ta/-kka	ussúpti-ta/-kka
PAST	usóssúpni-ta	usóssúpti-ta
REMOTE PAST	usóssóssúpni-ta	usóssóssúpti-ta
FUTURE	uskessúpni-ta	uskessúpti-ta
PAST FUTURE	usósskessúpni-ta	usósskessúpti-ta
PROPOSITIVE	usúpsi-ta	
IMPERATIVE	usú(si)psi-o	

INFORMAL *Familiar*

	INDICATIVE	RETROSPECTIVE
DECLARATIVE/ *INTERROGATIVE*		
PRESENT	us-ne/-núnka	us-te/-tónka
PAST	usóss-ne	usóss-te
REMOTE PAST	usóssóss-ne	usóssóss-te
FUTURE	uskess-ne	uskess-te
PAST FUTURE	usósskess-ne	usósskess-te
PROPOSITIVE	us-se	
IMPERATIVE	us-ke	

	INFORMAL *Intimate* INDICATIVE	INFORMAL *Casual* INDICATIVE
DECLARATIVE/ *INTERROGATIVE*		
PRESENT	us-ó	us-ci
PAST	usóss-ó	usóss-ci
REMOTE PAST	usóssóss-ó	usóssóss-ci
FUTURE	uskess-ó	uskess-ci
PAST FUTURE	usósskess-ó	usósskess-ci
PROPOSITIVE *IMPERATIVE*	us-ó	us-ci

CAUSATIVE: USKI.TA   *PASSIVE:*
to make (a person) laugh

to be funny. to be amusing   DESCRIPTIVE

FORMAL *Plain*

	INDICATIVE	RETROSPECTIVE
DECLARATIVE/ *INTERROGATIVE*		
PRESENT	usǔ-p.ta/-unya	usǔp-tóla/-tónya
PAST	usǔwóss-ta/-nǔnya	usǔwóss-tóla
REMOTE PAST	usǔwóssóss-ta	usǔwóssóss-tóla
FUTURE	usǔpkess-ta	usǔpkess-tóla
PAST FUTURE	usǔwósskess-ta	usǔwósskess-tóla

PROPOSITIVE
IMPERATIVE

FORMAL *Polite*

	INDICATIVE	RETROSPECTIVE
DECLARATIVE/ *INTERROGATIVE*		
PRESENT	usǔpsǔpni-ta/-kka	usǔpsǔpti-ta/-kka
PAST	usǔwóssǔpni-ta	usǔwóssǔpti-ta
REMOTE PAST	usǔwóssóssǔpni-ta	usǔwóssóssǔpti-ta
FUTURE	usǔpkessǔpni-ta	usǔpkessǔpti-ta
PAST FUTURE	usǔwósskessǔpni-ta	usǔwósskessǔpti-ta

PROPOSITIVE
IMPERATIVE

INFORMAL *Familiar*

	INDICATIVE	RETROSPECTIVE
DECLARATIVE/ *INTERROGATIVE*		
PRESENT	usǔp.ne/-unka	usǔp-te/-tónka
PAST	usǔwóss-ne/-nǔnka	usǔwóss-te
REMOTE PAST	usǔwóssóss-ne	usǔwóssóss-te
FUTURE	usǔpkess-ne	usǔpkess-te
PAST FUTURE	usǔwósskess-ne	usǔwósskess-te

PROPOSITIVE
IMPERATIVE

	INFORMAL *Intimate* INDICATIVE	INFORMAL *Casual* INDICATIVE
DECLARATIVE/ *INTERROGATIVE*		
PRESENT	usǔw-ó	usǔp-ci
PAST	usǔwóss-ó	usǔwóss-ci
REMOTE PAST	usǔwóssóss-ó	usǔwóssóss-ci
FUTURE	usǔpkess-ó	usǔpkess-ci
PAST FUTURE	usǔwósskess-ó	usǔwósskess-ci

PROPOSITIVE
IMPERATIVE

CAUSATIVE: *PASSIVE:*

FORMAL *Plain*

	INDICATIVE	RETROSPECTIVE
DECLARATIVE/ *INTERROGATIVE*		
PRESENT	ùlph-nùn.ta/-nùnya	ùlph-tóla/-tónya
PAST	ùlphóss-ta	ùlphóss-tóla
REMOTE PAST	ùlphóssóss-ta	ùlphóssóss-tóla
FUTURE	ùlphkess-ta	ùlphkess-tóla
PAST FUTURE	ùlphósskess-ta	ùlphósskess-tóla
PROPOSITIVE	ulph-ca	
IMPERATIVE	ulph-óla	

FORMAL *Polite*

	INDICATIVE	RETROSPECTIVE
DECLARATIVE/ *INTERROGATIVE*		
PRESENT	ùlphsùpni-ta/-kka	ùlphsùpti-ta/-kka
PAST	ùlphóssùpni-ta	ùlphóssùpti-ta
REMOTE PAST	ùlphóssóssùpni-ta	ùlphóssóssùpti-ta
FUTURE	ùlphkessùpni-ta	ùlphkessùpti-ta
PAST FUTURE	ùlphósskessùpni-ta	ùlphósskessùpti-ta
PROPOSITIVE	ùlphùpsi-ta	
IMPERATIVE	ùlphù(si)psi-p	

INFORMAL *Familiar*

	INDICATIVE	RETROSPECTIVE
DECLARATIVE/ *INTERROGATIVE*		
PRESENT	ùlph-ne/-nùnka	ùlph-te/-tónka
PAST	ùlphóss-ne	ùlphóss-te
REMOTE PAST	ùlphóssóss-ne	ùlphóssóss-te
FUTURE	ùlphkess-ne	ùlphkess-te
PAST FUTURE	ùlphósskess-ne	ùlphósskess-te
PROPOSITIVE	ùlph-se	
IMPERATIVE	ùlph-ke	

	INFORMAL *Intimate* INDICATIVE	INFORMAL *Casual* INDICATIVE
DECLARATIVE/ *INTERROGATIVE*		
PRESENT	ùlph-ó	ùlph-ci
PAST	ùlphóss-ó	ùlphóss-ci
REMOTE PAST	ùlphóssóss-ó	ùlphóssóss-ci
FUTURE	ùlphkess-ó	ùlphkess-ci
PAST FUTURE	ùlphósskess-ó	ùlphósskess-ci
PROPOSITIVE *IMPERATIVE*	ùlph-o	ùlph-ci

CAUSATIVE:　　　　　　　　　　　　　　*PASSIVE:*

FORMAL *Plain*

	INDICATIVE	RETROSPECTIVE
DECLARATIVE/ *INTERROGATIVE*		
PRESENT	yalp-ta/-ùnya	yalp-tóla/-tónya
PAST	yalpass-ta/-núnya	yalpass-tóla
REMOTE PAST	yalpassóss-ta	yalpassóss-tóla
FUTURE	yalpkess-ta	yalpkess-tóla
PAST FUTURE	yalpasskess-ta	yalpasskess-tóla

PROPOSITIVE
IMPERATIVE

FORMAL *Polite*

	INDICATIVE	RETROSPECTIVE
DECLARATIVE/ *INTERROGATIVE*		
PRESENT	yalpsúpni-ta/-kka	yalpsúpti-ta/-kka
PAST	yalpassúpni-ta	yalpassúpti-ta
REMOTE PAST	yalpassóssúpni-ta	yalpassóssúpti-ta
FUTURE	yalpkessúpni-ta	yalpkessúpti-ta
PAST FUTURE	yalpasskessúpni-ta	yalpasskessúpti-ta

PROPOSITIVE
IMPERATIVE

INFORMAL *Familiar*

	INDICATIVE	RETROSPECTIVE
DECLARATIVE/ *INTERROGATIVE*		
PRESENT	yalp-ne/-únka	yalp-te/-tónka
PAST	yalpass-ne/-núnka	yalpass-te
REMOTE PAST	yalpassóss-ne	yalpassóss-te
FUTURE	yalpkess-ne	yalpkess-te
PAST FUTURE	yalpasskess-ne	yalpasskess-te

PROPOSITIVE
IMPERATIVE

	INFORMAL *Intimate* INDICATIVE	INFORMAL *Casual* INDICATIVE
DECLARATIVE/ *INTERROGATIVE*		
PRESENT	yalp-a	yalp-ci
PAST	yalpass-ó	yalpass-ci
REMOTE PAST	yalpassóss-ó	yalpassóss-ci
FUTURE	yalpkess-ó	yalpkess-ci
PAST FUTURE	yalpasskess-ó	yalpasskess-ci

PROPOSITIVE
IMPERATIVE

CAUSATIVE: *PASSIVE:*

YATH.TA
to be shallow, to be low   DESCRIPTIVE   얕다

FORMAL *Plain*

	INDICATIVE	RETROSPECTIVE
DECLARATIVE/ *INTERROGATIVE*		
PRESENT	yath-ta/-únya	yath-tóla/-tónka
PAST	yathass-ta/-núnya	yathass-tóla
REMOTE PAST	yathassóss-ta	yathassóss-tóla
FUTURE	yathkess-ta	yathkess-tóla
PAST FUTURE	yathasskess-ta	yathasskess-tóla

PROPOSITIVE
IMPERATIVE

FORMAL *Polite*

	INDICATIVE	RETROSPECTIVE
DECLARATIVE/ *INTERROGATIVE*		
PRESENT	yathsúpni-ta/-kka	yathsúpti-ta/-kka
PAST	yathassúpni-ta	yathassúpti-ta
REMOTE PAST	yathassóssúpni-ta	yathassóssúpti-ta
FUTURE	yathkessúpni-ta	yathkessúpti-ta
PAST FUTURE	yathasskessúpni-ta	yathasskessúpti-ta

PROPOSITIVE
IMPERATIVE

INFORMAL *Familiar*

	INDICATIVE	RETROSPECTIVE
DECLARATIVE/ *INTERROGATIVE*		
PRESENT	yath-ne/-únka	yath-te/-tónka
PAST	yathass-ne/-núnka	yathass-te
REMOTE PAST	yathassóss-ne	yathassóss-te
FUTURE	yathkess-ne	yathkess-te
PAST FUTURE	yathasskess-ne	yathasskess-te

PROPOSITIVE
IMPERATIVE

	INFORMAL *Intimate* INDICATIVE	INFORMAL *Casual* INDICATIVE
DECLARATIVE/ *INTERROGATIVE*		
PRESENT	yath-a	yath-ci
PAST	yathass-ó	yathass-ci
REMOTE PAST	yathassóss-ó	yathassóss-ci
FUTURE	yathkess-ó	yathkess-ci
PAST FUTURE	yathasskess-ó	yathasskess-ci

PROPOSITIVE
IMPERATIVE

CAUSATIVE: *PASSIVE:*

to open, to hold (a party, etc.)

FORMAL *Plain*

	INDICATIVE	RETROSPECTIVE
DECLARATIVE/ *INTERROGATIVE*		
PRESENT	yŏ-n.ta/-nŭnya	yŏl-tóla/-tónya
PAST	yŏlóss-ta	yŏlóss-tóla
REMOTE PAST	yŏlóssóss-ta	yŏlóssóss-tóla
FUTURE	yŏlkess-ta	yŏlkess-tóla
PAST FUTURE	yŏlósskess-ta	yŏlósskess-tóla
PROPOSITIVE	yŏl-ca	
IMPERATIVE	yŏl-óla	

FORMAL *Polite*

	INDICATIVE	RETROSPECTIVE
DECLARATIVE/ *INTERROGATIVE*		
PRESENT	yŏpni-ta/-kka	yŏpti-ta/-kka
PAST	yŏlóssúpni-ta	yŏlóssúpti-ta
REMOTE PAST	yŏlóssóssúpni-ta	yŏlóssóssúpti-ta
FUTURE	yŏlkessúpni-ta	yŏlkessúpti-ta
PAST FUTURE	yŏlósskessúpni-ta	yŏlósskessúpti-ta
PROPOSITIVE	yŏpsi-ta	
IMPERATIVE	yŏ(si)psi-o	

INFORMAL *Familiar*

	INDICATIVE	RETROSPECTIVE
DECLARATIVE/ *INTERROGATIVE*		
PRESENT	yŏ-ne/-nŭnka	yŏl-te/-tónka
PAST	yŏlóss-ne	yŏlóss-te
REMOTE PAST	yŏlóssóss-ne	yŏlóssóss-te
FUTURE	yŏlkess-ne	yŏlkess-te
PAST FUTURE	yŏlósskess-ne	yŏlósskess-te
PROPOSITIVE	yŏ-se	
IMPERATIVE	yŏl-ke	

	INFORMAL *Intimate* INDICATIVE	INFORMAL *Casual* INDICATIVE
DECLARATIVE/ *INTERROGATIVE*		
PRESENT	yŏl-ó	yŏl-ci
PAST	yŏlóss-ó	yŏlóss-ci
REMOTE PAST	yŏlóssóss-ó	yŏlóssóss-ci
FUTURE	yŏlkess-ó	yŏkess-ci
PAST FUTURE	yŏlósskess-ó	yŏlósskess-ci
PROPOSITIVE *IMPERATIVE*	yŏl-ó	yŏl-ci

CAUSATIVE: *PASSIVE:* YŎLLI.TA
                                                  to be open,
                                                  to be held

This index includes all of the verbs found in the foregoing tables. Descriptive verbs and Intransitive verbs are marked by D and I respectively.

More selected BARRON'S titles:

DICTIONARY OF ACCOUNTING TERMS
Joel Siegel and Jae Shim
Approximately 2500 terms are defined for accountants, business managers, students, and small business persons.
Paperback, $8.95, Canada $12.95/ISBN 3766-9

DICTIONARY OF ADVERTISING AND DIRECT MAIL TERMS
Jane Imber and Betsy-Ann Toffler
Approximately 3000 terms are defined as reference for ad industry professionals, students, and consumers.
Paperback, $8.95, Canada $12.95/ISBN 3765-0

DICTIONARY OF BUSINESS TERMS
Jack P. Friedman, general editor
Over 6000 entries define a wide range of terms used throughout business, real estate, taxes, banking, investment, more.
Paperback, $8.95, Canada $12.95/ISBN 3775-8

DICTIONARY OF COMPUTER TERMS
Douglas Downing and Michael Covington
Over 600 key computer terms are clearly explained, and sample programs included. Paperback, $8.95, Canada $12.95/ISBN 2905-4

DICTIONARY OF INSURANCE TERMS, by *Harvey W. Rubin*
Approximately 2500 insurance terms are defined as they relate to property, casualty, life, health, and other types of insurance.
Paperback, $8.95, Canada $12.95/ISBN 3722-3, 448 pages

BARRON'S BUSINESS REVIEW SERIES
Self-instruction guides cover topics taught in a college-level business course, presenting essential concepts in an easy-to-follow format.
Each book paperback $9.95, Canada $13.95, approx. 228 pages
ACCOUNTING, by *Peter J. Eisen*/ISBN 3574-7
BUSINESS LAW, by *Hardwicke and Emerson*/ISBN 3495-3
BUSINESS STATISTICS, by *Downing and Clark*/ISBN 3576-3
ECONOMICS, by *Walter J. Wessels*/ISBN 3560-7
FINANCE, by *A. A. Groppelli and Ehsan Nikhbakht*/ISBN 3561-5
MANAGEMENT, by *Montana and Charnov*/ISBN 3559-3
MARKETING, by *Richard L. Sandhusen*/ISBN 3494-5
QUANTITATIVE METHODS, by *Downing and Clark.* $10.95, Canada $15.95/ISBN 3947-5

BARRON'S TALKING BUSINESS SERIES:
BILINGUAL DICTIONARIES
Five bilingual dictionaries translate about 3000 terms not found in most foreign phrasebooks. Includes words related to accounting, sales, banking, computers, export/import and finance.
Each book paperback, $6.95, Canada $9.95, approx. 256 pages
TALKING BUSINESS IN FRENCH, by *Beppie LeGal*/ISBN 3745-6
TALKING BUSINESS IN GERMAN, by *Henry Strutz*/ISBN 3747-2
TALKING BUSINESS IN ITALIAN, by *Frank Rakus*/ISBN 3754-5
TALKING BUSINESS IN JAPANESE, by *C. & N. Akiyama*/3848-7
TALKING BUSINESS IN KOREAN, by *Un Bok Cheong*/ISBN 3992-0
TALKING BUSINESS IN SPANISH, by *Fryer and Faria*/ISBN 3769-3

All prices are in U.S. and Canadian dollars and subject to change without notice.
At your bookseller, or order direct adding 10% postage (minimum charge $1.50), N.Y. residents add sales tax.

Barron's Educational Series, Inc.
250 Wireless Boulevard, Hauppauge, NY 11788
Call toll-free: 1-800-645-3476, in NY 1-800-257-5729
In Canada: 195 Allstate Parkway, Markham, Ontario L3R4T8